Guide for the Advancing Grammarian

An Exploration of English for Writers and Teachers

Kathleen Black
Northwestern College

Kitelko Publishing
St. Paul

Copyright © 2005 Kathleen Black

All rights reserved. No part of this book may be reproduced or transmitted in any form or by any means, electronic or mechanical, including photocopying, recording, or by any information storage and retrieval system without permission in writing from the publisher. For information, contact Kitelko Publishing.

Kitelko Publishing
1484 Arden View Dr.
St. Paul, MN 55112-1942

Library of Congress Control Number   2005906022

ISBN   0-9770834-0-3

Printed and bound in the United States of America.
Cover Design: John Printy
Second printing 2006

Contents

Preface vii
Chapter 1 Introduction to Grammar Study 1
    TRADITIONAL GRAMMAR 1
    STRUCTURAL GRAMMAR 14
    TRANSFORMATIONAL GRAMMAR THEORY 18
    SOME CONTEMPORARY APPROACHES 24
    A MODERN MELDING 25
    PRACTICE 25

Chapter 2 Basic Grammar Categories 27
    NOMINALS 27
    VERBS 30
    ADJECTIVES 32
    ADVERBS 33
    PREPOSITIONAL PHRASES 35
    WORDS CHANGING CATEGORIES 36
    GRAMMAR CATEGORIES AND STYLE 36
    PRACTICE 37

Chapter 3 Basic Sentence Patterns 41
    LINKING VERBS 41
    INTRANSITIVE VERBS 44
    TRANSITIVE VERBS 45
    REVIEW 50
    PRACTICE SENTENCES 52

Chapter 4 Noun Clusters 54
    DETERMINERS 54
    ADJECTIVE PHRASES 55
    NOUNS AND NOUN SUBSTITUTES 56
    ADJECTIVAL PREPOSITIONAL PHRASES 58
    PRE-DETERMINER AND POST-NOUN 60
    ADJECTIVAL OR NOMINAL GROUPINGS 60
    COMPOUNDS 62
    TREEING NOMINAL PHRASES 64
    PRONOUN USAGE 68
    QUALIFIERS AND USAGE 70
    NOMINAL PHRASE PUNCTUATION 70
    PRACTICE SENTENCES 71

Chapter 5 Adverb Choices 74
- ADVERB QUESTIONS AND MOBILITY 74
- ADVERB FORMS: ADVERBS WITH QUALIFIERS 75
- ADVERB FORMS: PREPOSITIONAL PHRASES 77
- ADVERB FORMS: NOUN CLUSTERS 78
- ADVERB FORMS: INFINITIVE PHRASES 79
- ADVERB FORMS: ADVERB CLAUSES 82
- COMPOUND ADVERB PHRASES 83
- ADVERB USAGE 85
- ADVERBS AND PUNCTUATION 86
- ADVERBS AND WRITING STYLE 87
- PRACTICE SENTENCES 88

Chapter 6 Verbs: Expansions and Variations 92
- VERB PARTICLES 93
- CONDITIONAL VERBS 95
- PERFECT VERBS 96
- PROGRESSIVE VERBS 96
- EMPHATIC VERBS AND NEGATIVES 97
- PASSIVE VERBS 99
- COMPOUND VERB PHRASES 103
- VERB USAGE 105
- VERBS AND WRITING STYLE 106
- PRACTICE SENTENCES 107

Chapter 7 Nominal Phrase Choices 110
- GERUND PHRASES 110
- NOUN CLAUSES 112
- NOMINAL INFINITIVE PHRASES 119
- EMBEDDED STRUCTURES 121
- NOMINAL PHRASE CHOICES AND USAGE 123
- NOMINAL PHRASE CHOICES AND PUNCTUATION 125
- NOMINAL PHRASE CHOICES AND STYLE 125
- PRACTICE SENTENCES 126

Chapter 8 Noun Cluster Expansions: Relative Clauses and Adjectival Infinitive Phrases 130
- RELATIVE CLAUSES 130
- RESTRICTIVE AND NONRESTRICTIVE RELATIVE CLAUSES 138
- ADJECTIVAL INFINITIVE PHRASES 141
- SIMILAR STRUCTURES WITH DIFFERENT FUNCTIONS 143

RELATIVE CLAUSES AND USAGE 144
ADJECTIVAL STRUCTURES AND PUNCTUATION 145
RELATIVE CLAUSES AND STYLE 146
PRACTICE SENTENCES 146

Chapter 9 Noun Cluster Expansions: Adjectival Participial Phrases and Adjectival Appositives 152

ACTIVE PARTICIPIAL PHRASES 152
PASSIVE PARTICIPIAL PHRASES 153
RESTRICTIVE AND NONRESTRICTIVE PARTICIPIAL PHRASES 154
ADJECTIVAL APPOSITIVES WITH ADJECTIVAL COMPLEMENTS 156
COMPOUND STRUCTURES 157
DISTINGUISHING BETWEEN ACTIVE PARTICIPIAL PHRASES AND GERUND PHRASES ... 161
NOUN CLUSTER EXPANSIONS AND PUNCTUATION 161
NOUN CLUSTER EXPANSIONS AND SENTENCE STYLE 161
NOUN CLUSTER EXPANSIONS AND USAGE 163
PRACTICE SENTENCES 163

Chapter 10 Adjectival and Adverbial Choices and Expansions 167

ADJECTIVAL COMPLEMENT INFINITIVE PHRASES 167
ADJECTIVAL COMPLEMENT CLAUSES 171
PREPOSITIONAL PHRASES AS PREDICATE ADJECTIVES 176
INFINITIVE PHRASES AS ADJECTIVAL OBJECT COMPLEMENTS 176
ADVERBIAL COMPLEMENT PHRASES AND CLAUSES 177
STRUCTURES THAT HAVE BECOME ADVERBIAL 179
MISPLACED OR DANGLING MODIFIERS 182
ADVERB STRUCTURES AND PUNCTUATION 183
USAGE IN ADJECTIVAL AND ADVERBIAL COMPLEMENT CLAUSES 183
PRACTICE SENTENCES 183

Chapter 11 Nominal Phrase Clarifications: Nominal Appositives and Nominal Complements 187

NOMINAL APPOSITIVES 187
NOMINAL COMPLEMENT INFINITIVE PHRASES 191
NOMINAL COMPLEMENT CLAUSES 194
NOMINAL APPOSITIVES AND WRITING STYLE 195
NOMINAL APPOSITIVES AND PUNCTUATION 196
A REVIEW OF PHRASES AND CLAUSES 196
PRACTICE SENTENCES 199

Chapter 12 Whole-Sentence Modifiers and Variations 203

COMPOUND SENTENCES 203

v

    Absolutes 204
    Adverbial Conjunctions 205
    Other Whole-Sentence Modifiers 207
    Relative Clauses with Whole-Sentence Heads 209
    Pro-Forms 210
    Ellipsis 212
    Notes about Punctuation 212
    Modifier Usage 214
    Sentence Modifiers and Style 215
    Practice Sentences 215

Chapter 13 Sentence Varieties 220
    Imperative Sentences 220
    Questions 221
    Extraposed Sentences 226
    Inverted Sentences 232
    Sentence Varieties and Usage 232
    A Note about Style 234
    Practice Sentences 234

Chapter 14 Launching Out 238
    Challenging Sentences 238
    Final Tree Assignment 245

Chapter 15 Applications of Grammar 246
    Applications for Writers and Students of Literature 246
    Applications for Teachers 250
    Applications for Students of Other Languages 265
    Applied Grammar Assignments 265

Index 270

Preface

I teach a course on the syntax of English. Year after year, frustrated by the textbooks I had them buy, my students asked me to write my own grammar book. I pointed out to them that I was too busy teaching a variety of courses, often an overload, to have time for that. Then they admitted that they never understood and finally quit trying to read the other textbooks; they simply waited until they came to class to have me explain the material and give them explanatory handouts. However, even though my former students were not reading the textbooks semester after semester, after I explained it to them, they grew to truly enjoy syntax analysis and to appreciate its application to their writing, reading, and teaching. So I finally decided to turn all the explanation into a book.

This is the textbook my students actually read.

Guide for the Advancing Grammarian is useful for students, writers, and teachers:
- students of linguistics or foreign languages who need to understand English syntax,
- students of literature who want to be able to analyze the writing of authors,
- writers who want more control over their writing style,
- writers who want to understand the grammar behind their punctuation and usage,
- teachers who need to understand English syntax before they can teach it (particularly to ESL students), and
- teachers who want guidelines for teaching and specific lesson planning ideas for teaching writing and reading.

Guide for the Advancing Grammarian will provide the reader with a strong foundation for understanding contemporary English syntax.
- The book is written in language that has been used successfully with the beginning grammarian.
- It is organized by grammatical function, not by structure, making the material easier to grasp and remember.
- *Guide for the Advancing Grammarian* is based upon years of teaching students of English grammar. My students need examples far more than they need intricate explanations. The book is a concise guide; it provides the reader with examples, illustrations, and visual aids.

- Chapters build on the previous material, dividing the learning into smaller increments.
- Each chapter has 50 practice sentences, containing new and review material, for students to practice their analysis. Readers also have practice opportunities to write sentences with the structures they are learning. I think of grammar as a skill, rather than a body of knowledge. When my students practice, they become proficient.
- Most grammar textbooks have sample sentences carefully crafted to conform to the standard structures. This book has sentences based on those I found in magazines and newspapers, in novels and other books, and on television. I haven't ignored "problem sentences." One of the chapters, "Launching Out," is specifically dedicated to the discussion of even more challenging sentences that we use but that do not fit the simple patterns. One of the goals of this book is to explain the sentences we actually find around us.
- I am not trying to adhere to any particular theory of grammar. My approach to explaining English syntax is as logical and as easily assimilated as possible; it is flexible enough for contemporary English.

Guide for the Advancing Grammarian emphasizes application of the material throughout the book.
- Each chapter has application sections so that the reader can see the use of the material for punctuation and usage. Because readers have, at that point, the grammatical understanding, these sections explain admonitions they have perhaps heard before but never understood.
- The book illustrates application of grammar study on writing style, a topic not often covered in other textbooks. Readers are invited to try out the various structures they are learning by writing their own sentences to become more comfortable with the new structures.
- It has detailed guidelines for students who want to analyze the writing of themselves or others. The "Applied Grammar Assignment" in Chapter 15 has been a good learning experience for my students.
- A major emphasis of *Guide for the Advancing Grammarian* is on teaching of grammar. The book has guidelines for teachers of English language arts and ESL teachers. It has specific lesson planning ideas for teaching writing and reading, including teaching new structures, adding of details to writing, parallelism, active and passive verbs, misplaced modifiers, subject and verb agreement, and sentence fragments.

- Each chapter has assignments so that the reader can immediately apply the learning to writing or to teaching.

My students insisted that I mention grammar t-shirts and grammar mascots. Mascots entered my Advanced Grammar classroom when, desperate for a sentence to illustrate a concept in class, I glanced out the window and saw the lake next to our campus. I imagined a family of beavers and went on from there. Now, each semester, I use a different small toy (unique and generally weird). Future teachers have proudly told me that they are ready for their own classrooms because they have a mascot. The t-shirts are custom made for the class; students all wear their shirts on t-shirt day (the first day they are allowed to wear the t-shirt). This comes at the end of the semester when they could tree the proverb that has been treed on the back of the shirt. We take pictures.

I would like to acknowledge my students. Their enthusiasm for the analysis of syntax feeds my own. They have "field tested" the book and have taken an active role in its writing by giving me suggestions and sentences. In particular, I would like to thank Deb Sullins, Laura Den Hartog, and Tia Martin for their particular contributions of sentences and especially Addic Zierman, Josh Dunn, Jessica Peterson, and Carrie Noennig for their help in proofreading at various stages of the writing. Finally, I would like to thank all of the students who have had fun exploring English with me and who were sad to have the class end.

Kathleen Black
Department of English and Literature
Department of Education
Northwestern College
St. Paul, Minnesota

Chapter 1
Introduction to Grammar Study

The Oxford English Dictionary indicates that the Old French word for grammar (*gramaire*) was used sometimes as a name for the occult sciences of astrology and magic. Modern students may find this definition appropriate in that grammar may seem like some magic trick that they can never quite understand. However, one does not need a magic potion to understand grammar. In fact, the analysis of English sentences (syntax) can be as satisfying (even fun) as completing a puzzle.

Simply stated, grammar is the system by which a language operates. When we study grammar, we analyze the various parts of the language and the relationship these parts have to each other.

Grammar is an important subject to study since the use of a language system sets humans apart as unique creatures. Scholars first developed grammar systems to explain and analyze language to teach to their students. Grammar study can also be used to understand the writing of others and to improve one's own writing. This study began hundreds of years ago and has undergone changes in perspective throughout that time. A survey of the history of grammar study would include a look at three systems (traditional grammar, structural grammar, and transformational grammar) that have been particularly important to the study of English.

Traditional Grammar

Historical Roots

The study of grammar goes back to the Greeks. Those scholars gave us terminology, established the practice of analyzing written text, and began the idea that there was a universally correct and acceptable logic of language for humans to use to express ideas. Plato and Aristotle formulated some of the basic terms of grammar study: *onoma* for the name of one who performs an action, *rhema* for the name of the action, and *syndesmoi* for "conjunction" or the words that connect *onoma* and *rhema*. Plato, in particular, thought that there were acceptable and unacceptable ways to express ideas. This concept is fundamental to traditional grammar. Around 100 B.C., Dionysius Thrax, a scholar of Alexandria, wrote *The Art of Grammar*--a grammar of written Greek, with eight parts of speech (noun, verb, participle, article, pronoun, preposition, adverb, and conjunction). Thrax is considered to be the first "real" grammarian.

For their study of Latin, the Romans took grammar terms and the method of description from the Greeks. They used the Greek classification system, but Latin had no articles, so they replaced that part of speech with one for interjections, in order to keep to a total of eight parts of speech, as the Greeks had. The Romans also used literary models (rather than the "Vulgar Latin" used by most people daily) for study, teaching their students to imitate the language of literature. One Latin scholar, Priscian, wrote 18 books on the parts of speech and 2 books on syntax. Although written in the sixth century, this was the basis for standard Latin grammars used throughout the medieval period in various countries.

During the medieval period, the church controlled the education of boys, and students studied Latin. Their religious teachers emphasized correction and wanted to stop "error" and "degeneration" in language, as they were trying to stop "error" in the lives of the people. So, teachers gave their students rules about the right way to use language and the wrong way. Language change or deviation was equated with sin. The teachers tried to fix language degradation by using rigid rules and classical models. Even when native languages in various countries began to be studied, rules were established that made languages adhere to strictly formulated logical principles dictated by Latin scholarship. Meanwhile, the native languages were changing in patterns developed by the users of these languages.

The emphasis on correctness and rules was reinforced during the eighteenth century (sometimes called the Age of Rationalism or the Neo-Classical Period). Grammarians wanted to make language logical or rational and were also heavily influenced by the classical Latin literature that was again being studied. The influence of logic is noticeable in rules formulated at this time such as "two negatives in language use make a positive" or "since the 'BE' verb is an 'equals sign', we need the nominative case for a pronoun predicate nominative." The Latin (classical) influence is noticeable in the use of Latin terms such as "antecedent," "intransitive," and "passive." Eighteenth century grammarians did study English as a language, but using Latin as a model, they equated English auxiliary verbs with Latin verb inflections and forced a future tense and a subjunctive mood onto English so that it more closely resembled Latin. They also wanted to stop degeneration and improve language, striving to establish "correct" usage and point out "errors." Some notable scholars during this time include Samuel Johnson, Robert Lowth, Lindley Murray, John Wallis, Joseph Priestly, and George Campbell. These **prescriptive grammarians**, especially Lowth and Murray, were widely used to establish rules of English grammar for several generations.

Characteristics of Traditional Grammar

Traditional grammar has the following characteristics:

- **Latin-based.** For example, we have eight parts of speech because there are eight parts of speech in Latin. Traditional grammarians created the strange category of "interjections" merely so that the total is eight. Also, verb labels are based on the verbs in Latin, rather than what actually appears in English.
- **Focused on written, not spoken, language.** As such, it includes only formal language use.
- **Prescriptive.** Traditional grammar describes what grammarians believe the language ought to be rather than what it is.
- **Proscriptive.** Certain constructions are condemned; they must be avoided. Traditional grammar texts place great emphasis on the correct or socially acceptable usage. Traditional grammar textbooks label these structures as WRONG or RIGHT. The emphasis is always on correctness in all language issues.
- **Rules-oriented.** This correctness is often based upon logic. For example, in English, we usually use the object form of pronouns after verbs. However, traditional grammarians point out that a sentence such as *"That's me"* should be *"That's I"* since the pronoun refers to the logical subject and so should be in nominative, not objective, form.
- **Characterized by defining, classifying, labeling, and diagramming.** These textbooks have drills and exercises asking students to do these.

Components of Traditional Grammar

Parts of Speech

In traditional grammar, a **noun** is defined as a person, place, thing or idea; it is used as a subject, direct object, indirect object, predicate nominative, appositive, and so on. The class of words that have typical noun functions, including nouns, pronouns, and gerunds, are called **substantive**. English nouns have a **common case** and **genitive (possessive) case**. They show singular and plural number. Plural nouns often end in *s*, but many nouns have irregular plural forms. Genitive case in English nouns is shown by adding an apostrophe to all plural words which end in *s* and adding an apostrophe and *s* to all other words.

An **Adjective** is defined as a word that modifies a noun or other substantive. Adjectives show degree (positive, comparative, or superlative) with a single word or a periphrastic comparison (more than one word to show the comparison). For example, a single adjective showing degree would be *short, shorter,* and *shortest,* whereas an example of a periphrastic comparison would be *perceptive, more perceptive,* and *most perceptive.*

Prepositions are words used to show a relationship between a noun or pronoun and some other word in a sentence. A **prepositional phrase** is the combination of a preposition plus the noun or pronoun and any modifiers the noun or pronoun may have. An object of the preposition is the noun or pronoun in the phrase.

Conjunctions are words used to connect words or groups of words in sentences. Types include **coordinating** to join groups of words that are equal in rank, **subordinating** to join words or groups of words that are unequal in rank with the idea said to be of lesser or lower rank joined to one of the greater rank by the subordinating conjunction, and **correlative** used to compare or contrast parallel words or groups of words.

An **adverb** modifies a verb, an adjective, or another adverb. Adverbs show positive, comparative, and superlative degrees with endings or with the use of periphrastic comparison, as do adjectives. Sometimes the word *not* is considered to be an adverb.

Introduction to Grammar Study 5

An **interjection** is a word or exclamatory sound that has no grammatical relationship to other words in a sentence. An example would be *"oh!"*.

Verbs are defined as words that express action or a state of being. Traditional grammar labels verbs in English as closely as possible using Latin forms.

> **Three types.** Transitive verbs express an action that must have an object. Intransitive verbs express an action that does not have an object. Linking verbs (copulative) are usually forms of the verb *to be* used as the main verb to connect subjects to predicate adjectives or predicate nouns.
>
> **Six tenses.** Present, past, and future refer to the time an action is performed. Present tense has singular and plural forms and is inflected for person (first person, second person, and third person). Past perfect indicates the definitive completion of an action in the past. Present perfect indicates the definitive completion of an action in the present. Future perfect tense indicates the definitive completion of an action in the future. Each tense has a progressive form, which indicates continuing action, and an emphatic form, which lays extra stress on the meaning of the verb.
>
> **Four principal parts.** The infinitive is the "base" form. The present participle form has *-ing* ending. The past form has *–d* or *-ed* ending in regular forms, and the past participle has *–en* ending in regular forms. (Irregular verbs do not have the endings listed above and are given in lists for students to memorize.)
>
> **Auxiliary verbs.** These "helping verbs" are used in combination with the principal parts of verbs to form the various tenses.
>
> **Three moods.** Imperative is used for requests or commands. Subjunctive is used for contrary-to-fact statements and in statements expressing a wish. Indicative is used for all other purposes.
>
> **Two voices.** Active expresses an action performed by the subject, and passive is used when the subject receives the action of the verb.

Verb conjugations are usually shown in charts such as the one that follows.

CONJUGATION OF THE VERB *SEE* (Indicative Mood)

Active Voice		Passive Voice	
Singular	*Plural*	*Singular*	*Plural*
Present Tense			
I see	we see	I am seen	we are seen
you see	you see	you are seen	you are seen
he/she/it sees	they see	he/she/it is seen	they are seen
Present Progressive		I am seeing (and so on)	
Present Emphatic		I do see (and so on)	
Past Tense			
I saw	we saw	I was seen	we were seen
you saw	you saw	you were seen	you were seen
he/she/it saw	they saw	he/she/it was seen	they were seen
Past Progressive		I was seeing (and so on)	
Past Emphatic		I did see (and so on)	
Future Tense			
I shall see	we shall see	I shall be seen	we shall be seen
you will see	you will see	you will be seen	you will be seen
he/she/it will see	they will see	he/she/it will be seen	they will be seen
Future Progressive		I shall be seeing (and so on)	
Present Perfect Tense			
I have seen	we have seen	I have been seen	we have been seen
you have seen	you have seen	you have been seen	you have been seen
he/she/it has seen	they have seen	he/she/it has been seen	they have been seen
Present Perfect Progressive		I have been seeing (and so on)	
Past Perfect Tense			
I had seen	we had seen	I had been seen	we had been seen
you had seen	you had seen	you had been seen	you had been seen
he/she/it had seen	they had seen	he/she/it had been seen	they had been seen
Past Perfect Progressive		I had been seeing (and so on)	
Future Perfect Tense			
I shall have seen	we shall have seen	I shall have been seen	we shall have been seen
you will have seen	you will have seen	you will have been seen	you will have been seen
he/she/it will have seen	they will have seen	he/she/it will have been seen	they will have been seen
Future Perfect Progressive		I shall have been seeing (and so on)	

Pronouns are defined as words that substitute for a noun. This class includes personal pronouns, possessive pronouns, relative pronouns,

Introduction to Grammar Study 7

interrogative pronouns, demonstrative pronouns, reflexive pronouns, and indefinite pronouns. **Personal pronouns** have **case** (nominative, objective, and possessive) and show **number** (singular and plural) and **gender** (male and female). **Demonstratives** and **reflexives** show **number** (singular and plural).

		Personal Pronouns			
		First Person	Second Person	Third Person	
Singular	Nominative	I	you	he	she	it
	Objective	me	you	him	her	it
	Possessive	my (mine)	your (yours)	his	her (hers)	its
Plural	Nominative	we	you	they	
	Objective	us	you	them	
	Possessive	our (ours)	your (yours)	their (theirs)	
Relative Pronouns	who, that, which, whose, whom				
Interrogative Pronouns	who, whom, which				
Demonstrative Pronouns	this, that, these, those				
Reflexive Pronouns	myself, yourself, himself, herself, itself, ourselves, yourselves, themselves				
Indefinite Pronouns	one, someone, something, anyone, no one (and so on)				

Phrases and Clauses

Phrases are a group of words that may function as a single part of speech.
- **Prepositional phrases** modify nouns (adjectival prepositional phrases) or verbs (adverbial prepositional phrases).
- **Participial phrases** begin with a present participle or past participial form of the verb and function as adjectives or adverbs. *-ing*
- **Gerund phrases** begin with a gerund and function as nouns. *-ing*

Trad. Grammar:
Absolute — Also nominative absolute, usually composed of noun/pronoun + a participle
Thought relationship — no direct grammatical relationship

- **Infinitive phrases** begin with the "sign of the infinitive" (*to*) and an infinitive form of the verb and function as nouns, adjectives, or adverbs.
- **Appositive phrases** are made up of nouns and their modifiers and can function as adjectives.

Clauses are a group of words that contain a subject or a verb and may function as a single part of speech.
- **An independent clause** can stand alone as a sentence.
- **A dependent clause (subordinate clause)** performs the function of a single part of speech.
    - **A nominal clause** functions as a noun.
    - **An adverbial clause** functions as an adverb.
    - **An adjectival clause** modifies nouns. **Relative clauses** are adjectival clauses, which may be restrictive or nonrestrictive, and are usually introduced by a relative pronoun.

Sentences

A sentence is defined in traditional grammar as a group of words expressing a complete thought. It contains a **subject** and a **predicate**. A subject is that about which something is said, and a predicate is whatever is said about the subject. Specific parts of the predicate may be **subject complements** (when a complement elaborates on the meaning expressed by the noun or pronoun of the subject) and **objective complement** (when a complement adds to or completes the meaning expressed by a verb). These include **predicate adjective** (when the subjective complement is an adjective), **predicate noun or nominal** (when the subjective complement is a noun), **direct objects** (which receive the action of the verb) and **indirect objects** (which are affected by the verb in a less immediate way).

Four Sentence Purposes:
- **Declarative** makes a statement.
- **Imperative** makes requests or gives commands.
- **Interrogative** asks a question.
- **Exclamatory** expresses strong feelings.

Four Structure Classifications:
- **Simple sentences** contain a single subject-predicate combination.

Introduction to Grammar Study

- **Compound sentences** contain two or more independent clauses.
- **Complex sentences** contain an independent clause plus at least one dependent clause.
- **Compound complex sentences** contain two or more independent clauses and at least one dependent clause.

Traditional Grammar Exercises

A traditional approach to grammar study is to provide students with definitions and charts and then ask them to do worksheets or exercises in which they identify and label words as illustrated below.

A. Traditional Parts of Speech. Identify the part of speech of each underlined word. Choose from noun, pronoun, verb, adjective, adverb, preposition, interjection, coordinating conjunction, and subordinating conjunction.

Cartoons, (1) drawings that (2) tell a story or express a message, may entertain, teach, (3) or comment (4) about a person, event, or (5) state of affairs. Most cartoonists do not draw things as (6) they appear in real life. (7) These artists (8) use fewer details (9) and may exaggerate (10) some feature (11) of a character, such as the head, hands, or feet. Oversized heads help (12) direct (13) attention to some important facial expressions, and (14) oversized hands and feet are (15) often drawn to stress action. (16) If the cartoonist wants to indicate a (17) bright idea, he or (18) she might use a light bulb above a character's head. A dark cloud (19) over a character's head may show (20) despair. (21) This (22) creative approach is (23) one of the reasons (24) that cartoons are (25) so popular.

B. Types of Pronouns. Find and list the 13 pronouns in the passage below. Label each pronoun as personal, possessive, reflexive, interrogative, demonstrative, indefinite, or relative.

Who gives us accurate information about nutrition? The advice which we hear and read is often contradictory and leaves us primarily confused. For example, a specialist may advocate eating eggs; another advises against them. Meat itself is supposedly nutritionally indispensable; however, studies suggest that it contributes to health problems. Nutritional controversies also exist over salt, sugar, fiber, and fat. These substances are usually recommended for our diets, but in different quantities. We can only await new studies that may provide answers.

C. Verbs
Using the verb *write*, fill in the blanks on your answer sheet.

1. third person, singular present
2. third person, singular past perfect passive
3. first person, plural present perfect
4. second person, future perfect
5. third person, future perfect progressive
6. first person, plural past
7. first person, future progressive
8. third person, singular past perfect progressive
9. third person, future

D. Verbs. Identify the tense of each verb and verb phrase (present, past, future, present progressive, past progressive, future progressive, present perfect, past perfect, future perfect, present perfect progressive, past perfect progressive, future perfect progressive, present passive, past passive, future passive, present perfect passive, past perfect passive, or future perfect passive).

1. He had hunted for one big white squirrel all his life.
2. On Herradura Beach, the young boy puts his hermit crabs in the shoes of crabby tourists.
3. Until the cement bags are delivered, the construction crew will be pilfering cement from a nearby sidewalk.
4. That lucky horseshoe had been worn by the Pegasus.
5. My roommate now does dental work on gerbils.
6. My siblings have been plotting mutiny in the bathroom.
7. The rum cake was enjoyed by succeeding generations until the prohibition of alcohol.
8. Before the famine, the population had been growing rapidly.
9. The dog is now considering new places for bone burial.
10. The Guatemalan City Dump has been housing the poor for the past ten years.
11. Chocolate will appease most roommates.
12. The aliens have arranged the museum's asteroid exhibit skillfully.

E. Sentences. Identify each sentence as simple, compound, complex, or compound-complex.
1) Plastic machine parts run silently, yet they need little or no oiling.
2) We arrived in Germany on June 27, and one of the first things that we did was head for the Mosel to taste the candy and eat fresh trout.
3) To tell the truth, most of the funds have already been spent.
4) To prevent piracy, manufacturers of computer programs have spent much time developing systems that have "copy protection."
5) Smith, who wrote his first novel at age fifteen, had made his reputation by age twenty, but he accomplished nothing after he turned forty.
6) After the new guidelines are established, the commission will be rating movies on a scale of one to four.
7) Before the recession, the company had been growing rapidly.
8) The state apartments are open to the public when the royal family is not in residence.
9) The director says that the actors had done a fine job interpreting their roles.
10) Audience members who stay to read them discover the names of people whose contributions are sometimes as important to the film as the actors are.

F. Clauses. Identify each subordinate clause as a nominal clause, adverbial clause, or adjectival clause.
(1) When squirrels become enraged, people (2) who sit in trees to hunt discover the dangers of these rodents (3) whose bark is sometimes as terrifying to hunters as the howl of a wolf. For instance, Andrew Potter went deer hunting one day last fall and came face-to-face with the squirrel (4) that will eventually go down in history. (5) That most gray squirrels are only a foot in length is well known, but many people do not realize (6) that there is at least one gigantic gray squirrel in every forest. (7) When Andy saw this squirrel in another tree, he did not realize its great size and shot at it with his bow and arrow out of sheer boredom. The squirrel, (8) who did not find this very amusing, leaped from his tree to the tree (9) which held Andy's tree stand. It yelled several unrepeatable squirrel profanities and raced straight down the branch at Andy's stand. Andy shot at the squirrel again and missed again. Realizing (10) that he only had one arrow left, he brandished it like a spear and pointed it at the charging squirrel, but the squirrel merely laughed, and without breaking stride charged to the underside of the branch. At this point, Andy's memory becomes hazy. He only remembers leaping and blocking and stabbing at a great gray mass of fur and then waking up on the ground a few hours later, alone with a long gray tail in his hand.

G. Phrases. Identify the following phrases (adjectival prepositional, adverbial prepositional, active participial, passive participial, gerund, infinitive, absolute, or appositive).

(1) Using six gallons of gasoline, a U.S. car (2) with a four-cylinder engine can run, (3) under ideal weather conditions, for almost 180 miles, but a car (4) built in Japan can run 200 miles.
(5) The pond having dried up, the fish slowly packed his bags and prepared to move on to wetter pastures.
(6) Confronted by financial difficulties, my friends are looking into the feasibility (7) of bank robbing, (8) a possible source of cold cash.
My cat is playing (9) with two mice, (10) the white laboratory mouse and the brown field mouse, which drive her nuts by twisting her whiskers (11) into little curls.
As the tide rises (12) over the pier, the tourists face the danger (13) of getting wet.
(14) Changing our phone company is not the answer (15) to our problems.
We dove from the tree, (16) each one aiming for a different squirrel.
(17) Solving their financial difficulties in this way would also be evidence (18) of their stupidity (19) to resort to crime (20) for fiscal purposes.
Such a scam, (21) being twenty times larger than any scam yet done by Al Capone, would be recorded in history as the scam (22) of the decade.
A strange method (23) to study is (24) to stand on your head and hold your book with your toes.
It is possible (25) to rob a bank which will supply enough money (26) to support three desperate people (27) for ten years.

Advantages and Disadvantages of Traditional Grammar

From traditional grammar we get the basic vocabulary with which we discuss syntax--*nouns, pronouns, verbs, adverbs,* and *adjectives,* in particular. We also use the traditional terms such as *gerund* and *participle* and some of the other classifications.

However, traditional grammar study has several limitations for a modern student of grammar.

- It focuses only upon written English and doesn't include spoken English, which is often contemporary usage.

- It doesn't recognize that language usage often changes in time as people use the language.

- It doesn't recognize any differences for audience appropriateness; all rules in traditional grammar dictate absolute right and wrong rather than distinguishing between various rhetorical situations.

- Some of the rules associated with traditional grammar were "forced" in by eighteenth-century grammarians based upon their reasoning rather than the language use. An example is the rule against double negatives. It is true that using double negatives might reflect upon one socially, but this should not be avoided for the typical reason given: "two negatives make a positive." I would not recommend trying to convince a class of ninth graders (as I attempted once) that if we said, "He ain't got no money," we were talking about a rich man! The ninth graders will merely stare at the teacher.

- It does not look at English as a unique language. Traditional grammar is based upon Latin, which was based upon Greek. Latin was enough like Greek so that using the Greek system worked for the Romans, but it doesn't work nearly as well for English, upon which it was imposed. Using the Greek/Latin system, traditional grammar includes categories we don't need and inappropriate rules. Latin has extensive sets of inflections. Nouns are inflected for subject, direct object, and indirect object. Verbs are inflected for person, number, tense, and mood. Order is not as important in Latin because of the inflections. However, English syntax is based upon word order. All of the categories used in Latin are not necessary for English. An example of a rule that comes from Latin is "Don't split an infinitive." In this language, the infinitive is a one-word verb, so one should not split it. There is no reason for this rule in English since infinitives are two words. The decision to split an infinitive or not is stylistic rather than grammatical in English, and some infinitives might be more effective if they are split.

- Exceptions to a "rule" are sometimes as numerous as instances of compliance. For example, one "rule" says that we form future tense with *shall* or *will*, but sometimes we do it with an adverb of time: *"The school musical opens next week."*

- The definitions in traditional grammar are not helpful to students. Some parts of speech are defined by meaning (noun and verb) and some by function (preposition and conjunction). The definitions are not consistent. Some definitions are vague. For example, "A sentence expresses a complete thought." What is an "incomplete thought"? In real-life situations, "ouch!" can be a complete thought, but it is not a sentence. Another interesting definition is that "a verb expresses action or a state of being." Most teachers know that explaining "state of being" to a 13-year-old is neither a fun nor generally successful experience! Also, not all words that traditional grammar would call pronouns "take the place of a noun." A final example is the circular definition: "An adverb modifies a verb, adjective, or another adverb." Traditional grammar uses the word "adverb" to define "adverb." Also, students can memorize this definition, but very few of them have any concept of what it might mean to "modify." Traditional grammar exercises such as those included in the section above are most often difficult and frustrating for students.

Structural Grammar

Historical Roots

Beginning roughly in the nineteenth century, linguists began to recognize that languages change over time and to study those changes. They also became interested in studying languages as they are used rather than as they "should be"; change in language use was viewed as a neutral. Linguists became **descriptive** rather than **prescriptive.** Comparative linguists studied the similarities and differences among languages whereas historical linguists looked at the development of various languages within common families over time.

These linguists did not want to establish rules of correctness. Rather, they gathered data, sorted it, and analyzed it. Their objective method looked at how languages were related to each other, not whether they were "correct" or not. For example, Rasmus Rask compared Icelandic and Scandinavian languages and dialects, and Jacob Grimm proposed a theory to account for the differences he found among related languages, showing that languages change gradually yet systematically over long periods of time.

Introduction to Grammar Study

These descriptive linguists (and others such as Ferdinand de Saussure, Henry Sweet, Franz Boas, and Edward Sapir) made several innovations in the study of grammar.

- They gathered data from many dialects, including those from secluded areas.
- They tried to develop methods of language study with scientific rigor.
- They looked more at the study of the sound of words.
- They began to see the importance of syntax and word order in English.
- They began to look at the context of language use within sentences.

Leonard Bloomfield, a prominent early American linguist, advocated a scientific approach to linguistic research using objectively verified data. Charles Fries also brought scientific descriptive methods to the study of modern American English in his books (*American English Grammar* and *The Structure of English*). Fries wanted to free himself of preconceived perceptions of traditional grammatical terminology and is a good example of a structural grammarian.

Description of Structural Grammar

Structural grammar is empirically based. These grammarians collected data and attempted to describe language as it actually exists. Structural grammar includes the following:

- The study of individual sounds (phonology)
- The study of groups of sounds that carry language meaning (morphology)
- The arrangement of words and their relationships to each other (syntax).

They began study with the primacy of speech (phonology and morphology). Structural grammar is characterized by the use of objective data, inductive process, and descriptive approach. A structuralist grammarian is trying to describe the language as it is used by speakers of English as precisely as possible.

Some structuralists wanted to start grammar study with a "clean slate" and so did not use the traditional grammar labels. Instead they used numbers or letters. Words were divided into two categories: **form class words** and **function words.**

Form Class Words	Function Words
1 Noun or Pronoun	D Determiner
2 Verb	A Auxiliary
3 Adjective	Q Qualifier
4 Adverb	P Preposition
	C Conjunction

The form class words are called that because they take certain forms and can be described. Form class words are characterized in certain ways. The structural criteria are **inflectional paradigms** (how words in that form class may be changed for meaning), **derivational affixes** (typical affixes which are associated with that form class), **intonation patterns** (which stress pronunciation), **position or word order** (which uses "test frames" for the position of that form class in an English sentence), and **function word markers** (that accompany a particular form class and distinguish it from the other form classes).

D Determiner	Words such as *the, a, my, his, her, this, that, these, those, each, either, many, several*, etc. which precede nouns
A Auxiliary	"Helper verbs" which precede the main verb: *may, could, should, might, have, had, is, was, were*, etc.
Q Qualifier	Words such as *very, rather, extremely*, etc. which precede adjectives and adverbs
P Preposition	Words used to show a relationship between a noun or pronoun and some other word in a sentence: *in, about, across, among, at, below, by, during, on, from, into, toward, through, under, with,* etc.
C Conjunction	Words used to connect words or groups of words in sentences: *and, but, or, because, if, while,* etc.

Traditionalists rely on notional or referential meaning; structuralists rely on descriptions based on these criteria. The method of explaining nouns,

Introduction to Grammar Study 17

verbs, adjectives, and adverbs in Chapter 2 of this book is primarily based upon structural methods.

The form class words (nouns, verbs, adjectives, and adverbs) are **open classes** because we add new words in these categories all the time.

The function words (determiners, auxiliary verbs, qualifiers, prepositions, conjunctions, subordinators, and interrogatives) do not have distinct characteristics and are simply tools for putting words together. They perform a function and have little meaning in themselves. The function words are usually **closed classes** because new words are rarely, if ever, added to their list.

Structuralists also do sentence analysis. In **phrase analysis,** structuralists look at word clusters or phrases (such as nominal phrase or verb phrase). The principal word in each cluster is called the headword. Phrases function generally as a type of one of the form classes. In **immediate constituent analysis**, sentences are divided into their principal parts or immediate constituents. Each of these is then divided and subdivided until the ultimate constituents are reached. One can identify structure and function at each cut.

Sometimes **sentence formulas** are used. For form class words, numbers are used, and for function words, letters are used. Basic sentence types are as follows: *1–2, 1-2-3, 1-2-1, 1-2-1-1*. An example of a sentence formula with function words added might look like *D-3-1-A-2-D-3-1-3-1-P-D-1*.

Uses and Limitations of Structural Grammar

Structural grammar has some advantages.

- Structural grammar is good for identifying the four main parts of speech. It is more objective, concrete, and descriptive than traditional grammar. Using the structural grammar "clues" and basic sentence patterns, one can identify nouns, verbs, adjectives,

and adverbs, even when they are "nonsense words." An example is the following nonsense sentence.
- *"The clodopty jillinglies fringeled a peducky on the zinction after an epituldum."*

Using structural grammar, one can tell that *"clodopty"* is an adjective, that *"jillinglies," "peducky," "zinction,"* and *"epituldum"* are nouns, and that *"fringeled"* is a verb.

- Structural grammar is good for understanding English as a distinct language, how it works, the word order of sentences, the inflections, and the relationships among the words and phrases.

- One can use structural grammar concepts in phonology and morphology to study ideolects and dialects.

- The inductive approach is a valid method of scientific study.

- One can use the sentence patterns for writing style.

- The descriptive approach is good for teaching. It does not make moral judgments about language use.

However, it does have limitations.

- It is limited to observable data.

- Using terms such as *"form class I words"* goes too far in an effort to reject traditional grammar; there is no reason not to use *"noun."*

- Structural grammar ignores meaning. It does not address the problems with a sentence such as "The house is painting a picture."

Transformational Grammar Theory

Description of Transformational Grammar

Transformational grammar is most often associated with Noam Chomsky, who found structuralism to be too limited. He believed that humans are "wired" for language, having an innate grammar ability, which enables them to naturally acquire a language code. **Competence** is the native speaker's knowledge and understanding of how the language works (conscious or unconscious), whereas **performance** is the production of sentences at any given time, which may show flaws. Therefore, grammar study looks at a speaker's competence and moves one from the subconscious to the conscious level. Transformationalists have also tried to describe degrees of grammaticality, sometimes using a different grammar for different dialects.

Chomsky attempted to explain the mental processes that take place when humans use a living language. He formulated the concept of **deep structure**, the underlying relationships in a sentence, and **surface structure**, the way the meanings and relationships may be expressed in speaking or writing. (For example, *"Peter performed the medical procedure"* and *"The medical procedure was performed by Peter"* have the same deep structure but different surface structures.) Thus, this grammar theory accounted for **synonymy**, similarities of deep structure that had differing surface structures. The theory also accounted for **ambiguity,** differences in deep structure but similar surface structures. Some study has also been done on the notion of language universals (deep structure features that are fundamental facts of human cognition and language, regardless of the particular language).

Phrase Structure Rules

A set of "rules" (phrase structure rules) describe the way basic sentences are put together. Transformationalists define the word "rule" to be a description of how the language operates. It is not like the "rules" in traditional grammar, which try to dictate how a language should operate. These rules are internal, not imposed externally by a teacher.

These formulas generate sentence patterns, so the grammar is sometimes called **generative grammar.** From a finite set of rules, one can generate an infinite set of sentences. Chomsky also created a second set of formulas to transform simple sentences into a variety of more complex forms. That is where the name **transformational grammar** came from. The terms are also combined: **transformational-generative grammar.**

The **phrase structure rules** (PS rules) were designed to explain, as simply as possible, the underlying structure of simple declarative sentences. The rules use abbreviations for traditional or structural terminology (*S* for sentence, *NP* for nominal phrase, *VP* for verb phrase, *D* for determiner, *N* for noun, *t* for tense, *Aux* for auxiliary, *BE* for be-type verbs, V_T for transitive verb, V_I for intransitive verb, V_L for linking verb, etc.) and have options or choices involved (shown by braces for choices and parentheses for optional elements). The rules show order, but some rules are also recursive (a rule such as the NP rule may be used more than once in a sentence). Phrase structure rules produce basic sentences. Two sample PS rules are given below merely as examples.

Aux → t (M) (HAVE -en) (BE -ing)

$$V \longrightarrow \begin{Bmatrix} V_I \\ V_T \ NP \ (NP) \ (Av\text{-}m) \\ V_L \ \{Adj\} \ \{NP\} \\ Vh \ NP \end{Bmatrix}$$

Phrase markers (tree diagrams) demonstrate the order and relationships between the parts of the sentence.

Syntactic Features

Transformational theory also involves **subcategorization of nouns, verbs, adverbs, and adjectives** to explain how these words are used. For example, transitive verbs were subcategorized into Vc (for "consider"-type verbs) and Vg (for "give"-type verbs). These verbs will be explained later in this textbook. Another subcategory that has been used for verbs is Vh, for "have" verbs. Also, verb particles are included in the verb cluster. Nouns also had to be subcategorized since all nouns do not fit into the nominal phrase locations. For example, one cannot say, *"The taco ate the child."*

Adjectives also had to be subcategorized to account for contextual considerations. For example, a painting can be fascinating to an artist, but the artist cannot be fascinating to a painting. Even adverbs are subcategorized. For example, some adverbs of manner (which answer "how") aren't used with some verbs *("the teacher has a notebook quietly")*. Also, one can say, *"The grocer weighed the produce carefully"* but not

Introduction to Grammar Study 21

"The man weighed 180 pounds carefully." Subcategorization problems were solved in part by the **syntactic feature** method.

Lexical insertion is putting in appropriate selections from the dictionary (lexicon), using distinctive features of the words. These features show the characteristics of a word that make it appropriate or inappropriate in a slot of PS rules. Simple lexical insertion following the PS rules may produce nonsense (or at least whimsical) sentences. For example, a *house* is not animate (-animate) so it can't *paint a picture* because *paint* as a verb requires an animate subject. These features are put into a **distinctive feature matrix.**

Sample Distinctive Feature Analysis

[+ Common]   girl, car, anger, mush, dog, love
[- Common]   Dr. Black, Los Angeles, France
[+ Count]   book, pen, man, cat
[- Count]   sand, love, mush, joy
[+ Abstract]   love, honesty, fear, hope
[- Abstract]   girl, pizza, sand, freckles
[+ Animate]   dog, girl, princess, president
[- Animate]   rock, roof, lake, paper
[+ Human]   dad, brother, aunt, stranger
[- Human]   chicken, elephant, goose, pig
[+ Masculine] ram, father, grandpa, rooster, bull
[- Masculine]   woman, mother, ewe, mare

Some of the features are redundant. One might leave out some features that are unnecessarily repetitive. For example, all [+ Count] nouns are [+Common] and all [+ Human] nouns are [+ Animate] and [- Abstract]. After eliminating redundancy, the noun *girl* would be

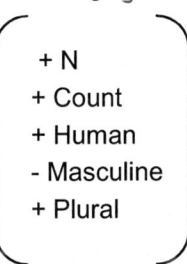

$$\left\{ \begin{array}{c} + N \\ + \text{Count} \\ + \text{Human} \\ - \text{Masculine} \\ + \text{Plural} \end{array} \right\}$$

One can also make a syntactic feature matrix for determiners. Notice the samples which follow.

The	A	Some	This	That	These	Those
+ Det	+ Det	+ Det	+ Det	+ Det	+ Det	+ Det
+ Def	- Def	- Def	+ Def	+ Def	+ Def	+ Def
- Dem	- Dem	+ Dem	+ Dem	+ Dem	+ Dem	+ Dem
	- Plural		- Plural	- Plural	+ Plural	+ Plural
			+ near		+ near	

	a girl			these boys	
+ N			+ N		
+ Common			+ Common		
+ Count			+ Count		
- Abstract		+ Det	- Abstract		+ Det
+ Animate		- Def	+ Animate		+ Dem
+ Human		- Dem	+ Human		+ Near
- Masculine			+ Masculine		
- Plural			+ Plural		

Transformations

Transformations modify a sentence's underlying structure in a specific way. They add or combine, delete, substitute, and reorder. Transformations are indicated by a double-shafted transformation arrow. The transformation rule notations are difficult to interpret without training. For example, the transformation that creates the passive would be as follows.

NP1 Aux Vt NP2 => NPs Aux *be* -en Vt by NP1

Heidi cooked Thanksgiving dinner.
Thanksgiving dinner was cooked by Heidi.

Other examples include transformations that move adverbs, create questions, create contractions, create a command, create lists of items, or create and insert relative clauses, adverb clauses, appositives, gerunds, noun clauses, infinitives, and participial phrases. A few transformations are illustrated with the sentences below.

The troll crossed the bridge slowly.	
The troll slowly crossed the bridge.	Transformation to Move Adverb
Did the troll cross the bridge slowly?	Yes/No Question Transformation
The troll didn't cross the bridge slowly.	Negative Transformation
The troll does cross the bridge.	Emphasis Transformation
What does the troll cross?	Wh-Question Transformation

The troll fought a giant.	
The troll fought a giant to recover the treasure.	Infinitive Formation Transformation
The troll fought a giant when he recovered the treasure.	Adverb Clause Formation Transformation
The troll who fought a giant recovered the treasure.	Relative Clause Formation Transformation
Fighting the giant was important to the troll.	Gerund Phrase Formation Transformation
That he fought the giant was important to the troll.	Nominal Clause Formation Transformation

Some transformations are **context sensitive.** For example, some pronouns are only used in "object" positions (*me, him, her,* and *us*), and reflexive pronouns are used after a transitive verb when the subject matches the direct or indirect object (*"The hunter shot himself in the foot"* rather than *"The hunter shot the hunter in the foot"*).

Most transformations are **optional,** but some transformations are **obligatory** under certain conditions. For example, if one has a sentence such as *"The operator looked up the phone number in the directory,"* the verb particle (*up*) can be moved in an optional transformation: *"The operator looked the phone number up in the directory."* However, the transformation is obligatory if the direct object is a pronoun: *"The operator looked it up in the directory."* **Single-base transformations,** such as the verb particle moving in the sentences above, involve one sentence. **Double-base (or multiple-base) transformations** involve embedding. Finally, some transformations need to be done in a certain order.

Uses and Limitations of Transformational Grammar

The emphasis on a native speaker's previous knowledge can be used while teaching native speakers of English; a teacher can use this innate knowledge as a base. However, the greatest use of transformational grammar has been for teaching creativity and sentence style. Transformational grammar has been used as the basis for **sentence combining** exercises to improve sentence style. This helps writers with variation and fluency in their writing. Transformational grammar can also be used to teach students to build cumulative sentences by adding and modifying material.

However, the PS rules are not particularly helpful to students, and students find the notion of transformations confusing. Even Chomsky has departed from the concepts of deep structure and transformations, now emphasizing universal grammar and grammar as a function of the brain.

Some Contemporary Approaches

Beginning in the 1980's, linguists began to criticize transformational grammar, saying, for example, that the rules don't account for the errors people make and that it is a big and not necessarily correct assumption that people induce rules based on the language data they receive. New theorists have emerged.

For example, some linguists are particularly interested in how language is acquired, saying that we learn language by matching, similar to the way we learn animal species ("if it barks like a dog and walks like a dog, it must be a dog "). We compare and match new information with old. In learning syntax, children don't induce rules; they identify a pattern. Therefore, grammar is not a set of rules that govern mental operations. Instead, we associate new language encounters with the old. These grammarians emphasize language environment. Our previous encounters with language affect our current uses, and we in turn affect the language of those around us. Language is not an isolated activity; it is interacting with others.

Cognitive grammarians study thinking and language function, and semanticists think that semantics (study of meanings of utterances and written text), rather than syntax (sentence structure), is the most fundamental aspect of human language. Therefore, they study semantics and semantic relationships rather than syntax and syntactic relations.

These linguists propose theories about how language works and how it is acquired. Therefore, they are not focusing on new sentence diagrams, new classifications, or new analysis systems.

A Modern Melding

As is obvious in the account above, the approach to grammar study and even the definitions of grammar study have varied widely.

At this point in the long tradition of grammar study comes this textbook. While acknowledging the validity of phonology and morphology, in this study we will look at words as the basic parts of the English language and focus on syntax (sentences) in English. Our goal in this textbook is not to follow any particular grammar theory and not to speculate on topics such as language acquisition. Rather, our primary goal is to attempt to explain the sentences in English that we use and find around us. Our goal in this textbook, as readers, writers, and future teachers, is to understand sentences in English, to be more effective language users ourselves, and to be able to help others become more proficient language users. Therefore, for this study, we will use a melding of any useful aspects of any of the approaches to grammar study along with some original ideas that seem to explain the sentences we find.

Practice

Part I: Traditional Grammar

Do the traditional grammar exercises included in this chapter. Were you, as a college student (perhaps majoring in English or some type of English Education), able to do the exercises well? How did you feel as you did these? Give your analysis of this approach.

Part II: Structural Grammar

Give a sentence that matches these formulas.

1. 1-2-3
2. D-1-A-2-D-3-1
3. D-3-1-A-2-D-3-1-3-1-P-D-1
4. 3-1-2-4
5. ~~4-D-2-1-2-D-1~~
   4-D-3-1-2-D-1

Part III: Transformational Grammar

1. Do a distinctive feature analysis of the following:
   a. those girls
   b. these roosters
   c. the desk

2. Look at the list of examples of transformations in this chapter.
   - Transformation to move adverb
   - Yes/no question transformation
   - Negative transformation
   - Emphasis transformation
   - Wh-question transformation
   - Infinitive formation transformation
   - Adverb clause formation transformation
   - Relative clause formation transformation
   - Gerund phrase formation transformation
   - Nominal clause formation transformation

Try at least 5 of these transformations using the basic sentence below. You will need to add words to do some of the transformations.

The girl threw a ball with power.

3. Give an example of a context-sensitive transformation.

Chapter 2
Basic Grammar Categories

All of these structures will be examined in more detail in later chapters. Our purpose here is to take an initial look at the four basic grammar functions (nominal, verb, adjective, and adverb) and prepositions. In this chapter, we are identifying characteristics of the basic structures that do these functions, sometimes called **parts of speech**. However, words should never be labeled as one of these parts of speech apart from their use in a sentence. Some words can fall into more than one of these categories, depending upon the use.

Nominals

In grammar, a nominal is a noun or a group of words that functions as a noun. Common noun functions include subject, predicate nominative, direct object, indirect object, and object of the preposition. In later chapters, we will look at these functions and at more complicated structures that have a noun function. Our purpose here is to see the characteristics of nouns and pronouns themselves.

Noun Suffixes

One possible indicator of nouns can be the suffixes. Certain suffixes may be added to "base" words to create nouns. Some of these suffixes are listed below.

Derivational Suffix	Example
-ster	youngster
-ment	government
-tion	imagination
-ness	goodness
-er, -or	governor, teacher
-ity	superficiality

Determiners with Nouns

The best indicator of a noun is that it may be preceded by a determiner. In English, we have five types of determiners: articles, demonstratives, possessive pronouns, quantifiers, and genitive nouns. If one of these can be put in front of a word, that word is functioning in that sentence as a noun. Lists of the five types of determiners follow. Note, determiners are not used in front of pronouns or many other nominal structures. However, they are a clue for nouns.

Determiner Quantifiers (Quant)
(representative list)
most   some   any   no
each   every   either   many
neither   few   several   all
more   enough   much   another

Articles (Art)
a
an
the

Demonstratives (Dem)
this
that
these
those

Possessive Pronouns (Poss)
my, your, his, her,
our, their, its

Genitive Noun (GenN)

This stands for genitive (possessive) noun. It can be either a proper noun (Peter's) or a common noun (the tall man's). Look for a noun with an apostrophe (usually *'s,* sometimes *s'*).

Noun Inflections

In English, nouns are inflected (changed to add meaning) to show plurality and possession. Sometimes the noun has an irregular inflection for plural.

Regular Inflection of a Noun		Sample Irregular Inflection	
Base Word	girl	Base Word	child
Plural	girls	Plural	children
Possessive	girl's	Possessive	child's
Plural Possessive	girls'	Plural Possessive	children's

Basic Grammar Categories

Noun Test Frames

A "test frame" can be used to help determine if a word is acting as a noun. If a word or group of words makes sense in the blank of the following sentences, it is acting as a noun.

"The ____ is here."   "These ____ are here."

Nominal Pronouns

Some pronouns are like nouns in that they perform similar functions in the sentence (subject or direct object, for example.) Pronouns that can be considered nominals are illustrated below. Since there is a finite number of pronouns in English, and since we are not adding new pronouns to our language (as we do with nouns), the best way to learn pronouns is simply to learn the lists, rather than to look for other characteristics.

Types of Pronouns

Personal Pronouns : Pro$_P$

she	he	it	they	I	we	her	him	them	me
us	you	one*	(*Sometimes used as a personal pronoun)						

Reflexive Pronouns: Pro$_{REF}$
(These end in *–self* or *-selves*.)

myself	ourselves
itself	yourself
yourselves	herself
himself	themselves

Demonstrative Pronouns: Pro$_{DEM}$

This is the same list as the demonstrative determiners. However, if the word is acting as a determiner, it comes *before* the noun. If the word is acting as a demonstrative pronoun, it **is** the nominal.

| this | that | these | those |

Indefinite Pronouns: Pro_IND						
everybody	anyone	anybody	someone	nobody		something
anything	everything	nothing	no one	another		somebody

Quantifier Pronouns : Pro_Q

This is the same list as the determiner quantifiers. However, if the word is acting as a determiner, it comes *before* the noun. If the word is acting as a quantifier pronoun (Pro_Q), it *is* the nominal. This is a representative list.

most	some	any	no	each
every	neither	many	few	several
all	either	enough	more	much

Pronoun Inflections

Personal pronouns are inflected for number (plurality) and possessive case, but they are also inflected for gender and subject and object cases. Indefinite pronouns are inflected like nouns for possession.

	Subject Forms			Object Forms		
Singular	it she he	I	you	it her him	me	you
Plural	they	we	you	them	us	you

Verbs

Verb Inflections

Perhaps the best test to see if a word is acting as a verb is to try inflecting (changing) it.

A regular verb in English can take five forms. This can be illustrated with the verb *give: give, gives, gave, giving, given*. Of course, there are irregular verbs in English as well. Some of the irregular forms follow some patterns; for example, the passive participle form may be the same as the past form, as in *walk, walks, walked, walking, walked*. However, for the most part, these irregular forms must simply be learned.

Basic Grammar Categories

Conjugation and Verb Test Frames

Generally, to test if a word is a verb, try conjugating it to convey present or past. Putting the word in the blank, say,

"Today they _____."
" Yesterday they _____."

If the word can't be inflected in this way and make sense, it isn't a verb.

Test frames may also be useful in identifying a verb. If a word or group of words makes sense in the blank of one of these test frames, it is probably being used as a verb. You would need to try all of these test frames since certain types of verbs would go into only one of them.

"The creature(s) _____ something."
"The creature(s) _____ friendly."
"The creature(s) _____."

Auxiliaries with Verbs

Another test for a verb might be to see if it <u>has or could</u> have auxiliaries. Just as nouns may be preceded by determiners, verbs may be accompanied by auxiliaries. A complete discussion of these is in Chapter 6, but the list below can be used as "verb markers." If a word has or could have one or more of these words directly in front of it, it is being used as a verb. However, a verb need not have an auxiliary. English verbs indicate simple present and past tense without auxiliaries.

Some words that Can Function as Auxiliaries

can	could	shall	should	will	would	may	might	must	has
have	had	be	been	is	was	were	are	am	

Verb Affixes

There are a few suffixes and prefixes that signal that a word is being used as a verb. Some examples are given in the chart which follows.

Derivational Affix	Example
-ate	accentuate
-ize	itemize
-fy	quantify
en-	enclose
-en	strengthen

Adjectives

Adjective Test Frame

Adjectives are sometimes called "describing words." They are used in English sentences to add descriptive detail to a nominal. They can stand alone as predicate adjectives, or they are attached in some way to a nominal structure. If a word makes sense in either blank of this test frame, the word is an adjective.

"The _____ creature was very _____."

Qualifiers with Adjectives

Words which may "signal" adjectives are qualifiers, such as *very*. The qualifier comes in front of the adjective. However, qualifiers are also used in front of adverbs, so inserting a qualifier signals that a word is either an adjective or an adverb.

Adjective Suffixes

There are some suffixes that provide "adjective clues." Some of these are given in the following chart.

Suffix	Example	Suffix	Example
-y	pretty	-(i)al	congenial
-ic	frantic	-ish	skittish
-ous	ridiculous	-able	amenable
-less	joyless	-ive	responsive
-ent	prudent	-ful	fruitful

Adjective Inflections

Adjectives are inflected for comparative and superlative degrees. The regular pattern for this uses –er and –est (*happy, happier, happiest*), but we also use *more* and *most* in front of some adjectives to signal comparative and superlative (*more responsive, most responsive*). The same patterns of inflections are used in English for adverbs.

Adverbs

Qualifiers with Adverbs

Words which may "signal" single-word adverbs are qualifiers, such as *very*, which may come before adverbs. However, as noted above, qualifiers are also used before adjectives.

Adverb Suffixes

There are a few suffixes that can signal a single-word adverb.

Suffix	Example
-ly	bravely
-ward	heavenward

However, even "-*ly*" (the most commonly given adverb suffix) can also be found on an adjective (*lovely*). Therefore, affixes are not a very reliable test for adverbs.

Adverb Test Frame and Adverb Mobility

A test frame for adverbs is below. If a word or group of words could fit in that blank, it is acting as an adverb.

"The creature did it _____."

Another possible indicator of an adverb is that it might be able to be moved to another location in the sentence without changing the meaning. Nominals, verbs, and adjectives do not "travel" in this way, but **adverb phrases are highly mobile.** They can appear almost anywhere in the sentence.

*He cleared the table and washed the dishes **efficiently**.*
*He **efficiently** cleared the table and washed the dishes.*
***Efficiently**, he cleared the table and washed the dishes.*

Adverb Questions

The best indicator that a word or group of words is acting as an adverb is that it will answer an adverb question. Below is a chart of most of the adverb questions. This is not a complete list, and you can often argue that an adverb could be labeled more than one way. Notice that an adverb can be a word or a group of words.

ADVERB QUESTION	ADVERB LABEL	EXAMPLE
How?	Adverb of manner	swiftly
When?	Adverb of time	in the afternoon
Where?	Adverb of place	at the lake
Why?	Adverb of reason	to restore order
Through what means?	Adverb of means	with his talent for flying
To what extent?	Adverb of extent	throughout the galaxy
How often?	Adverb of frequency	frequently
How far?	Adverb of distance	for seven miles
Under what condition?	Adverb of condition	with a shortage of food
To whom? To what?	Adverb of recipient	to the best singer
How long?	Adverb of duration	for several days
With what instrument?	Adverb of instrument	with a snow blower
By whom?	Adverb of agency	by the committee
With whom?	Adverb of association	with the rest of the clowns
From where?	Adverb of origin	from Minneapolis
From whom or what?	Adverb of source	from my parents
In what order?	Adverb of order	first
Compared to what?	Adverb of comparison	quicker than the turtle
To where?	Adverb of destination	to England
In what direction?	Adverb of direction	forward, to the left
How near or far?	Adverb of proximity	close to the garage

Basic Grammar Categories

Adverb Inflections

Single-word adverbs can be inflected for the comparative form and superlative form as adjectives are (*carefully, more carefully* and *fast, faster*). Therefore, this test would indicate either an adverb or an adjective.

Prepositional Phrases

Prepositional phrases will have either an adjectival or adverbial function, and therefore, they do not constitute a separate category of grammatical function. However, they are included in this chapter because sentences in English often have prepositional phrases (some languages do not have prepositional phrases at all), and it is helpful to be able to identify prepositional phrases from the beginning of a study of English. Prepositional phrases begin with a preposition and end with some type of nominal.

Common Prepositions					
about	above	across	after	against	among
around	as*	at	before	behind	below
beneath	beside	between	beyond	by	despite
down	during	except	for*	from	in
including	inside	into	like	near	of
off	on	out	outside	over	past
since	throughout	through	to	toward	up
upon	under	with	without		
* These words are sometimes used as prepositions.					

Sometimes a cluster of words acts together as a preposition.

Some Cluster Prepositions		
except for	in regards to	in spite of
as far as	instead of	next to
outside of	out of	

The important part of identifying prepositional phrases for students and writers is that neither the subject nor the verb will be in a prepositional phrase. When students are trying to make sure that subjects and verbs match in number, they should ignore all prepositional phrases.

Words Changing Categories

Remember, specific words could be in more than one category. For example, *run* seems like a typical verb, but it can be a noun, as it is in the context of a baseball game: *she scored a run in the second inning.* Sometimes a word such as *progress* is pronounced differently if it is a noun than if it is used as a verb. A word such as *convict* has a different syllable stressed if it is used as a verb than if it is used as a noun. The word *down* can be used in a variety of ways:

- *I went down the street.* (a preposition)
- *The football team ran the ball for the first down.* (a noun)
- *The quarterback downed the ball.* (a verb)
- *Not knowing the language was the down side.* (an adjective)
- *We looked down.* (an adverb)

Particularly in informal usage, we coin new words by using a word in a different grammatical way. Therefore, words should never be analyzed for their category apart from use in a sentence.

Grammar Categories and Style

Writers can manipulate their style by paying attention to their usage of words in these basic categories. For example, consider these sentences, which convey much the same information in different ways. Pay particular attention to the form of the root word *amaze*.
- *The lion's roar amazed the children.* (used as a verb)
- *The children heard the amazing lion's roar.* (used as an adjective)
- *The amazement of the children at the lion's roar was obvious.* (used as a noun)

In the first sentence, the emphasis is on the children, and the second sentence changes the emphasis to the roar itself, not the response of the children. So, expressing concepts using different grammar categories can change the emphasis. The third sentence uses the noun form and tends to make the sentence more abstract and definitely longer, maybe more formal. Notice that in this third version, there are two prepositional phrases added, and the verb is linking (without much meaning in itself). When verbs carry more of the meaning, the writing style tends to be more direct and active.

Basic Grammar Categories

Practice

I. Short Answer

1. Identify which grammar function(s) each of these "clues" identifies: noun, verb, adjective, or adverb.
    a) Fit this test frame: "*The creature _____ something.*"
    b) Can make use of *more* and *most* for compound comparative and superlative degrees
    c) Have suffixes such as *–y, –c, –ous*
    d) Have suffixes such as *-ment, -tion,* and *–ness*
    e) Can generally be moved to another location in the sentence
    f) Can be preceded by a determiner
    g) Can be changed into present and past tense
    h) Can be preceded by auxiliaries
    i) Answer questions such as *How? When? Where? Why?*

2. Which do you consider to be the best "clue" or "clues" for each of the following? Write out explanations of the clues as if you were teaching them to someone else.
    a) nouns — determiners (art, dem, quant, poss, genN)
    b) verbs — inflecting
    c) adjectives
    d) adverbs

3. What is the best way to learn prepositions, pronouns, and determiners?

II. Converting to other categories.
Convert each of these words to other categories by adding suffixes or prefixes. See if there is a form for each of the categories (noun, verb, adjective, and adverb). List each form and label the category for each, including the one listed.

   a) active
   b) work
   c) stupid
   d) add
   e) light
   f) magnet
   g) code

h) weak
i) destroy
j) sympathy

III. Prepositional phrases. Put parentheses around each prepositional phrase. (Remember that the subject and the verb are not going to be found in a prepositional phrase.)

1. I expected a poke (in the ribs) (from my brother).
2. Most people speak (without thinking).
3. (During that decade), the greatest threat was the American passion (for urban development).
4. The fog (of cigarette smoke and stale beer) encompassed the usual Wednesday crowd (at their favorite table) (in the middle) (of the bar).
5. The craze (for Native American art) became very popular (among the North Oaks crowd).
6. You contribute money (to the account) (in regular payments).
7. (Like humans), chimps get malaria and pneumonia (from parasites).
8. (Throughout the 56 years) (since the attacks), critics, scholars and members (of the public) scrutinized the decision (under the magnifying glasses) (of hindsight and revisionism).
9. The murderer evaded capture (for five long years) (in the woods) (of western North Carolina).
10. Part (of the pattern) (of his behavior) (with his friends) was telling the punch line (to the joke).

IV. Adverbs. Identify each adverb in these sentences with the <u>adverb question</u> that it answers. List the adverb phrase in one column and the adverb question across from it. Note, some adverb phrases are embedded within another adverb phrase. Watch for this and list them all.

1. I expected a kiss <u>on the cheek</u> <u>from my sister</u>.
2. That international spy dressed <u>in jeans</u> <u>to remain inconspicuous</u>.
3. We are here to learn English grammar.
4. Her son ran the marathon <u>very consistently</u>.
5. She purchased the gown <u>to look elegant</u>.
6. Most people speak <u>without thinking</u>.

Basic Grammar Categories

7. Several soldiers gave their lives to protect our country during the war.
8. The six sailors struggle to survive a violent storm among the whitecaps.
9. Throughout that century, typhoid fever, cholera, botulism, and trichinosis were common.
10. To finance his re-election campaign, the mayor made some questionable deals.
11. We look forward to the coming years and the changes in activities.
12. I went outside to walk the dog.
13. You make spreadsheets for the marketing department with that software.
14. With its island facility, Lion Country provided the chimps sanctuary for years.
15. Ryan ran the race to show his speed and agility.
16. By the next day, her mother disguised herself differently.
17. The judges chose Daisy to represent the country at the international competition.
18. To thank him for his kindness, Sage sent Tom a note.
19. Here the villagers learn healing from the jungle medicine men.
20. Like humans, chimps get malaria and pneumonia from parasites.
21. The orange and yellow leaves fell fast during the autumn months.
22. The new president later added difficulty to an already complex situation.
23. Dr. Humania went far into the jungle for ten years to research monkeys.
24. All summer, they ride bikes to save the environment.
25. Women served well in combat positions in the Balkans and the Middle East.
26. To catch the thief, the police officers waited for several hours outside in the freezing cold.
27. You add honey to tea and soymilk to make a savory treat.
28. Last week, the horse ran considerably slower.
29. Yesterday, Jason cleaned the garage to receive his weekly allowance.
30. The woman washed the dishes daily to reduce the number of ants in her kitchen.

31. That extremely diligent child worked quickly to get his dying brother's approval.
32. To build endurance for next month's race, the cross-country skier increased her practice time.
33. Every year, the lions survive rather well with the droughts.
34. To feel healthy during her pregnancy, the young woman daily walked for four miles.
35. Naomi rather quickly took the elephant's picture.
36. The young boy brought the feed to the quarter horse every day.
37. Jodie, to travel with her friends, saved through the school savings plan.
38. Joachim received his violin from The National Orchestra Association.
39. The journalism majors studied to report effectively with computer technology.
40. With her efficiency and intelligence, Heidi Erickson rose to the supervisor level, despite her lack of experience.

Chapter 3
Basic Sentence Patterns

Sentences in English have two basic components: a subject and a predicate. Generally, we will begin to analyze sentences by drawing a grammar tree as shown below.

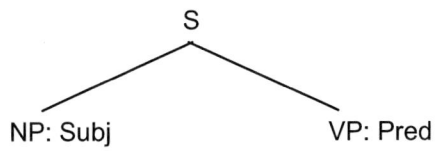

```
         S
        / \
       /   \
   NP: Subj   VP: Pred
```

The NP stands for nominal phrase. The VP stands for verb phrase. *NP:Subj* indicates that there is a nominal phrase functioning as a subject, and the *VP:Pred* indicates that there is a verb phrase functioning as a predicate. The notation in front of the colon indicates the structure. The notation after the colon indicates the function.

We will begin our study by identifying the basic patterns of sentences. These patterns are determined by the type of verb used. To show the patterns, we will be using some grammatical notation. Basic notation meaning is shown below.

⟶	Consists of
{ }	Indicates choice of elements
+	Can have more than one of these elements
( )	Indicates optional element

We identify basic sentence patterns by looking at the type of verb in the sentence and by looking at what follows the verb. In fact, to determine the type of verb in the sentence, one must look at what comes after the verb within that sentence. Each of the types will be explained below.

Linking Verbs

The first pattern has a **linking verb** (V_L). The notation which follows says that the verb phrase in this type of sentence consists of a linking verb (V_L) followed by either a nominal phrase (NP) or an adjective phrase (AdjP).

The braces indicate that there is a grammatical choice of required elements (either NP:PredN or AdjP:PredAdj). This formula also says that there could be any number of optional Adverb Phrases (AdvP) in the sentence. We will discuss adverbs later in this chapter and much more in Chapter 5.

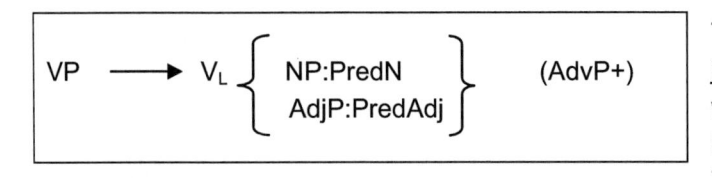

$$VP \longrightarrow V_L \begin{Bmatrix} NP:PredN \\ AdjP:PredAdj \end{Bmatrix} (AdvP+)$$

The linking verb joins the subject with an element in the predicate. This type of verb indicates a state of being. Many times the linking verb is a form of the verb *be* (*is, was, were, are, am*, etc.), but other words can also function as linking verbs if they are indicating a state of being.

Verbs that Can Function as Linking Verbs					
is	be	seem	are	being	smell
was	feel	sound	were	look	been
become	am	remain	appear	taste	stay
grow	turn				

Predicate Nominative

One structure that can follow a linking verb is a predicate nominative. The predicate nominative (nominal structure) renames the subject. It might help to think of the linking verb as an *equals* sign (=). The following are examples of sentences with linking verbs and predicate nominatives.
- *The new software is a complete publishing package.*
- *My son is a student of veterinary medicine.*
- *The college catalog remains the best guide to your classes.*
- *Corporate tax avoidance seems a complicated issue.*
- *The coaches and athletes were the heart of the program.*

Notice that in each case, the predicate nominative renames the subject.
- *The new software = a complete publishing package.*
- *My son = a student of veterinary medicine.*
- *The college catalog = the best guide to your classes.*
- *Corporate tax avoidance = a complicated issue.*
- *The coaches and athletes = the heart of the program.*

Basic Sentence Patterns

To tree sentences, you will need to divide them up into their major components. This pattern looks like the following.

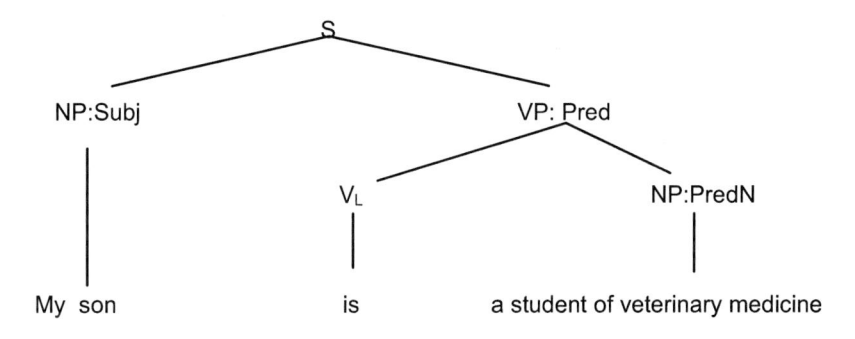

```
                         S
              _____|_____
             |                       |
          NP:Subj                 VP: Pred
             |                 _____|_____
             |                |             |
             |               V_L         NP:PredN
             |                |             |
          My son              is      a student of veterinary medicine
```

Predicate Adjective

The second structure that can follow a linking verb is a predicate adjective. The predicate adjective describes the subject. See the following examples.
- The achievement record of the team is outstanding.
- Some of the company's troubles are external.
- His apology sounded hollow.
- The toddler feels tired.
- The Justice Department's handling of the interrogation remains baffling.
- The apple cider tastes bitter.

Qualifiers

The Adjective Phrase (AdjP) can have an optional qualifier. Qualifiers can come in front of the adjective and change the adjective somewhat by intensifying it or diminishing it. Some examples include *very, rather, incredibly, really,* and *somewhat.*
- The achievement record of the team is **really** outstanding. *(Note that the qualifier is *really* not *real.*)*
- Some of the company's troubles are **somewhat** external.
- His apology sounded **incredibly** hollow.
- The toddler feels **very** tired.
- The Justice Department's handling of the interrogation remains **rather** baffling.
- The apple cider tastes **distinctly** bitter.

You would tree this type of sentence as follows.

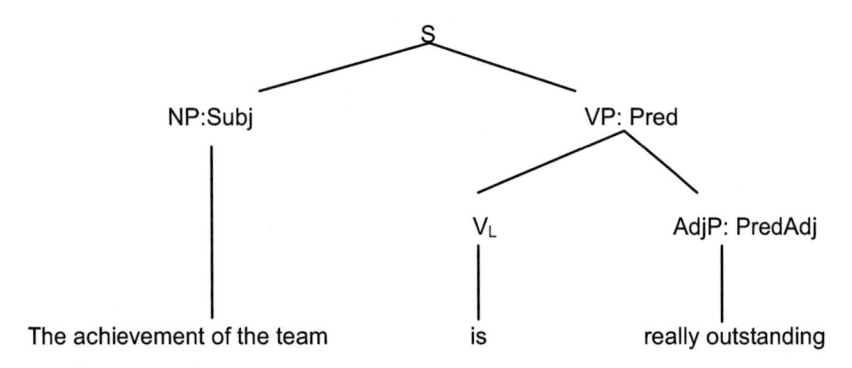

```
                    S
           ┌────────┴────────┐
        NP:Subj            VP: Pred
           │           ┌──────┴──────┐
           │           V_L        AdjP: PredAdj
           │           │             │
The achievement of the team   is    really outstanding
```

Intransitive Verbs

> VP ⟶ V_I (AdvP+)

The next sentence pattern we will look at is a subject and intransitive verb. In this type of sentence, the action is not carried to a direct object. As with the other sentence types, it can have one or more adverb phrases added. Some examples without adverb phrases are below.

- *The leaves blew.*
- *The Ents slept.*
- *The missiles exploded.*

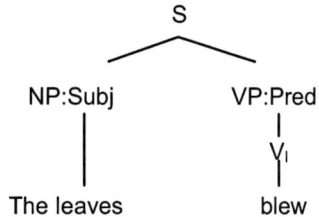

```
            S
       ┌────┴────┐
    NP:Subj    VP:Pred
       │         │
       │        V_I
       │         │
   The leaves  blew
```

Remember, adverb phrases can be single words or a group of words, often prepositional phrases. They answer adverb questions such as *where, when, how,* or *why.*

> Note: <u>Adding adverbs does not change the type of verb</u>. For purposes of figuring out the verb type, ignore the adverbs (any structure that answers questions such as *where, when, how,* or *why*).

The following sentences still have intransitive verbs even though adverb phrases have been added. The adverb phrases are in bold.

- *The leaves blew **from the trees**.*

Basic Sentence Patterns

- The Ents slept **in the old forest**.
- The missiles exploded **on the rooftop**.
- Your future is **in her hands**.
- The software industry moves **at warp speed**.

A sentence with an adverb phrase added would look like this.

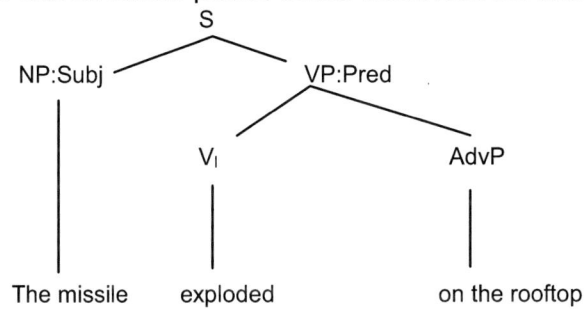

```
              S
      ┌───────┴───────┐
   NP:Subj         VP:Pred
      │          ┌────┴────┐
      │         V_I       AdvP
      │          │          │
  The missile  exploded  on the rooftop
```

Words such as *look* or *appear* can be either linking verbs or intransitive verbs, depending upon how they are used. Remember, adverb phrases (answering *where* or *when*, for example) do not affect the verb type.

Intransitive Verb V_I	Linking Verb V_L
She looked into the box.	The statue looked lumpy.
The ghost appeared at the end of the play.	The students appeared listless.

In the intransitive verb sentences, the phrases *in the box* and *at the end of the play* are both adverb phrases, so the verbs remain intransitive. The phrase *in the box* answers the adverb question *where*, and the phrases *at the end of the play* answer the adverb question *when*.

Transitive Verbs

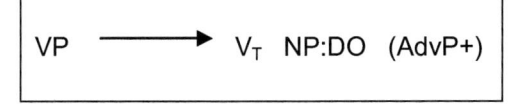

VP ⟶ V_T NP:DO (AdvP+)

In this pattern, the verb is **transitive**. It carries the action over to a **direct object**. The direct object is a nominal phrase (NP). There could be optional adverb phrases also with a transitive verb.

Many of the sentences we use in English have transitive verbs. Some examples are below.
- *The toddler picked a bunch of dandelions.*
- *The college learning center needs tutors.*
- *The anthropologist studied the isolated tribe.*
- *Bilbo took the ring of power.*

The tree for this type of sentence is shown below.

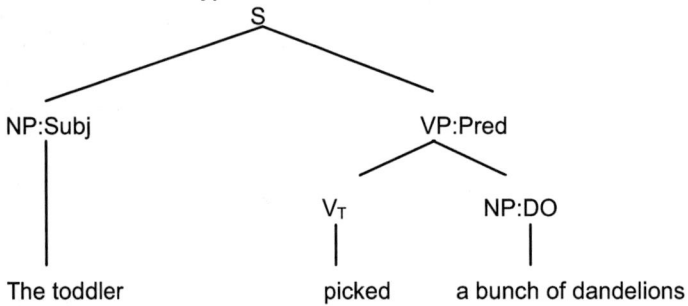

```
              S
       /            \
   NP:Subj         VP:Pred
      |           /       \
      |          V_T       NP:DO
      |          |          |
  The toddler  picked  a bunch of dandelions
```

Remember, adverb phrases may be attached to any sentence.

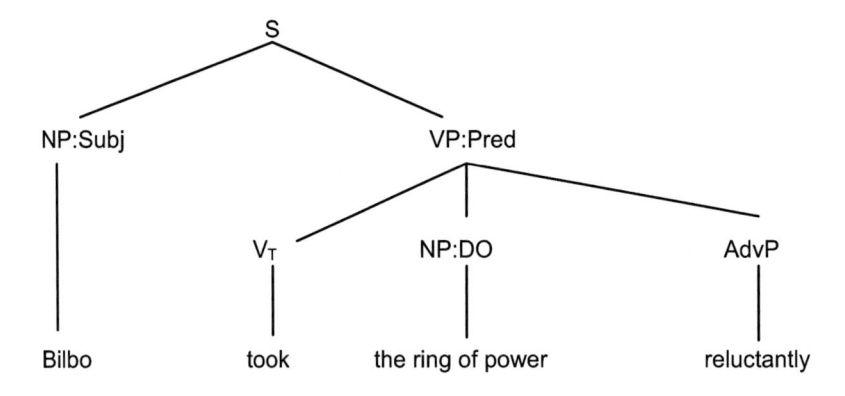

```
              S
       /            \
   NP:Subj         VP:Pred
      |        /     |       \
      |       V_T   NP:DO    AdvP
      |       |      |        |
    Bilbo   took  the ring  reluctantly
                  of power
```

Words such as *smell, sound,* or *feel* can be either linking or transitive verbs, depending upon how they are used. If they describe the subject, they are linking. If they carry the action of the subject to an object, they are transitive. Some examples are in the chart.

Basic Sentence Patterns 47

Linking Verb V_L	Transitive Verb V_T
The kitchen smelled rancid.	The child smelled the flower.
The piano sounds melodious.	The leader sounds the warning bell.
She felt exhilarated.	We felt the rough surface.

Vg Verbs Bitranstive

VP ⟶ Vg   NP:IO   NP:DO   (AdvP+)

The verb in this sentence pattern is labeled *g* for *give*. It is a type of transitive that has both an indirect object (IO) and a direct object (DO). To find these elements, you can say the verb, then ask the question *what*. The answer to the question is the direct object. Then ask *to whom, to what, for whom,* or *for what*. The answer to one of these will be the indirect object. The IO comes before the DO. See the examples for illustrations.

- *The students gave the grammar teacher chocolate candy to impress her.*

gave what?	chocolate candy	DO
to whom?	the grammar teacher	IO

Notice in the sentence above, the phrase *to impress her* is an adverb phrase.

Vg Sentence	IO	DO
The quaking scientist handed the thief a new microscope.	the thief	a new microscope
The reporter asked the egotistical actor a question.	the egotistical actor	a question
The sales manager sent that customer a five-year guarantee.	that customer	a five-year guarantee

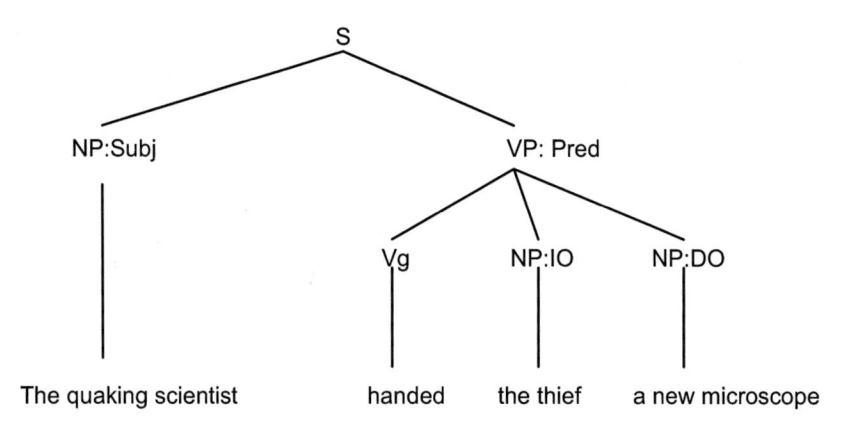

```
                        S
                  /           \
            NP:Subj           VP: Pred
               |            /    |    \
               |           Vg  NP:IO  NP:DO
               |           |    |      |
      The quaking scientist handed the thief a new microscope
```

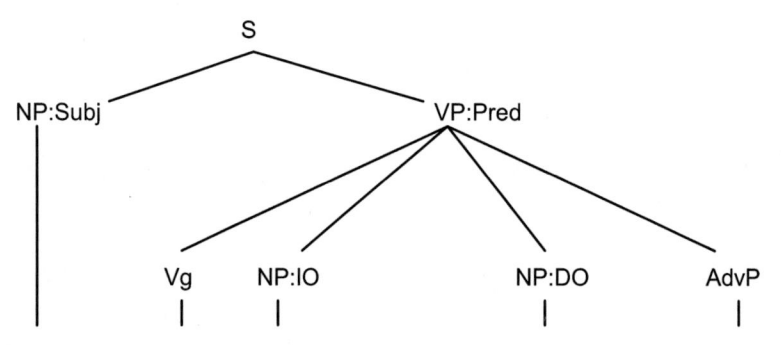

```
                        S
                  /           \
            NP:Subj           VP:Pred
               |         /   |     |      \
               |        Vg NP:IO NP:DO   AdvP
               |        |   |     |       |
       The students  gave the grammar teacher chocolate candy to impress her
```

Note: Some grammarians label some prepositional phrases indirect objects. However, I would argue that a *to* or *for* prepositional phrase that comes after the direct object is not an indirect object and does not make the verb into a Vg. This labeling is based upon the structure of the sentence, not the meaning. Remember, the IO comes before the DO.

The quaking scientist handed a new microscope **to the thief.** (V$_T$ not Vg)
The sales manager sent a five-year guarantee **to the customer.** (V$_T$ not Vg)

Vc Verbs

The verb in this sentence pattern is labeled *c* for *consider*. It is a type of transitive verb that has a direct object (DO) and an object complement (OC). The object complement completes the object and is either an NP or

Basic Sentence Patterns

an AdjP. If the object complement is an NP, it renames the direct object. If the object complement is an AdjP, it describes the direct object.

| VP ⟶ V_C NP:DO { NP:OC / AdjP:OC } (AdvP+) | To check this type out, try to insert "to be" or "to have been" |

have been" in front of the object complement (OC). The sentence should still make sense if it is a V_C type of sentence.

NP:OC

Here are some examples in which the object complement is an NP (NP:OC).
- *The sophomores elected Ophelia class president.*
- *The critics considered the song a sure hit.*
- *The press named Peter athlete of the week.*

Try the *to be/to have been* insertion test on these.
- *The sophomores elected Ophelia (to be) class president.*
- *The critics considered the song (to be) a sure hit.*
- *The press named Peter (to have been) athlete of the week.*

Notice that in these sentences, the NP:OC renames the NP:DO. In this respect, it is similar to the NP:PredN. However, the predicate nominative renames the subject of the sentence, and the nominal phrase object complement (NP:OC) renames the direct object of the sentence.
- *Ophelia = class president*
- *The song = a sure hit*
- *Peter = athlete of the week*

AdjP:OC

Here are some examples in which the object complement is an AdjP (AdjP:OC). In these cases, the AdjP:OC describes the NP:DO.
- *The young men find first dates awkward.*
- *The royal family deemed her worthy of utmost respect.*

Try the *to be/ to have been* insertion test on these.
- *The young men find first dates (to be) awkward.*
- *The royal family deemed her (to have been) worthy of utmost respect.*

Notice that the AdjP:OC is similar to the PredAdj. However, the predicate adjective describes the subject of the sentence, and the adjective phrase object complement (AdjP:OC) describes the direct object.

Here is a sample tree with an NP:OC.

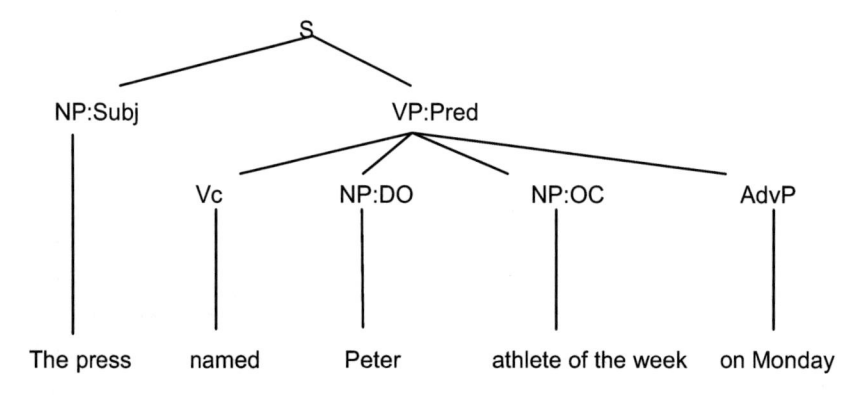

```
                            S
              ┌─────────────┴─────────────┐
           NP:Subj                     VP:Pred
              │          ┌────────┬────────┬────────┐
              │          Vc     NP:DO    NP:OC     AdvP
              │          │        │        │         │
          The press    named    Peter  athlete of  on Monday
                                        the week
```

Here is a sample tree with an AdjP: OC. This one doesn't have an AdvP.

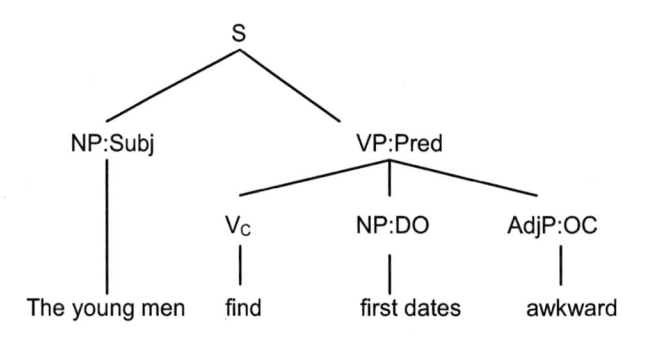

```
                       S
              ┌────────┴────────┐
           NP:Subj           VP:Pred
              │          ┌──────┼──────┐
              │          Vc   NP:DO  AdjP:OC
              │          │      │      │
        The young men   find  first  awkward
                              dates
```

Review

Look for the number of "countable elements" after the verb. Remember, adverbs (answering questions such as *when, where, why,* or *how*) don't count when you are determining the basic sentence pattern.

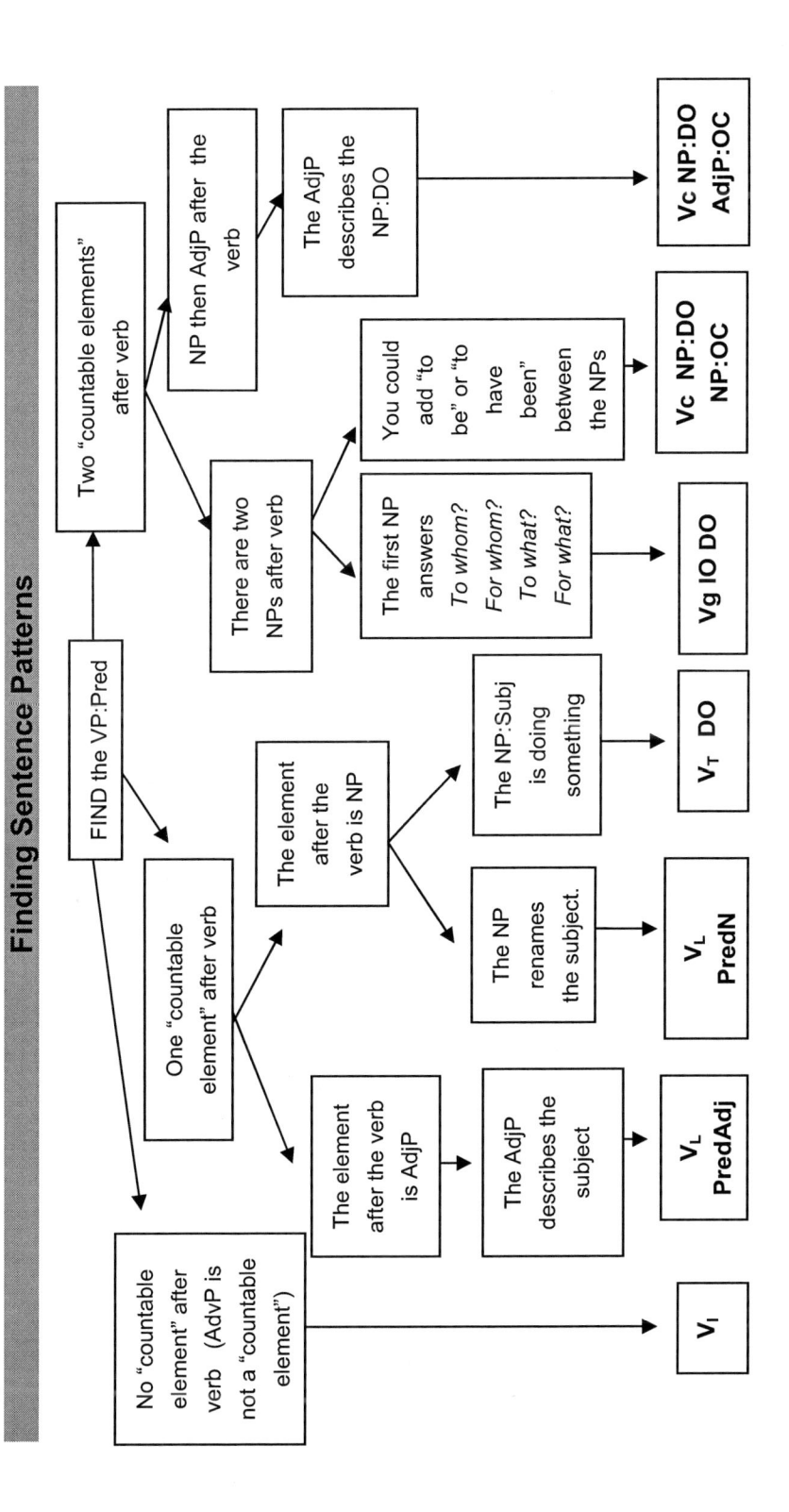

Finding Sentence Patterns

FIND the VP:Pred

- **No "countable element" after verb** (AdvP is not a "countable element") → **V_I**

- **One "countable element" after verb**
  - The element after the verb is AdjP
    - The AdjP describes the subject → **V_L PredAdj**
  - The element after the verb is NP
    - The NP renames the subject. → **V_L PredN**
    - The NP:Subj is doing something → **V_T DO**

- **Two "countable elements" after verb**
  - There are two NPs after verb
    - The first NP answers *To whom? For whom? To what? For what?* → **Vg IO DO**
    - You could add "to be" or "to have been" between the NPs → **Vc NP:DO NP:OC**
  - NP then AdjP after the verb
    - The AdjP describes the NP:DO → **Vc NP:DO AdjP:OC**

Practice Sentences

I. Tree the following sentences, showing the major elements of each sentence. Label any adverb phrases as simply AdvP. Remember, adverb phrases do not change the type of verb.

1. Her frail elderly mother remained in her house until her death.
2. We consider the spinning wheel a family heirloom.
3. Some of the construction workers punched a hole in the wall.
4. The power of the sun is very evident on radar systems.
5. The warrior sounded the alarm to warn the others.
6. The professor offered her students a place for the party.
7. That game was a challenge this morning.
8. Deb became a principal of a prominent middle school.
9. My grandpa has his own website.
10. The kind husband bought his wife an opal ring.
11. The man with a cigar twirled the pen with finesse.
12. Regret remains a waste of time.
13. The veterinary medical student fed his alligator frozen mice last week.
14. Somebody cleaned the stains from the wall.
15. Hexaba believed herself superior to all others.
16. Caffeine gave everybody insomnia throughout the night.
17. Thom found the wood duck's behavior peculiar.
18. The best proposal came from the executive council.
19. The history of modern Israel is unique.
20. The baby boomers sound somewhat older now.
21. The next generation created even more legends.
22. The bicycle delivery boys need firm guidance to remain conscientious.
23. The respected landscaper found the cold May weather incredible.
24. This skeptical novice practiced the sport of curling.
25. Brightly colored glass chips adorned the lamp in the living room.
26. The thunder rumbled during the night.
27. They called it a disaster.
28. The college student sounded rather excited during the class.
29. The anthropologist studied the isolated tribe for several years.
30. The future of technical writers appears promising.

Basic Sentence Patterns 53

31. The patient supervisor explained the procedure to the yawning worker.
32. The torch illuminated everything in the cave with its powerful beam.
33. Something felt very wrong.
34. The bedraggled woman drove herself to the hospital.
35. The killer was behind her.
36. The Victorian doctors considered the inventor insane.
37. The department believed her a hostile force.
38. The riders of Rohan joined the defense.
39. The college graduate mailed the university her grad school application this morning.
40. The handsome man went to the job interview.
41. The nasty woman is an evil presence in the village.
42. The old diplomat bequeathed his niece a substantial collection of miniature swords.
43. The book contains four of Erma Bombeck's most popular works.
44. Nothing bothered those museum guards.
45. The helicopter swerved around the building.
46. This painting is truly irreplaceable.
47. The harbor seals adorned the shoreline.
48. Nothing made a difference on the team.
49. The designer added a touch of luxury.
50. The clairvoyant seemed upset.

II. Write sentences to illustrate the basic sentence patterns. Write 3 sentences for each of the 7 patterns.

1. NP:Subj   Linking Verb   AdjP: PredAdj   (Add qualifiers to the PredAdj. Use *really* and other correct forms of qualifier.)
2. NP:Subj   Linking Verb   NP:PredN
3. NP:Subj   Intransitive Verb   (Add adverb phrases of *when, where, how,* or *why.*)
4. NP:Subj   Transitive Verb   NP:DO
5. NP:Subj   Vg   NP:IO   NP:DO
6. NP:Subj   Vc   NP:DO   NP:OC
7. NP:Subj   Vc   NP:DO   AdjP:OC

Chapter 4
Noun Clusters

As we saw in Chapter 3, nominal phrases are key components in English sentences. So far, we have seen that they can function as subjects, predicate nouns, direct objects, indirect objects, object complements or objects of prepositions. Primarily in this chapter, we will look at the elements that make up a noun cluster, the most common type of nominal phrase. Before we look at each element, notice what the diagram below is saying.

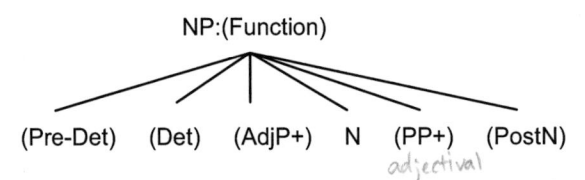

NP:(Function)

(Pre-Det) (Det) (AdjP+) N (PP+) (PostN)
                                    adjectival

In this diagram for a noun cluster, the N (noun or noun substitute) is required. All of the other elements are in parentheses, indicating that they are optional. However, they will appear in this order if they are present. Also, the formula tells us that there could be more than one adjective phrase (AdjP+), and there could be more than one prepositional phrase (PP+) in the noun cluster.

Remember, in a grammar tree we indicate the function of the NP after the colon (NP:Subj, NP:PredN, NP:DO, NP:IO, NP:OC, for example).

Determiners

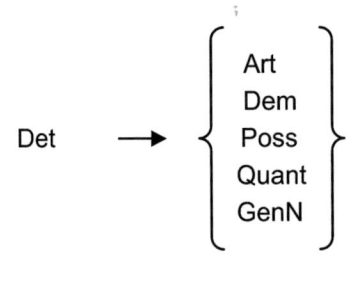

Det ⟶ { Art, Dem, Poss, Quant, GenN }

The determiner (Det) of a nominal phrase could be any of five types of determiner. Notice the braces indicate a choice. However, if there is a determiner, there is only <u>one</u> determiner for each distinct NP. (Notice that in the formula above, there is no + after the Det.) The five types of determiners follow.

Noun Clusters

Determiner Quantifiers (Quant)
(representative list)
most   some   any   no
each   every   either   many
neither few   several all
more   enough much   another

Articles (Art)
a
an
the

Demonstratives (Dem)
this
that
these
those

Possessive Pronouns (Poss)
my, your, his, her,
our, their, its

Genitive Noun (GenN)
This stands for genitive (possessive) noun. It can be either a proper noun (Peter's) or a common noun (the tall man's). Look for a noun with an apostrophe (usually *'s;* sometimes *s'*).

In each of the five cases, you draw a line from the NP to the determiner and then label the type of determiner. The GenN will take some additional labeling. Treeing GenN determiners is illustrated later in this chapter.

Adjective Phrases

The adjective phrase (AdjP) comes before the noun, and there could be more than one adjective phrase in the NP. (Notice the + in the diagram in the beginning of the chapter.) The AdjP comes after the determiner and before the N. There are three options for the adjective phrase, as indicated by the formula below.

$$\text{AdjP} \longrightarrow \begin{Bmatrix} \text{(Qualifier) Adj} \\ \text{OrdN} \\ \text{CardN} \end{Bmatrix}$$

Notice that there are three choices for an adjective phrase before a noun. The first choice has an optional qualifier (such as *very*). The OrdN stands for ordinal number; these numbers indicate order (*first, second, third, fourth*). The CardN stands for cardinal number (*one, two, three, four*).

the very big book   *my second attempt*   *seven brothers*

```
      NP                      NP                    NP
    / | \                   / | \                  / \
  Det AdjP N              Det AdjP N             AdjP  N
   |  / \  |               |   |   |              |    |
  Art Qual Adj            Poss OrdN              CardN
   |   |   |               |   |   |              |    |
  the very big  book       my second attempt    seven brothers
```

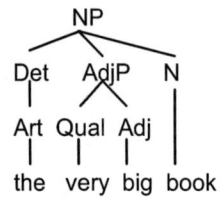

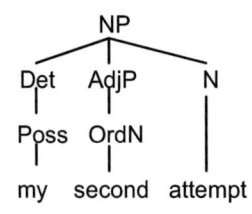

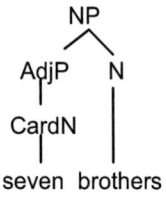

Each AdjP is a choice of one of these three, but you could have as many AdjPs before a noun as you want. Each AdjP gets a separate line down from the NP.

a rather reserved hesitant smile

```
                    NP
         /       /      \      \
       Det    AdjP      AdjP    N
        |     / \        |      |
       Art  Qual Adj    Adj     |
        |    |    |      |      |
        a  rather reserved hesitant smile
```

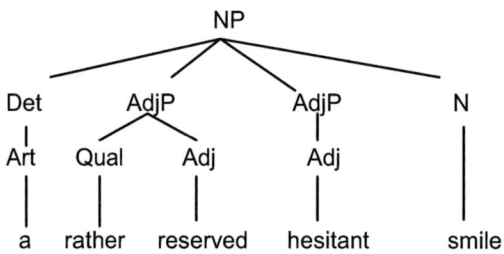

Proper Adjective

You might also have an adjective that is capitalized. We can call this a proper adjective (Adj$_{PR}$): *British* cuisine.

Nouns and Noun Substitutes

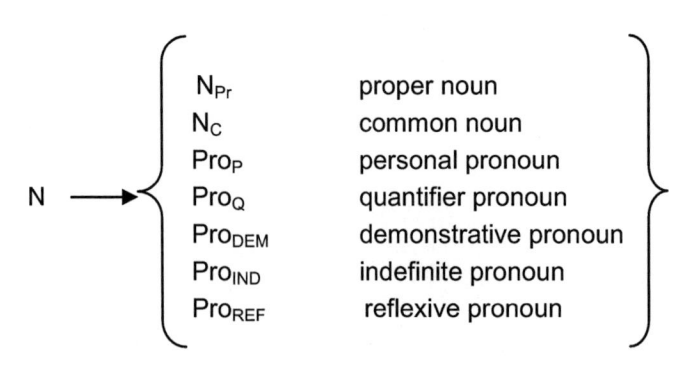

N → { N$_{Pr}$ proper noun
      N$_C$ common noun
      Pro$_P$ personal pronoun
      Pro$_Q$ quantifier pronoun
      Pro$_{DEM}$ demonstrative pronoun
      Pro$_{IND}$ indefinite pronoun
      Pro$_{REF}$ reflexive pronoun }

The N is the one required element in the noun cluster. Every noun cluster has an N. In this chapter, we will discuss seven possible types of N. The nominative pronouns were also listed in Chapter 2.

Proper Nouns / Common Nouns:
N_{PR} and N_C

These are easy to recognize. The proper nouns are capitalized and are specific names.

Personal Pronouns : Pro_P

| she | he | it | they | I | we | her | him | them | me |

us   you   one*   (*Sometimes used as a personal pronoun)

Reflexive Pronouns: Pro_{REF}
(These end in *–self* or *-selves*.)

myself	ourselves
itself	yourself
yourselves	herself
himself	themselves

Demonstrative Pronouns: Pro_{DEM}

This is the same list as the demonstrative determiners. However, if the word is acting as a determiner, it comes *before* the noun. If the word is acting as a demonstrative pronoun, it *is* the nominal.

| this | that | these | those |

Indefinite Pronouns: Pro_{IND}

everybody	anyone	anybody	someone	nobody	something
anything	everything	nothing	no one	another	somebody
everyone	others

Quantifier Pronouns : Pro_Q

This is the same list as the determiner quantifiers. However, if the word is acting as a determiner, it comes *before* the noun. If the word is acting as a quantifier pronoun (Pro_Q), it *is* the nominal. This is a representative list.

most	some	any	no	each
every	neither	many	few	several
all	either	enough	more	much

Here is an illustration of some subject NPs in the following sentences:
- *Some flying dragons breathe fire.*
- *Those are my favorite books.*
- *Everybody seems tired.*
- *They gave themselves a break.*

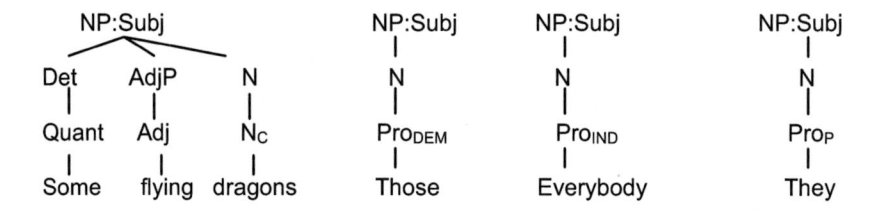

```
      NP:Subj                  NP:Subj        NP:Subj        NP:Subj
     /   |   \                    |              |              |
  Det  AdjP   N                   N              N              N
   |    |    |                    |              |              |
 Quant Adj   N_C                Pro_DEM       Pro_IND         Pro_P
   |    |    |                    |              |              |
 Some flying dragons            Those        Everybody         They
```

A note about how pronouns work in English

In the sentence, if there are two identical NPs, the second NP or the embedded NP changes to a personal pronoun or a reflexive pronoun. If there are two identical NPs in the same clause of a sentence, the second NP becomes a reflexive pronoun (*The man gave himself a party*).

Adjectival Prepositional Phrases

After the N in the NP, there could be a prepositional phrase acting as an AdjP (PP:AdjP). As we saw in an earlier chapter, prepositional phrases begin with a preposition, either a single word or a cluster of words. Tree the cluster prepositions as one unit.

Some Cluster Prepositions			
except for	in regards to	out of	in spite of
as far as	instead of	outside of	next to

Noun Clusters

Common Prepositions					
about	above	across	after	against	among
around	as*	at	before	behind	below
beneath	beside	between	beyond	by	despite
down	during	except	for*	from	in
including	inside	into	like	near	of
off	on	out	outside	over	past
since	throughout	through	to	toward	up
upon	under	with	without		

* These words are <u>sometimes</u> used as prepositions.

A prepositional phrase consists of a preposition and an NP functioning as the object of the preposition (NP:OP). An example of an NP with a prepositional phrase (PP) is below.

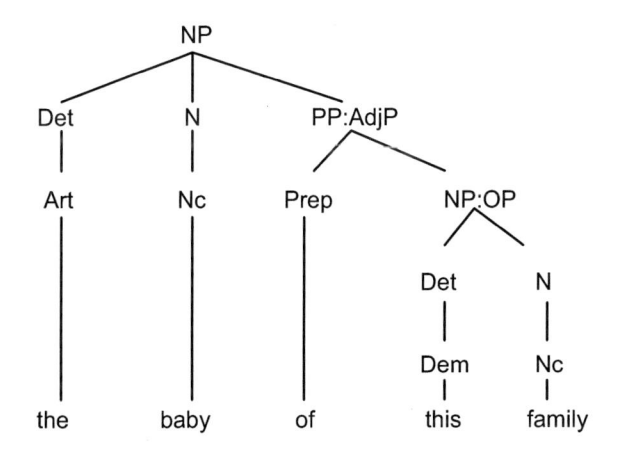

```
              NP
       _____/|_____
      Det     N       PP:AdjP
       |      |       /     \
      Art     Nc    Prep    NP:OP
       |      |      |      /   \
                           Det    N
                            |     |
                           Dem    Nc
                            |     |
      the   baby    of    this  family
```

Quantifier pronouns (ProQ) are generally followed by a prepositional phrase. Remember, quantifier pronouns are a noun substitute--a type of N. An example is below.

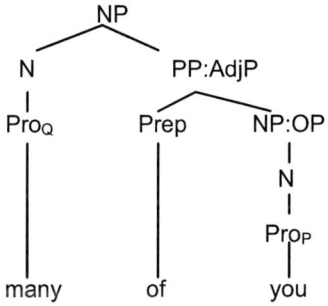

```
              NP
             /  \
            N    PP:AdjP
            |    /     \
          ProQ  Prep   NP:OP
                        |
                        N
                        |
                       ProP
                        |
          many    of   you
```

Next is an example with a cluster preposition. Notice that an adjectival prepositional phrase can come within another prepositional phrase.

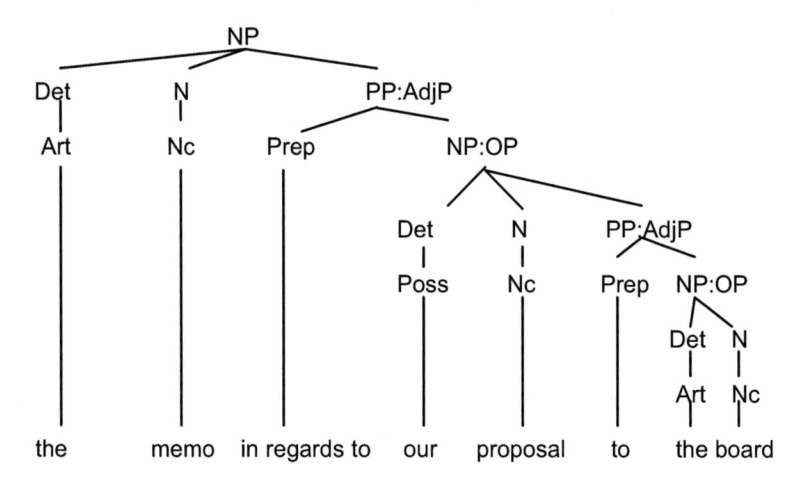

```
                         NP
      ┌──────────┬───────────┴──────┐
      Det        N              PP:AdjP
      │          │          ┌───────┴────┐
      Art        Nc         Prep       NP:OP
                                   ┌─────┼──────────┐
                                   Det   N       PP:AdjP
                                   │     │      ┌────┴────┐
                                   Poss  Nc    Prep     NP:OP
                                                       ┌──┴──┐
                                                       Det   N
                                                       │     │
                                                       Art   Nc
      │          │          │        │     │      │    │     │
      the      memo   in regards to  our  proposal to  the  board
```

Pre-Determiner and Post-Noun

Sometimes a single word precedes the determiner or follows the noun. A pre-determiner (Pre-Det) comes in the NP *all the boys.* A post-noun comes in the NP *you all*. Pre-determiners and post-nouns are generally words such as *both* and *all*. They are not very common but do appear more often in some dialects of American English.

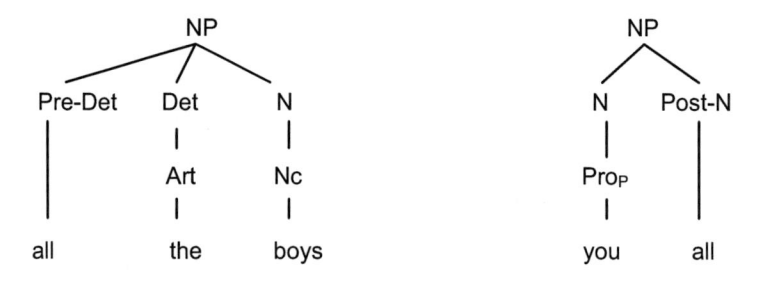

```
              NP                              NP
      ┌───────┼─────────┐             ┌───────┴───────┐
    Pre-Det  Det        N             N            Post-N
              │         │             │               │
              Art       Nc           Prₒp             │
              │         │             │               │
      all    the      boys           you             all
```

Adjectival or Nominal Groupings

Sometimes an NP functions as an AdjP.

When the AdjP is a single word, it really doesn't matter if you label it an NP:AdjP or simply as an adjective. However, if the AdjP is two or more words acting as one unit to describe an N, you must label it NP:AdjP. An

Noun Clusters

example of an **embedded NP:AdjP** is below. In this instance, the words *sea* and *turtle* work together as a unit. They are not two separate adjective phrases. Words acting as an adjective cluster before a noun are usually hyphenated.

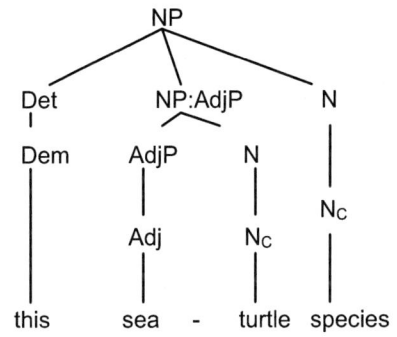

```
                    NP
         _____|_____
        |           |           |
       Det        NP:AdjP       N
        |        ___|___        |
       Dem      AdjP    N       Nc
        |        |      |       |
        |       Adj    Nc       |
        |        |      |       |
       this     sea  - turtle species
```

Notice that the NP:AdjP comes in the AdjP position between the determiner and the N. However, you must tree the structure of the NP:AdjP with its own AdjP and its own N.

Two or more words can also function as an N. In the example below (*the worst Italian hotel*), it is the group of Italian hotels that is being evaluated, and this one is the worst of that group. *Italian* and *hotel* work together as a cluster.

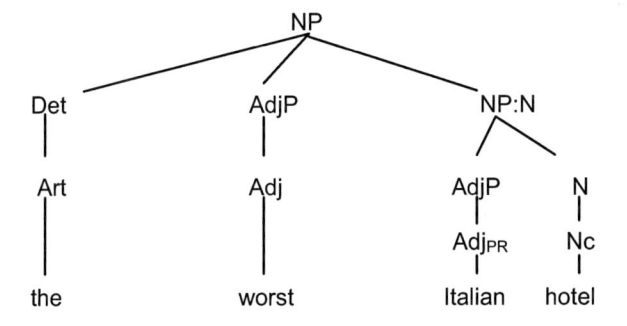

```
                    NP
         _____|_____
        |           |           |
       Det         AdjP        NP:N
        |           |         ___|___
       Art         Adj       AdjP    N
        |           |         |      |
        |           |        AdjPR  Nc
        |           |         |      |
       the        worst    Italian  hotel
```

Sometimes a hyphen is used to clear up ambiguity In a sentence such as "*He is an ancient history professor,*" how the words are grouped into a unit makes a difference in meaning. Does the professor teach ancient history or is he a really old professor of history? Treeing the sentence would clear up the meaning, of course, but to make the meaning clear in writing, one could use a hyphen to connect the adjective: *he is an ancient-history professor.*

Compounds

In English, we join like elements using coordinating conjunctions (Cjc).

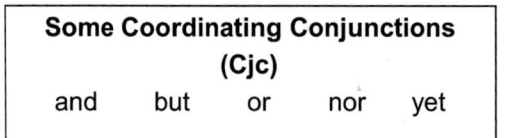

Some Coordinating Conjunctions (Cjc)
and   but   or   nor   yet

So, we could have two NPs joined by a coordinating conjunction.

the Chinese dragon and his companion

```
                    NP
         ┌──────────┼──────────┐
         NP         Cjc         NP
      ┌──┼──┐                 ┌──┴──┐
     Det AdjP  N             Det    N
      │   │    │              │     │
     Art AdjPR Nc            Poss   Nc
      │   │    │              │     │
     the Chinese dragon      and   his companion
```

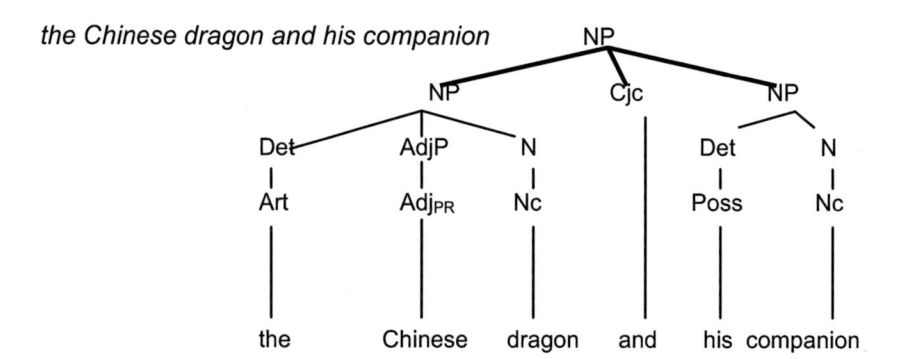

Notice, the Cjc connects two NPs under an NP. All 3 points of the Cjc triangle must match.

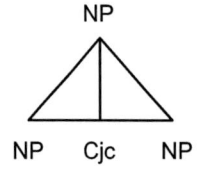

Sometimes the Cjc connects a group of items.

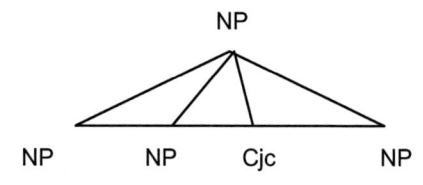

We could also join AdjPs with a Cjc.

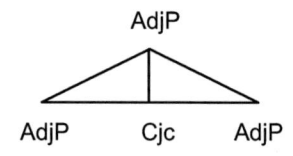

Noun Clusters

the rugged and isolated interior of the country

```
                              NP
        ┌──────────┬──────────┴──────┬─────────────────┐
       Det        AdjP               N              PP:AdjP
        │     ┌────┼────┐            │          ┌──────┴─────┐
       Art  AdjP  Cjc  AdjP          Nc        Prep       NP:OP
        │    │         │             │          │        ┌───┴──┐
        │   Adj        Adj           │          │       Det     N
        │    │         │             │          │        │      │
        │    │         │             │          │       Art     Nc
        │    │         │             │          │        │      │
       the rugged and isolated    interior       of      the  country
```

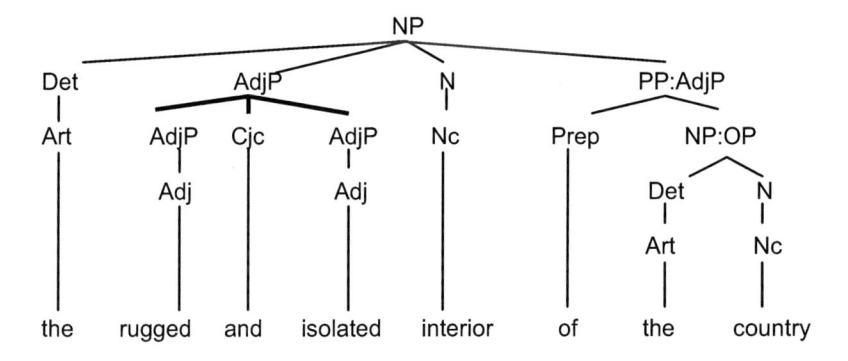

Again, notice the Cjc triangle with the matching points of AdjP.

Correlative Conjunctions

We can also join elements with correlative conjunctions. These conjunctions come in pairs.

Correlative Conjunctions (Cjcorr)
both/and either/or
neither/nor not only/but also

We put both pairs in the position of the second of the two and label them both Cjcorr. Then we show that the first element of the pair has been moved to a position in front of the compound NP. See the sample trees.

either the manatee or the dolphin
```
              NP
      ┌───────┼───────┐
     NP     Cjcorr    NP
   ┌──┴─┐          ┌──┴─┐
  Det   N         Det   N
   │    │          │    │
  Art   Nc        Art   Nc
   │    │          │    │
   │    │          │    │
  the manatee │either/ or the dolphin
```

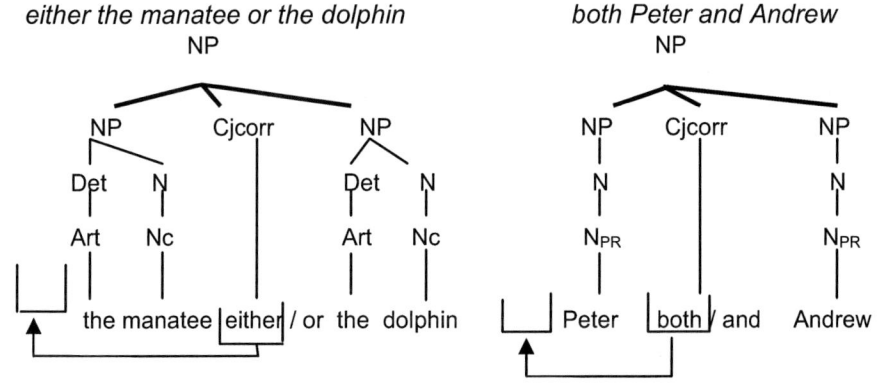

both Peter and Andrew
```
             NP
      ┌──────┼──────┐
     NP   Cjcorr    NP
      │             │
      N             N
      │             │
     N_PR          N_PR
      │             │
     │Peter   │both│/ and Andrew
```

Notice that, like the Cjc, the Cjcorr makes a triangle with like elements at all three points of the triangle. Don't forget to show that the first word (or set of words) of the correlative conjunction is moved to the front.

Treeing Nominal Phrases

- First, divide the sentence into its major components as you did in Chapter 3. Then, each time you have an NP, label the parts of that NP.
- **Look to see if the NP has an apostrophe.** If it does, you have a GenN determiner. Write the following. This part should be automatic if there is an apostrophe.

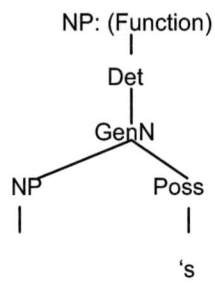

```
              NP: (Function)
                    |
                   Det
                    |
                  GenN
                 /     \
              NP        Poss
              |          |
                         's
```

Tree the NP under the GenN. Then, tree the rest of the main NP.

- **If there is no apostrophe, tree each word as you get to it.**
- Whenever you come to a preposition in an NP, write

```
        PP:AdjP
        /      \
      Prep   NP:OP
```

- Then tree the NP:OP under the PP. Remember that the NP:OP could also have a PP:AdjP in it.

Examples of NP trees

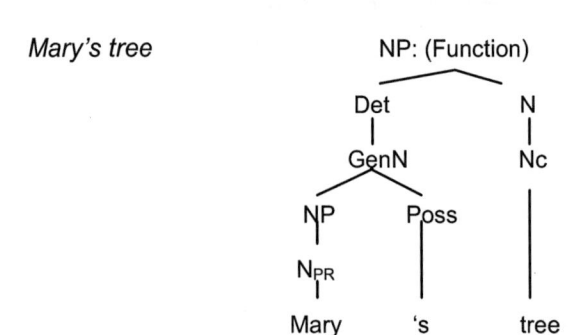

Mary's tree

```
              NP: (Function)
              /            \
            Det             N
             |              |
           GenN            Nc
          /    \            |
        NP     Poss          |
        |      |             |
       N_PR                  |
        |     's           tree
      Mary
```

Noun Clusters

the old man's problem

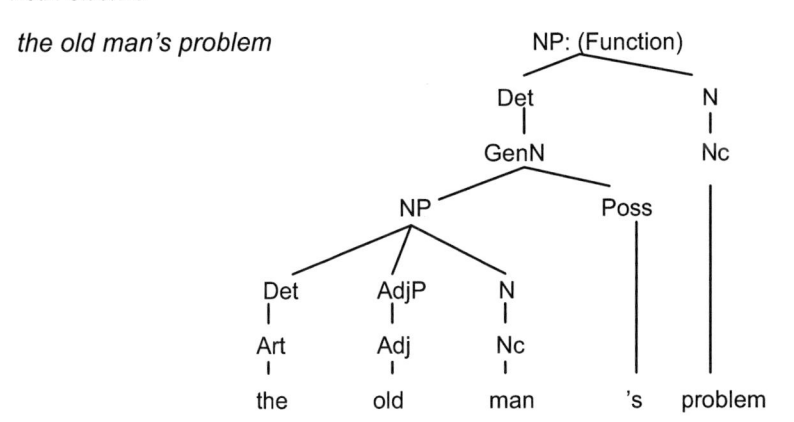

```
                         NP: (Function)
                        /              \
                     Det                N
                      |                 |
                    GenN                Nc
                   /     \
                 NP      Poss
               / | \
            Det AdjP N
             |   |  |
            Art Adj Nc
             |   |  |
            the old man    's    problem
```

both our dorky dog and cat

```
                    NP: (Function)
          /      |      |         \
       Pre-Det  Det    AdjP        N
                 |      |        / | \
                Poss   Adj      N Cjc N
                                |     |
                                Nc    Nc
         both   our   dorky    dog and cat
```

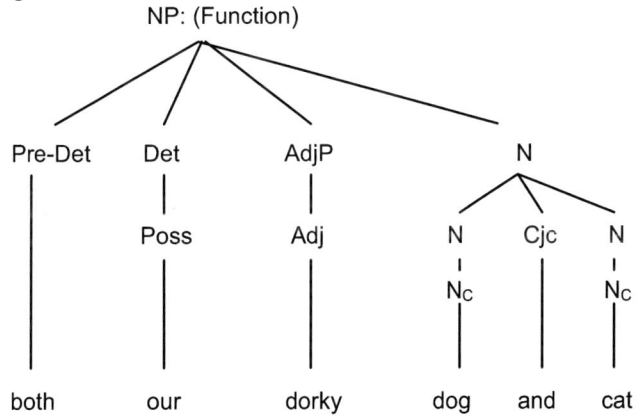

the executive director's impressive work on the procedures of the program

```
                          NP: (Function)
         /          |         |       \
       Det        AdjP        N      PP:AdjP
        |          |          |      /     \
      GenN        Adj        Nc   Prep    NP:OP
     /    \                       /    |      \
   NP    Poss                   Det    N    PP:AdjP
  / | \                          |     |    /     \
Det AdjP N                      Art   Nc  Prep  NP:OP
 |   |  |                                        /  \
Art Adj Nc                                     Det   N
                                                |    |
                                               Art   Nc

The executive director 's impressive work on the procedures of the program
```

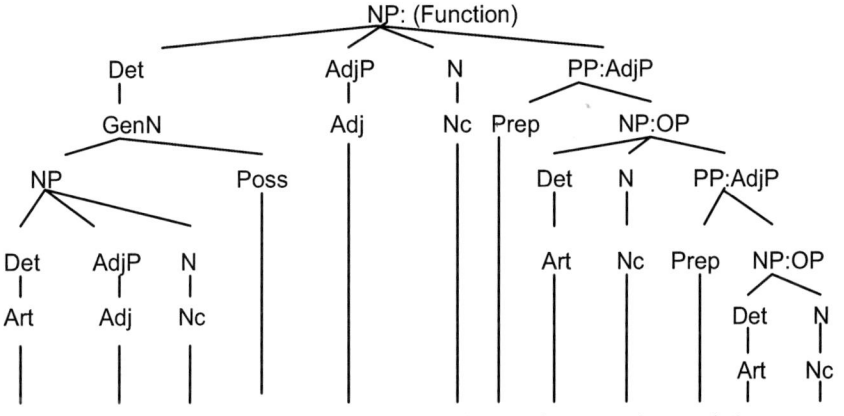

Checking your Answers

- Make sure that whenever you have a noun cluster, you have an N underneath. (Review the 7 types of N.) Every noun cluster has an N.

- There is only one N for each noun cluster, but remember that you can have an NP embedded within an NP. The embedded NP also has an N. At this point, each time you write NP, there should be only one line drawn down to an N.

- There is only one determiner for each noun cluster. (Review the 5 types of determiner.)

- Remember that the GenN determiner has an embedded NP.

- Each AdjP has a separate line down from the NP, unless it has a qualifier with it.

- Remember that if there is a prepositional phrase functioning as an adjective, it will come after the N.

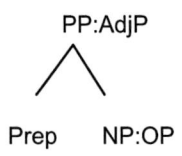

```
        PP:AdjP
         /\
        /  \
      Prep  NP:OP
```

Noun Clusters 67

Treeing the Full Sentence

That precocious child handed our second daughter several old books with Egyptian hieroglyphics.

```
                                            S
                    ┌───────────────────────┴───────────────────────┐
                  NP:Subj                                         VP:Pred
                ┌───┬───┐                          ┌────────┬────────┬──────────┐
               Det AdjP  N                         Vg     NP:IO    NP:DO
                │   │   │                                ┌──┬──┐   ┌──┬───┬──────┐
               Dem Adj  Nc                             Det AdjP N  Det AdjP N  PP:AdjP
                                                        │   │   │   │   │   │    │
                                                       Poss OrdN Nc Quant Adj Nc  ┌───┬──┐
                                                                                 Prep NP:OP
                                                                                      ┌──┐
                                                                                     AdjP N
                                                                                      │   │
                                                                                    Adj_PR Nc

That precocious child   handed   our second daughter   several old books   with Egyptian hieroglyphics
```

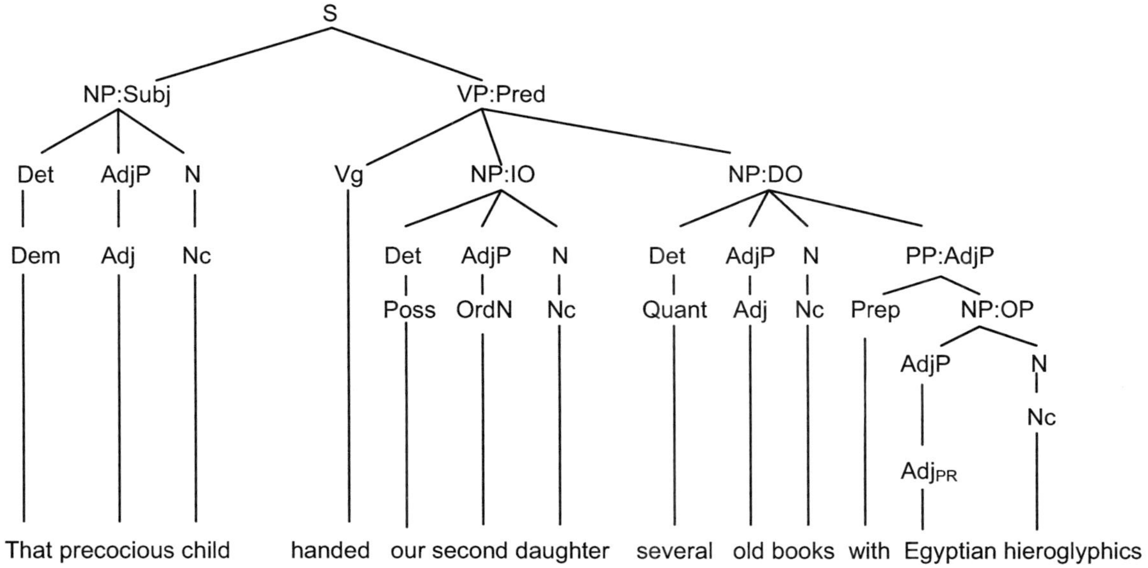

Pronoun Usage

Pronoun Clarity and Consistency

The noun cluster or other nominative structure to which the pronoun refers is called its **antecedent**. A pronoun should agree with its antecedent and should be consistent with other pronouns in the sentence. Also, the pronoun reference should be clear. Note the following examples.

- *The counselors learned that if a camper does not clean up for inspections,* **he or she** *(not* **they***) may be penalized.*
- *After the guests enter,* **they are** *(not* **he or she is***) given a program.*
- *Extra study sessions given by the teacher assistant help the student learn, but not if* **he or she** *does not attend* **them** *(not* **it***).*

The following examples show a shift in pronoun use.

- *I love to walk at least three miles each morning because it can really help you keep in shape.* (The word should be **me** not **you**.)
- *Everyone likes to be fit, but you do not always like to exercise.* (The second half of the sentence should be **everyone does not always like to exercise**.)

The pronoun in the following sentence has an unclear pronoun reference.

- *Moving the book from the shelf, Herbert dusted it.* (Did Herbert dust the book or the shelf?)

Sometimes a demonstrative pronoun does not have a definite antecedent.

- *Jessica had already typed and organized the information.* **This** *amazed her boss.*

In this set of sentences, the antecedent, while not directly stated, is fairly clear: *that Jessica had already typed and organized the information amazed her boss.*

However, with intervening sentences, the antecedent is less clear.

- *Jessica had already typed and organized the information. It was arranged by subject matter and date and put into a template chart. This amazed her boss.*

Noun Clusters

Now the antecedent to the pronoun *this* is less clear. Many teachers of writing suggest that their students put a noun or noun cluster and use *this* as a determiner.
- *This efficiency amazed her boss.*
- *This ingenuity amazed her boss.*

Pronouns and Case

Most of the personal pronouns in English have a subject form and an object form. In Standard English, if the personal pronoun has a subject function (NP:Subj), we use *she, he, they, I,* or *we*. If the personal pronoun has an object function (NP:DO, NP:IO, NP:OP), we use *her, him, them, me,* or *us*. The reflexive pronouns (such as *myself, himself,* or *themselves*) are used for object functions. Sometimes speakers of a nonstandard dialect have trouble when the NP is compound. For example, they might say "*Him and me went to the mall*" (object form for a compound NP:Subj) or "*The gift was given to my sister and I*" (subject form for NP:OP).

Further examples are below.
- **We** *(not **Us**) tennis players must practice every day.*
- *The inheritance of the lost treasure was to be given to the professor and* **me.** *(not **I** or **myself**)*
- *The students, the tour guide, and I (not **myself** or **me**) will join you later at the Pantheon in Rome.*

Even more troublesome is when the personal pronoun is used as a predicate nominative (NP:PredN). Grammarians of the eighteenth century dictated that predicate nominatives should be in subject form. For example, a person was taught to say "This is she" when identifying herself rather than "This is her." Many modern speakers of English find the use of the subject form of personal pronouns for predicate nominatives awkward and use the objective form. The subjective form continues to convey more formality.

Singular and Plural Pronouns

In formal language situations, the indefinite pronouns are considered singular and are used with singular verbs. (Review the list of indefinite pronouns.) Quantifier pronouns are more varied.

Quantifier Pronouns	
Singular	each, neither, either, none
Plural	many, several, both
Depends upon the usage	some, most, any, few, all, enough, more, much

Here are some examples.
- *Either of those gifts **is** (not are) appropriate to give as a wedding gift. (Either is singular and so needs a singular verb.)*
- *Every one of those trees had a layer of frost across **its** (not their) leaves.*
- *Someone may win the big prize if **she or he is** (not they are) lucky enough. (Someone is singular and needs a singular pronoun to accompany it.)*
- *Enough of the building **was** saved. (singular)*
- *Enough of the books **were** saved. (plural)*

Although the traditional usage rule says that the word *everybody* is singular, it seems as if it should be plural. In fact, in everyday usage, many people treat it as if it were plural.

- Standard formal usage: *Everybody should complete his or her assignment on time.*
- Informal usage: *Everybody should complete their assignment on time.*

Qualifiers and Usage

Sometimes people use the nonstandard form of qualifier when they are using words such as *real* as the qualifier. The standard form is *really,* as in the following: *the diamond ring is **really** expensive.*

Nominal Phrase Punctuation

You can use a hyphen to connect one or more words that are being used as an adjective unit.
- *Rogness Mercantile carries even those hard-to-find items.*

Also, students and some writers often confuse the possessive pronoun *its* with a contraction *it's*. Look again at the list of possessive pronoun determiners (Poss). We do use apostrophes to show possession with nouns (*Carrie's*), but none of the possessive pronouns has an apostrophe. *It's* is a contraction for *it is*.

- This tree lost all of its leaves before October 1. It's a shame.

Practice Sentences
I. Tree the following sentences.
1. This is the beginning of the first local politician's ad campaign.
2. Nobody ate the three decaying chunks of fish.
3. The ambitious political candidate met not only the organization's president but also the chairman of the board.
4. The state visit days allow everyone access to the queen.
5. Kris Erickson is a true believer in beneficial forest conservation.
6. Those are always interesting.
7. That brown and white rabbit is the best one of the bunch.
8. The witness for the defense cried in court during the trial.
9. We collected Herbert's old baseball cap and his mother's five purple candles.
10. Hundreds of workers died in either the accident or the aftermath.
11. The tourist demand for eucalyptus-wood didgeridoos raised the price for everyone.
12. This golf ball equalizes the density of the solid core and cover materials.
13. Those really strange students in her advanced grammar class wrote sentences for that first exam.
14. The very old fan's six rusty blades broke in our hands.
15. Both our agitated dogs barked at the third intruder.
16. The company's lawyer is a former federal prosecutor and a rather experienced manipulator.
17. Those stories from Ground Zero are a mix of horror and heroism.
18. The herpetologist sent herself a nonvenomous constrictor in the mail.
19. Several of the researchers delivered those to the chief biologist's main office.

20. Something about the undeniable advantages of the procedure clicked with the bureaucrats.
21. That third version of the Senate bill passed.
22. The first line of defense against rising sea levels and storms is these sand dunes.
23. Many of the trips include the amenities of maid service and private chefs.
24. Melody's fantasy novel is brilliant.
25. The funny, likable romantic comedy opened yesterday.
26. Few dedicated divers know enough about underwater archaeology as an academic discipline.
27. Neither of their crowded shops contained flawless black diamonds.
28. Astute observers consider the growing popularity of M-rated games a sign of cultural decline.
29. She gave herself orders for the evening's entertainment of guests.
30. The new polyurethane suit's lining keeps some of the explorers dry.
31. Everybody gathered some very rotten yellow apples.
32. State officials brought one hundred potential investors to the meeting.
33. Our game show contestants seem relaxed and very eager.
34. Many of the exact details of the plan are sketchy.
35. Most of the artists studied his fascinating picture's colors.
36. Gunter Grass gives his readers a look at the events at the end of WWII.
37. Both reading and writing are a major part of my life.
38. Many of them chose this extremely fun activity.
39. The forensic anthropologists all had enough of all this.
40. Neither his key nor the map was available during the trip.
41. The glow from the moonlight cast a soft shine over my baby's features.
42. Their repertoire includes not only other birdcalls but also sirens, chain saws, and horses' whinnying.
43. Those bright hues of a poison-dart frog advertise its toxicity.
44. That is a sarcophagus.
45. All ten men hunt the golden seals.
46. South Africa has one of the world's largest populations of white sharks.

Noun Clusters

47. Each of her students wrote five papers.
48. The first candidate nominated himself.
49. The four detectives suspected nothing.
50. We refreshed ourselves with cold water.

II. Pronoun Practice:
1. Reread the section on "Singular and Plural Pronouns." Write 10 sentences in which the N element is an indefinite or quantifier pronoun and the verb is present rather than past tense. Use a different pronoun for each sentence. Then reread your sentences to make sure that you have used the correct verb form for formal standard usage. (These can be used as models for your future students if you will be a teacher.)

2. Reread the section on "Pronoun Clarity and Consistency." Using both singular and plural, write 5 sentences in which the pronoun agrees with its antecedent and is consistent with all other pronouns in the sentence. Use the examples given as models.

3. Reread the section on "Pronouns and Case." Write paragraphs in which you use all of the possible personal pronouns and reflexive pronouns. Assume a formal language situation and choose the standard pronoun form in each sentence. Reread the section on pronoun usage and incorporate those situations into your sentences. Underline all pronouns. (Note: This can be turned into an exercise for students if you give them choices for each of the pronouns and have them choose the standard form.)

III. For more practice with noun clusters, go back to the sentences in Chapter 3 and tree each NP.

Chapter 5
Adverb Choices

Adverbs can be added to any sentence to include valuable information. They are labeled to show the adverb question that they answer. Adverb phrases come in a variety of forms, which we will examine in this chapter. Generally, the structure notation is written in front of the colon, and the function is written after the colon. For example, *PP:AdvP-time* indicates a prepositional phrase functioning as an adverb phrase of time, and *InfPh:AdvP-reason* indicates an infinitive phrase functioning as an adverb phrase of reason.

Adverb Questions and Mobility

ADVERB QUESTION	ADVERB LABEL	EXAMPLE
How?	Adverb of manner	swiftly
When?	Adverb of time	in the afternoon
Where?	Adverb of place	at the lake
Why?	Adverb of reason	to restore order
Through what means?	Adverb of means	with his sewing talent
To what extent?	Adverb of extent	throughout the galaxy
How often?	Adverb of frequency	frequently
How far?	Adverb of distance	for seven miles
Under what condition?	Adverb of condition	with a food shortage
To whom? To what?	Adverb of recipient	to the best singer
How long?	Adverb of duration	for several days
With what instrument?	Adverb of instrument	with a snow blower
By whom?	Adverb of agency	by the committee
With whom?	Adverb of association	with the clowns
From where?	Adverb of origin	from Minneapolis
From whom or what?	Adverb of source	from my parents
In what order?	Adverb of order	first
Compared to what?	Adverb of comparison	quicker than the turtle
To where?	Adverb of destination	to England
In what direction?	Adverb of direction	forward, to the left
How near or far?	Adverb of proximity	close to the garage
With what result?	Adverb of result	to no avail

Adverb Choices

Remember, this is not a complete list, and you can often argue that an adverb could be labeled more than one way.

To check for an adverb phrase, say the verb, then ask one of the adverb questions. The answer to the question will be the adverb phrase; the adverb phrase might be a single word or a group of words.

| They quickly extinguished the candle. | extinguished how? | Quickly | AdvP-manner |

Remember, adverb phrases are highly mobile. They can appear almost anywhere in the sentence.

- The conservation crew collected the accumulated debris of road trash **for seven miles.**
- **For seven miles**, the conservation crew collected the accumulated debris of road trash.
- The conservation crew, **for seven miles,** collected the accumulated debris of road trash.
- The conservation crew collected, **for seven miles,** the accumulated debris of road trash.

When we tree the sentence, we place adverb phrases at the end of the VP:Pred, with the adverb label attached. Then we draw arrows to show the current location of the AdvP, if it isn't at the end of the sentence. See the example on the next page.

Adverb Forms: Adverbs with Qualifiers

Adverbs can also have a **qualifier (Qual)** in front. Like adjective qualifiers, adverb qualifiers come in front of the adverb and change the adverb somewhat, typically by intensifying it or diminishing it: *very, rather, incredibly, really.*

| They very quickly extinguished the candle. | Extinguished how? | very quickly | AdvP-manner |

Adverb Choices

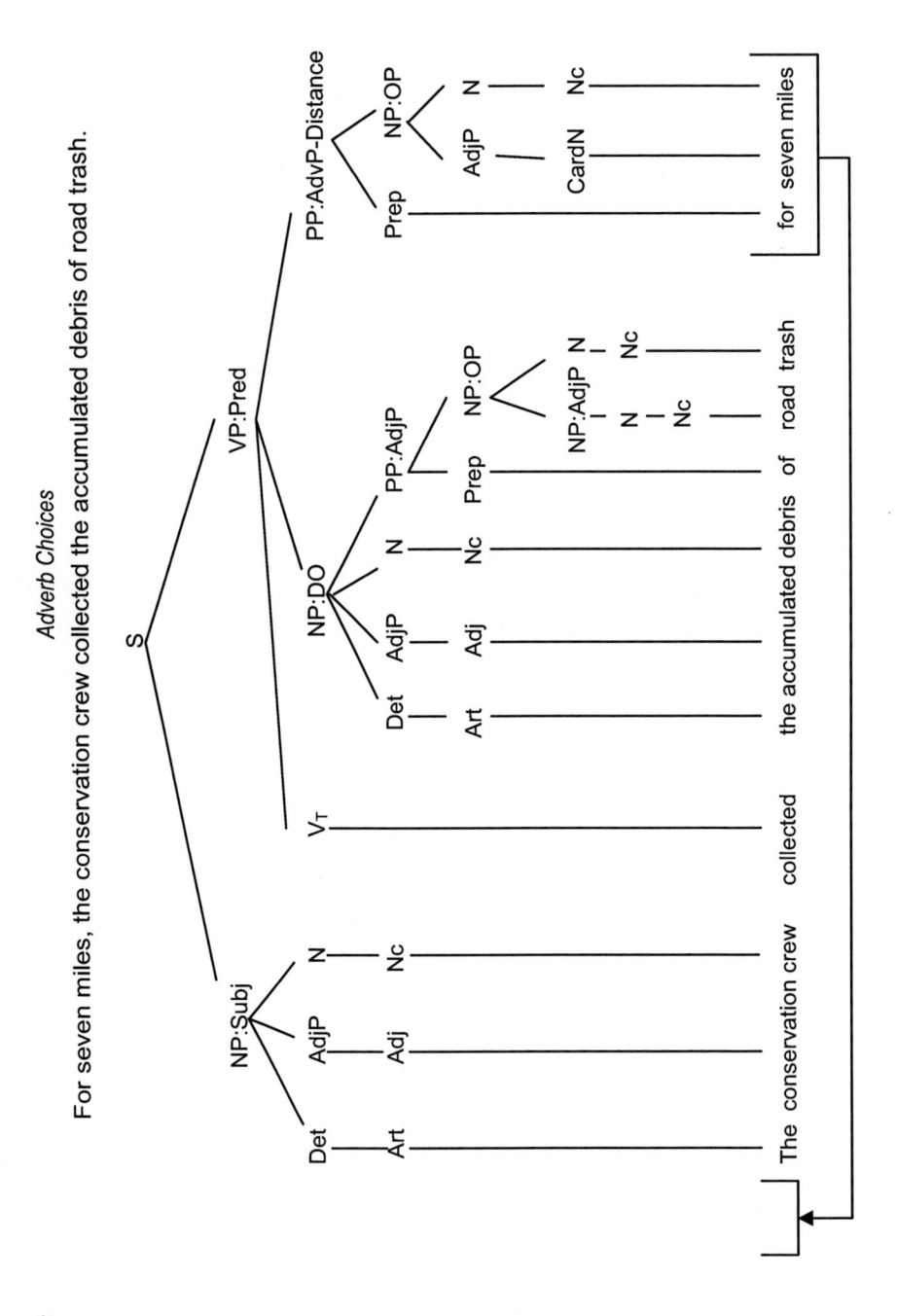

For seven miles, the conservation crew collected the accumulated debris of road trash.

They very quickly extinguished the candle.

```
                        S
         ┌──────────────┴──────────────┐
      NP:Subj                       VP:Pred
         │           ┌─────────────────┼──────────────┐
         N          V_T              NP:DO         AdvP-Manner
         │           │           ┌─────┴─────┐      ┌────┴────┐
        Pro_P        │          Det          N     Qual      Adv
         │           │           │           │      │         │
         │           │          Art          Nc     │         │
         │           │           │           │      │         │
        They    extinguished    the       candle   very    quickly
```

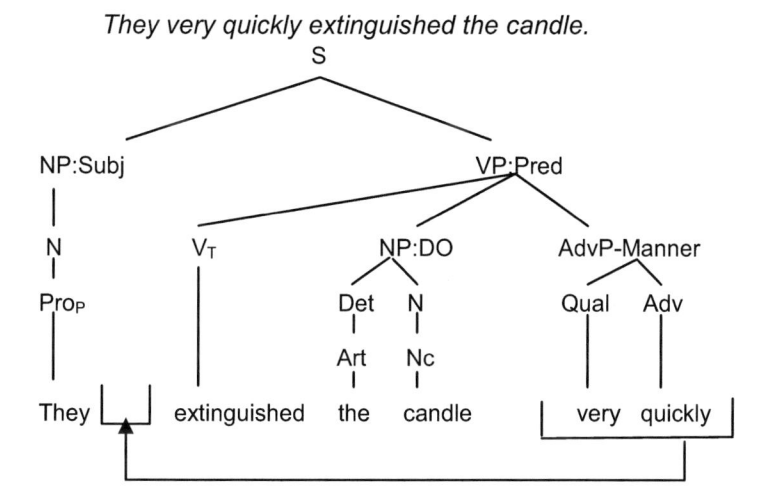

Adverb Forms: Prepositional Phrases

Adverb phrases frequently have the form of a prepositional phrase (**PP:AdvP**). Remember that a prepositional phrase begins with a preposition and ends with a nominal phrase functioning as the object of the preposition. The NP:OP can include any of the elements of an NP, which we studied in Chapter 4. If you need a review, see the list of common prepositions in previous chapters.

Difference between PP:AdjP and PP:AdvP

Adjectival prepositions come after the N in an NP and tell something about the N. Adverbial prepositions answer the adverb questions. As with other adverb phrases, you should say the verb and ask the question; the answer is the PP:AdvP. All PP:AdvP are treed at the end of the VP:Pred and then shown to be moved, if necessary, as illustrated in the example above.

When a prepositional phrase follows a direct object, it sometimes takes a bit more analysis to determine if the PP is adjectival or adverbial. Look at the following prepositional phrases to determine if they are adjectival or adverbial.

1) Meshugana is a monkey with an attitude.
2) Herbert shoveled the snow with gusto.
3) Petunia's strange cousin planted a tree in the living room.
4) Jeffrey painted the picture in the museum.

In number l), the PP (*with an attitude*) is adjectival (PP:AdjP). It describes the monkey. In number 2), the PP is adverbial (PP:AdvP). It answers the adverb question *how* Herbert shoveled the snow (with gusto). In number 3), the PP is adverbial (PP:AdvP). It answers the adverb question *where* Petunia's strange cousin planted a tree. In number 4), the PP function is ambiguous. If Jeffrey is painting a copy of a picture that is in the museum, then the PP is adjectival (PP:AdjP), giving more of a description of the picture. However, if Jeffrey was physically in the museum when he was painting the picture, then the PP is adverbial (PP:AdvP), answering the adverb question *where* Jeffrey painted the picture.

Adverb Forms: Noun Clusters

We have seen that noun clusters generally function as a subject, predicate nominative, direct object, indirect object, object complement, or object of the preposition. However, noun clusters can also function as adverb phrases (**NP:AdvP**). As do the other adverb phrase structures, these noun clusters answer the adverb questions.

The team from Minnesota finished the dog sled race this afternoon.	finished when?	this afternoon	NP:AdvP- time
This medical insurance covers expenses the best.	covers how?	the best	NP:AdvP- manner

Of course, this form of adverb phrase is also mobile: *this afternoon, the team from Minnesota finished the dog sled race.*

Remember, all adverb phrases should be treed at the end of the VP:Pred and then, if necessary, shown to be moved to a different location in the sentence.

Notice in the sample tree which follows, an NP is functioning as a cluster AdjP: *dog sled*.

Adverb Choices

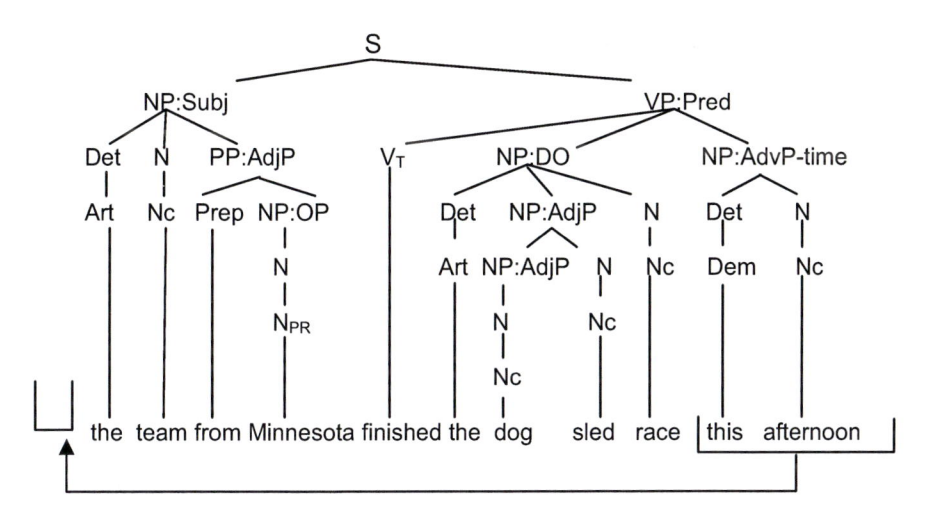

```
                                    S
              _____|_____
          NP:Subj                                  VP:Pred
      _____|_____              _____|_____
    Det   N    PP:AdjP      V_T       NP:DO              NP:AdvP-time
     |    |     __|__        |      ____|____              __|__
    Art   Nc  Prep  NP:OP              Det  NP:AdjP  N    Det    N
                     |                  |    __|__    |    |     |
                     N                 Art  NP:AdjP  N    Nc   Dem   Nc
                     |                        |      |
                    N_PR                      N      Nc
                                              |
                                              Nc

    the  team from Minnesota  finished  the  dog  sled  race | this  afternoon |
```

Adverb Forms: Infinitive Phrases

An infinitive begins with the word *to* followed by a verb (*to run, to smile, to tickle, to become, to award*). An <u>infinitive phrase</u> usually begins with the word *to* followed by a VP (*to run a marathon race, to smile appropriately at the wedding, to tickle my little cousin's tummy, to become an expert calligrapher, to award Hettie the grand prize*).

Adverbial infinitive phrases usually answer the adverb question <u>why.</u> You can usually insert *in order to* in place of the word *to* without changing the meaning of the sentence.
- *We trained vigorously* **to run a marathon race***.*
- *The nervous groom practiced grinning* **to smile appropriately at the wedding***.*
- **To tickle my little cousin's tummy***, I catch him first.*
- *My aunt,* **to become an expert calligrapher***, took a class at the local school.*
- **To award Hettie the grand prize***, the judges manipulated the scores.*

As you can see in the examples above, infinitive phrases functioning as adverb phrases are also highly mobile. As with the other forms of adverb phrases, tree adverbial infinitive phrases at the end of the sentence and then show that they have been moved to a different location, if necessary.

Infinitive Phrase Form

An infinitive phrase consists of a **subordinator followed by a VP.** The VP in the infinitive phrase is <u>not</u> functioning as a predicate. There is no subject in an infinitive phrase; therefore, there is no predicate. The VP here is merely a part of the infinitive phrase.

The VP can have any elements that we have been seeing in the VP:Pred. Also, the examples of infinitive phrases that follow show that the V element within the infinitive phrase can be any of the five main types we examined earlier. As you look at each grammar tree, notice the VP of the infinitive phrase. The infinitive phrases are inserted into partially treed sentences to indicate location. The MV:inf label identifies the verb form as infinitive.

In the first example, the verb is a V_T followed by an NP:DO and a PP:AdvP-manner: *To complete the assignment with ease, the students assembled their research sources.*

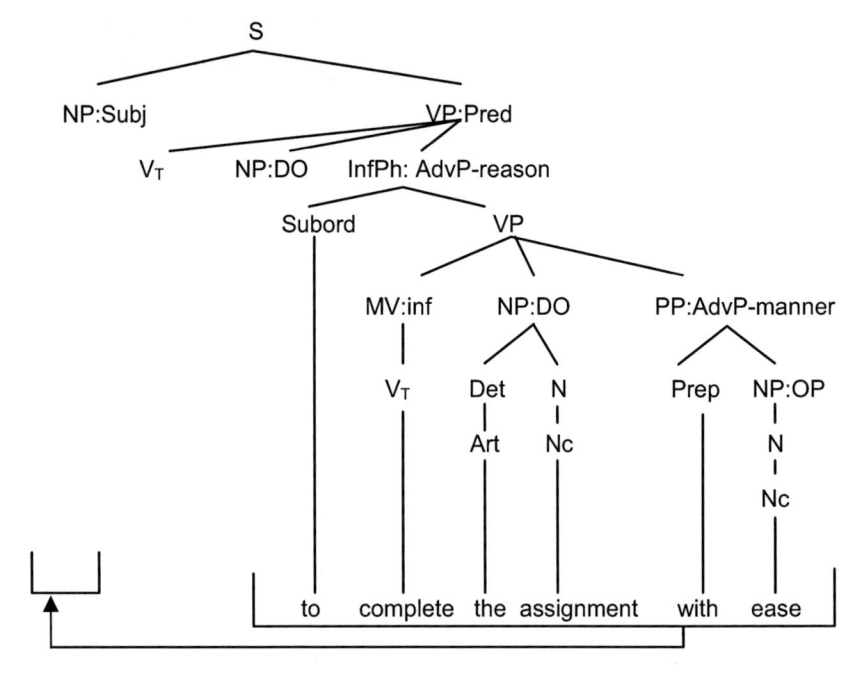

In the next example (*The nervous groom practiced grinning to smile appropriately at the wedding*), the VP in the infinitive phrase has a V_I with an AdvP-manner and a PP:AdvP-place: *to smile appropriately at the*

wedding. Again, the infinitive phrase is inserted into a partially treed sentence to indicate its location. Only the infinitive phrase in the sentence is completely treed.

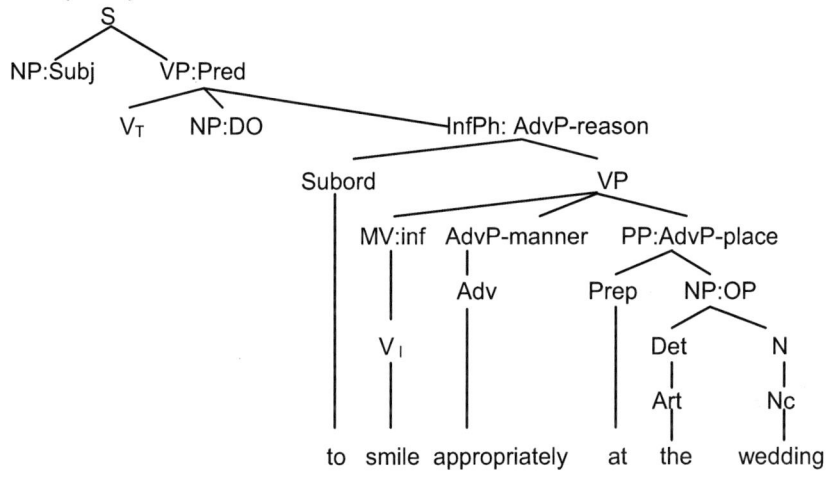

```
                    S
           ┌────────┴────────┐
        NP:Subj           VP:Pred
                  ┌──────────┼──────────────────────┐
                 VT        NP:DO            InfPh: AdvP-reason
                                          ┌──────────┴──────────┐
                                       Subord                   VP
                                                 ┌──────────────┼──────────────┐
                                              MV:inf       AdvP-manner    PP:AdvP-place
                                                 │              │         ┌─────┴─────┐
                                                 VI            Adv       Prep       NP:OP
                                                                                  ┌────┴────┐
                                                                                 Det        N
                                                                                  │         │
                                                                                 Art        Nc
                                                                                  │         │
                                              to smile    appropriately    at   the     wedding
```

In this last example (*My aunt, to become an expert calligrapher, took a class at the local school*), the VP in the infinitive phrase has a V_L followed by a NP:PredN: *to become an expert calligrapher.* Again, the sentence is partially treed with the infinitive phrase completely treed.

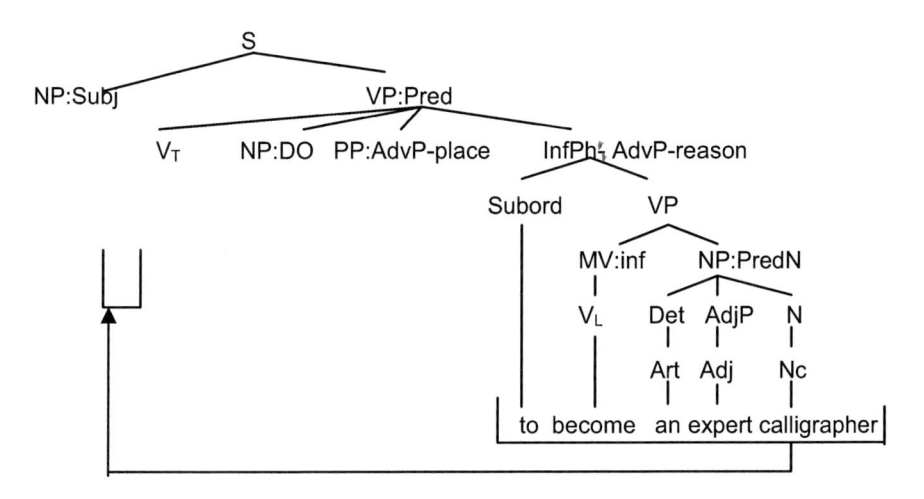

```
                          S
           ┌──────────────┴──────────────┐
        NP:Subj                       VP:Pred
                     ┌────────┬────────────┬──────────────┐
                    VT      NP:DO    PP:AdvP-place   InfPh: AdvP-reason
                                                     ┌─────┴─────┐
                                                  Subord         VP
                                                          ┌──────┴──────┐
                                                       MV:inf       NP:PredN
                                                          │       ┌────┼────┐
                                                         VL      Det  AdjP  N
                                                                  │    │    │
                                                                 Art  Adj  Nc
                                                                  │    │    │
                                                        to become  an expert calligrapher
```

Occasionally, you might see an infinitive phrase that answers another type of adverb question. An example is in the following sentence:
- *That child was raised to respect her elders.*

One might object to the term "*raised*" rather than "*reared*"; nonetheless, the infinitive phrase "*to respect her elders*" seems to answer the question *how* rather than *why*, and so it is an adverb of manner rather than an adverb of reason.

Adverb Forms: Adverb Clauses

Adverb clauses (Cl:AdvP) are like other adverb phrases.
- They answer the same adverb questions as other adverb phrases, such as manner, place, time, reason, frequency, or condition.
- They have the same adverb labels.
- We will also tree adverb clauses in the same place as we have been treeing adverb phrases: at the end of the VP:Pred.
- Like other adverb phrases, adverb clauses are mobile. They can appear at various points in the sentence. If the adverb clause is not at the end of the sentence, we will tree it there and show that it has been moved to its present location.

Adverb clauses differ from other adverb phrases only in their structure. An adverb clause consists of a subordinating conjunction (Cjs) followed by a subject and predicate. Subordinating conjunctions can be single words or a cluster of words acting as one unit.

Some of the words that function as a subordinating conjunction (Cjs) can also function as a preposition. The difference between a prepositional phrase acting as an adverb and an adverb clause is that the preposition is followed only by an NP:OP whereas the subordinating conjunction (Cjs) is followed by a complete NP:Subj and VP:Pred.

PP:AdvP-time	Cl: AdvP-time
The quiz team was nervous **before the tournament**.	The quiz team was nervous **before the tournament started**.

Words that Can Function as Subordinating Conjunctions Cjs							
after	although	as	because	before	if		once
provided	since	though	unless	until	when		lest
whenever	wherever	while	whether	for	where		till

Adverb Choices

Words that Can Function as Cluster Subordinating Conjunctions Cjs			
as if	as long as	as soon as	as though
even though	in order that	no matter how	even if
in as much as	so that	in so far as	whether or not

As long as these rebels are willing, we wait on this line all summer.

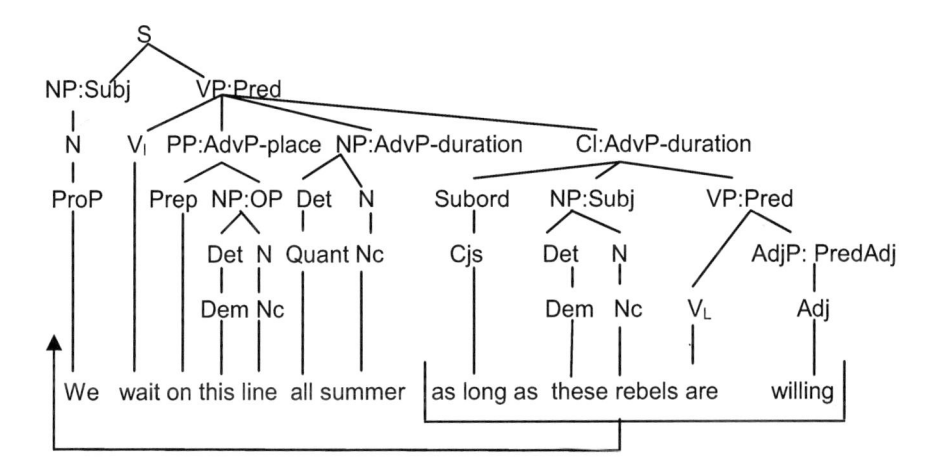

```
                    S
           ┌────────┴────────┐
        NP:Subj           VP:Pred
           │        ┌────────┼──────────────────┐
           N       Vᵢ  PP:AdvP-place  NP:AdvP-duration   Cl:AdvP-duration
           │        │    ┌───┴──┐      ┌────┴───┐      ┌─────┼─────┐
         ProP     Prep  NP:OP  Det  N         Subord  NP:Subj   VP:Pred
           │        │   ┌─┴─┐   │    │          │     ┌──┴──┐      │
           │        │  Det  N  Quant Nc         Cjs  Det    N    AdjP: PredAdj
           │        │   │   │                    │    │     │      │
           │        │  Dem  Nc                   │   Dem    Nc    Adj
           │        │   │   │       │            │    │     │   Vₗ │
          We   wait on this line  all summer  as long as these rebels are   willing
```

Subjunctive Mood

The subjunctive mood in everyday English seems to be dying off. However, one sometimes still sees the subjunctive in an adverb clause introduced by *if* when the subject is singular. The subjunctive mood is used to describe hypothetical situations or imaginary events that have not actually happened. The verb does not follow its "normal forms." The most common example comes in adverb clauses such as *If I were you* (*If I were you, I would do what he says*). *(*Normally we say *"I was"* not *"I were."*) We tree adverb clauses with subjunctive mood the same way we tree all others.

Compound Adverb Phrases

We have seen that it is possible in English to have compound nominal phrases and compound adjective phrases. These sentence elements are joined by coordinating conjunctions (Cjc) such as *and, nor, but, or*. We also occasionally use compound adverb phrases.

- The woman **quickly and efficiently** gutted the salmon.
- **Through the influence of his father-in-law and with his talent**, the painter should go far.
- We answered the question **one way or another**.
- The university coaches united **to show support for the programs and to request more time to raise money**.

Notice that in these examples, both adverb phrases in a compound adverb pair have the same structure and answer the same adverb question. Although this is usual, this isn't always the case.

An example of "mixed" adverb phrases would be the following: *she arrived at the theater **unemotionally** and **on time***. In this example, the first AdvP answers *how* and is a single word adverb. The second AdvP is a prepositional phrase and answers *when*.

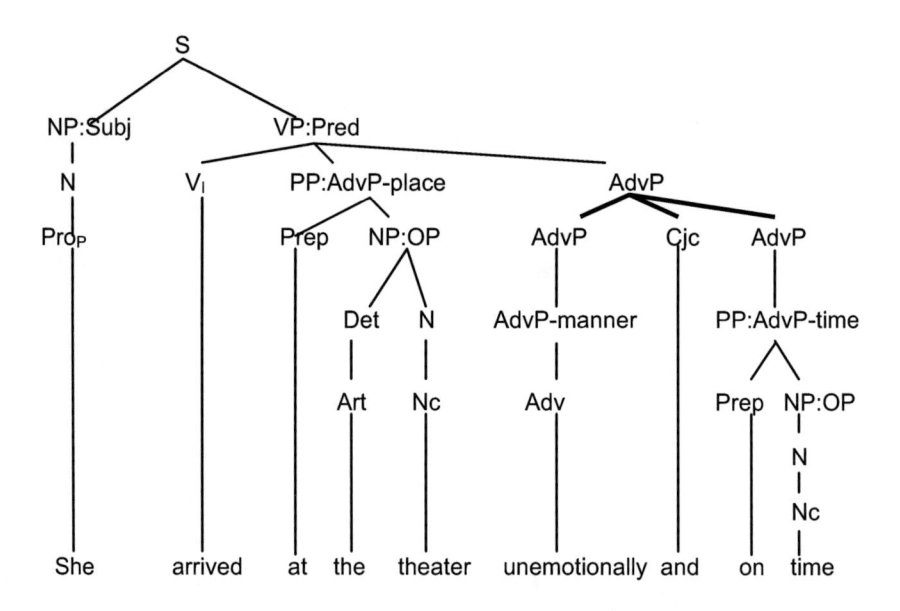

Notice that the Cjc still makes a triangle connecting the same kind of elements.

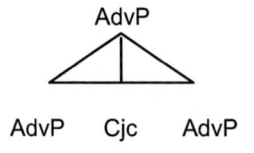

Adverb Choices

We can also join AdvP with correlative conjunctions (Cj$_{corr}$): *both/and, either/or, neither/nor, not only/but also.*
- The woman gutted the salmon **both quickly and efficiently.**
- **Either through the influence of his father-in-law or with his talent**, the painter should go far.
- The university coaches united **not only to show support for the programs but also to request more time to raise money.**

Adverb Usage

PredAdj or AdvP?

In English, the appropriate word for a predicate adjective is often not the same word that is appropriate for an adverb. This causes confusion when the verb can be either linking or intransitive, depending upon its use. Consider the following examples which show a common confusion.
- *I feel bad.* In this sentence the verb is linking, and the word *bad* is a predicate adjective describing the subject *I*.
- *I feel badly.* In this sentence, *badly* is an AdvP-manner. If you say this sentence, you are saying that your sense of touch is impaired. (Perhaps your fingers have been burned, and you have lost your sense of touch.)
- *He looks good.* Here *looks* is a linking verb, and the word *good* is a predicate adjective. The word *good* is **not** an adverb. Therefore, if the subject is doing something, we say *well* rather than *good*.
- *They eat well. She jumps the hurdles well. He draws well.* The word *well* is an AdvP-manner.

Placement of Adverbs

Adverb phrases are highly mobile, but they can have consequences for the meaning in a sentence if they are misplaced. For example, consider the following.
- *He **only** wants to spend ten dollars.* In this sentence, the word *only* is an AdvP-extent. You are saying that his sole desire is to spend the money.
- *He wants to spend **only** ten dollars.* In this sentence the word *only* is a quantifier determiner. Here, you are saying that he may have more money, but he wants to spend just that amount of money. Therefore, where you place the word makes a difference.

Standard Usage of Subordinating Conjunctions

Some adverb forms are considered to be nonstandard English. For example, for most language situations, you would want to use *"because"* instead of *"being that"* for a subordinating conjunction.

Standard English:
- *Because she was chosen as president, she had more work.*

Nonstandard English:
- *Being that she was chosen as president, she had more work.*

Also, some people use *"as"* when the meaning is *"since"* or *"because"* or use *"while"* when the meaning is *"whereas."* In formal, Standard English, *"as"* and *"while"* should be used to introduce adverbs of time.

Standard English:
- *The polar bear continued to pace, because (or since) the treatment of the altered diet had no effect.*
- *Bears in zoos exhibit this repetitive behavior whereas wild bears do not do so.*

Nonstandard English:
- *The polar bears continued to pace, as the treatment of the altered diet had no effect.*
- *Bears in zoos exhibit this repetitive behavior while wild bears do not do so.*

Adverbs and Punctuation

Sentence Fragments

<u>Also, an adverb clause sometimes ends up as a sentence fragment</u>. If the clause begins with a Cjs (subordinating conjunction), the clause cannot be punctuated as an independent clause. Watch for the subordinating conjunctions listed in the box earlier in this chapter. They signal an adverb clause, not an independent clause.

Examples of adverb clauses as fragments:
- *The elephant traveled for hours. So that it could get to water to drink.*

Adverb Choices 87

- *The tech writer had to work all night. Because the instruction manual was due to be shipped with the project the next day.*

Commas

The longer, more complex adverb structures are often set off from the rest of the sentence by commas. For example, adverb clauses appear at various locations in the sentence. This determines whether you use a comma or not.

Adverb clause comes at the beginning of the sentence.	Put a comma after the adverb clause.	**Before the night is over,** they will have finished the task.
Adverb clause comes in the middle of the sentence.	Put a comma both before and after the adverb clause.	The students, **if they have studied**, will do well on the next test.
Adverb clause comes at the end of the sentence.	The comma is optional.	They were allowed to pick the flowers **whenever they wanted.**

Adverbs and Writing Style

Adverb Phrases for Details

Adverbs can add a richness of detail to your writing. Try reviewing the list of adverb questions when you are writing a narrative, for example, to see if you could improve your writing by incorporating details using adverbs. On the other hand, if you find yourself using too many adverbs, look at your verbs. Perhaps a more specific verb choice can convey some of the information that was being carried by an adverb. For example, if you used *shuffled* rather than *walked*, you could use various structures to answer adverb questions, but you might not need a further adverb of manner.

Adverb Placement for Emphasis

Also, as we have seen, adverbs are highly mobile. Moving an adverb structure within the sentence can change the rhythm, the intonation pattern, and even the emphasis. Here is an example.

- *Her nephew started his own business as a master of ceremonies for weddings two years ago.* (Emphasis is on the time he did this: *two years ago.*)
- *Two years ago, her nephew started his own business as a master of ceremonies at weddings.* (Emphasis is on the action: starting his own business as a master of ceremonies at weddings.)
- *Her nephew, two years ago, started his own business as a master of ceremonies at weddings.* (Emphasis is on the nephew.)

When you write, try moving the adverbs to different locations in the sentence to achieve different effects.

Practice Sentences

Tree the following sentences. Remember to tree adverbs at the end and show that they have been moved, if necessary.

1. All winter, they eat canned fruit to save money.
2. She anticipated an award during the assembly from the principal.
3. While we are in this class, we are here to learn English grammar.
4. This famous actress rode on the subway to stay humble.
5. His grandmother ate flaxseed quite regularly.
6. She purchased the gown to look elegant when she went to the party.
7. Several girls gave their phone numbers to ensure a call after the concert.
8. By noon, the vociferous complaints of the children made the cafeteria extraordinarily loud.
9. Most seagulls honk without ceasing.
10. During the trip, the greatest frustration was the incessant construction on the interstate.
11. To feel better during his illness, the old man daily sang for one hour.
12. Those three women fought to grab the beautiful bouquet from the air.
13. Throughout that century, typhoid fever, cholera, botulism, and trichinosis were common because the sanitation was poor.
14. To convince her stubborn father, the girl made some delicious peach pie.

Adverb Choices 89

15. The glimmer of fireflies and moonbeams surrounded the busy Illinois toll way at the long tollbooth line outside of Rockford.
16. The obsession with Beanie Baby dolls became quite consuming among Mr. Smith's class.
17. I go to the hills to walk the dog unless it rains.
18. You contribute money to the account in regular payments or lump sums.
19. The nanny was good to her if she behaved.
20. With its island facility, Lion Country provided the chimps sanctuary for years.
21. Ryan ran the race to show his speed and agility.
22. Since the race was next month, the cross-country skier increased her practice time to build endurance.
23. By the next day, her mother disguised herself differently.
24. To become the top salesman, Thom worked hard for many years.
25. The judges chose Daisy to represent the country at the international competition.
26. To reward her for her honesty, Eleanor gave Judith ten dollars.
27. Although their methods seem strange, here the villagers learn healing from the jungle medicine men.
28. Like Susan, I get dizzy and weak from heights.
29. Over the seven days since the hazing, reporters, teachers, and members of the school board buried the girls' team under a dozen lectures of discipline and remediation.
30. The entrance of a new president later added difficulty to an already complex situation.
31. Even though she sacrificed, Dr. Humania went far into the jungle every morning for ten years to research monkeys.
32. The young boy brought the feed to the quarter horse whenever he came to the stable.
33. The water smacks against the pot as she rinses the rest of the apple butter down the mouth of the drain.
34. Because they trained well, women served well in combat positions in the Balkans and the Middle East.
35. To catch the thief, the police officers waited for several hours outside in the freezing cold.
36. Even if they are poor, the villagers add honey to tea and soymilk to make a savory treat.

37. Last week while I was on vacation, the hours went considerably faster.
38. Friday, Angela washed the pig to receive first prize at the fair.
39. The murderer washed the knife completely to eliminate any possibility of fingerprints on the weapon.
40. The United States rose against the odds to overcome terrorism.
41. That extremely skinny woman ate quickly to avoid her boss's rude comments.
42. The lions survive rather well each year in spite of the droughts in the area.
43. Once they began their studies, the naturalists found elephant companionship essential.
44. You place the ball where you want it with a seven iron.
45. Whether or not others understood her, Naomi rather quickly considered the elephants a part of her family.
46. With its daily rigor, that discipline made me a stronger person every day.
47. The San Diego Zoo conscientiously and very enthusiastically sent The Minnesota Zoo a breeding pair of takin because they wanted the animals.
48. If he wins the competition, Joachim receives his violin from The National Orchestra Association.
49. The next morning, the teenage girl planned excellent parties with the cheerleaders.
50. With her grace and elegance, the ballerina rose to the challenge of the dance, despite her fear of the audience.

II. Write Sentences.

1. Write one sentence for each of the seven basic sentence patterns.
    a. Intransitive verb
    b. Linking verb with predicate adjective
    c. Linking verb with predicate noun
    d. Transitive verb
    e. Vg verb
    f. Vc verb with an NP:OC
    g. Vc verb with an AdjP:OC

Adverb Choices

2. Now add adverb phrases to the seven basic sentences that you wrote. Use the chart on page 27 and add at least one adverb phrase for each of the adverb questions to at least one of your seven sentences. Label the types of adverbs in each sentence. Also, make sure that you have some simple adverbs, some NP:AdvP, some PP:AdvP, some InfPh: AdvP and some Cl:AdvP. Make sure that you use a comma after long adverb phrases that come at the beginning.

3. Write adverb clauses to answer the following adverb questions. Use the lists given in the chapter for ideas for the Cjs. Then write a main clause for each one and attach your adverb clauses. Remember that an adverb clause without the main clause is a fragment.
   a. AdvP-time
   b. AdvP-reason
   c. AdvP-condition
   d. AdvP-duration

4. Now move the adverb clauses that you wrote for #3 into various positions in the sentence and use commas to punctuate them correctly, depending upon where the adverb clause is located in the sentence. Put some adverb clauses at the beginning of the sentence, some in the middle, and some at the end. Review the section on "Adverbs and Punctuation."

5. Reread the section on "Adverb Usage and Writing Style." Use the examples given in this section to write 5 original sentences illustrating standard usage. Make sure you have sentences with *good* and *well* and *bad* and *badly*.

Chapter 6
Verbs: Expansions and Variations

Up to this point, we have been looking at sentences with single words as the verbs. In this chapter, we will look at verb expansions and variations.

The main verb of a sentence (MV) may have an optional auxiliary (Aux) with the required verb (V). The Aux can have a number of elements, as indicated in the formula below.

$$\text{Aux} \longrightarrow \begin{Bmatrix} \text{(Emph-DO)} \\ \text{(neg) (Supp-DO)} \\ \text{(neg) (modal) (HAVE) (BE)} \end{Bmatrix}$$

We will examine these elements individually below, but notice what the formula tells us. First we have a choice of the first line [(Emph-DO)], the second line [(neg) (Supp-DO)], or the third line [(neg) (modal) (HAVE) (BE)]. This tells us that the optional negative element can be added to either of the last two choices of verb clusters. It also tells us that if we have the Emph-DO element, we will not have any of the other verb cluster elements. Finally, the formula tells us that if we have the various elements (such as a *modal, HAVE,* and *BE*), they will appear in that order.

A tree representation would look like the following:

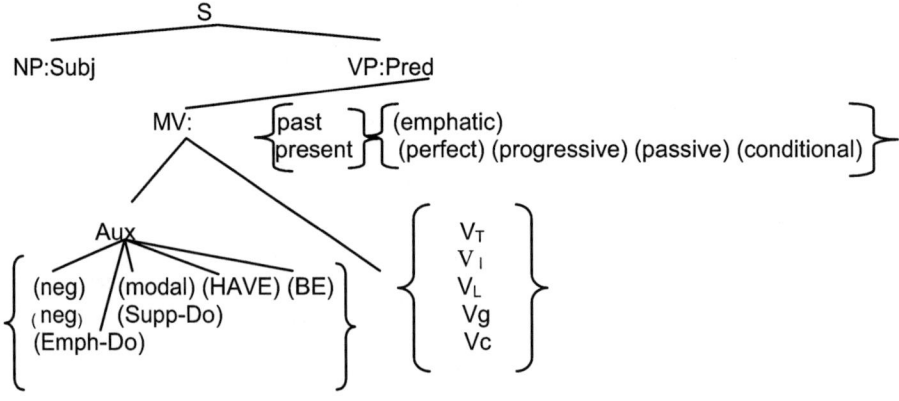

```
                           S
         _____
NP:Subj                           VP:Pred
                      MV:   {past    } {(emphatic)
                            {present }  (perfect) (progressive) (passive) (conditional)}
              _____
             Aux
        _____
    {(neg)  /(modal) (HAVE) (BE)}    { V_T }
    {(neg) / (Supp-Do)          }    { V_I }
    {(Emph-Do)                  }    { V_L }
                                     { Vg  }
                                     { Vc  }
```

Notice that we label the main verb (MV). The first word in the label is either past or present. One of those two forms is required. To determine if it is past or present, look at the first word in the verb cluster. That determines whether the first word in the MV label is past or present. In English, we can show the future with verbs, but we do not have a verb form that is future. We do have verb forms that are past or present. These are form labels, not meaning labels. When you label a verb cluster, look at the form the words are taking; do not try to determine the shades of meaning that the verb cluster is conveying. So, the very least an MV label will have is *past* or *present,* indicating the form of the first word in the verb cluster. The other labels will be discussed below.

Verb Particles

Speakers of modern English occasionally use a verb particle with the verb. In this instance, two words are acting as a single verb constituent. Examples are in bold below.
- We **looked up** the reference in the book.
- John will **toss in** his cheese sticks for free.
- It **shows up** as a blue line on the radar.
- The sun **came out** today.

When the sentence has a verb particle and a direct object, the verb particle may move to a position behind the direct object, as in the examples below. The verb particle is usually moved if the direct object is a pronoun.
- John will toss his cheese sticks **in** for free.
- We looked the reference **up** in the book.
- The librarian looked it **up** in Who's Who.

Sometimes there are two verb particles in the verb cluster. In the example which follows, both *up* and *on* are verb particles.
- The interior decorator **gave up on** the idea of natural wood trim.

A style of usage rule tells us not to end a sentence with a preposition. However, often what people think is a preposition is actually a verb particle. It is acceptable to end a sentence with a verb particle.
- We **looked** it **up.**
- She **copied** the assignment **down.**

We tree these as follows. *We looked the reference up in the book.*

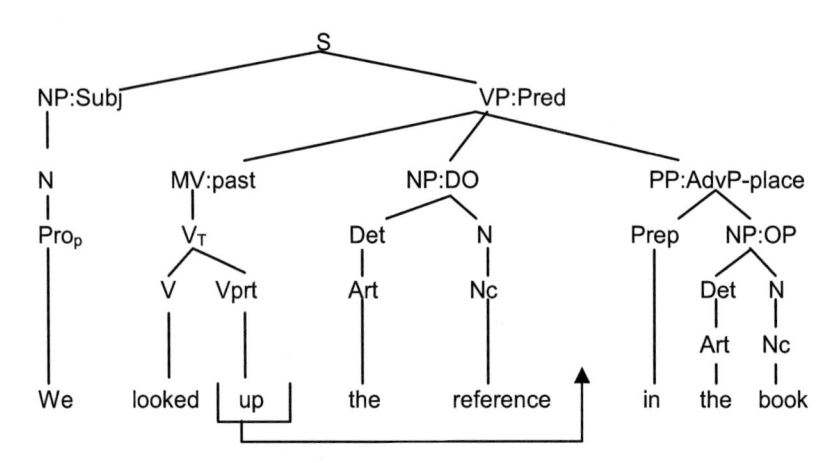

```
                                    S
        ┌───────────────────────────┴──────────────────────┐
    NP:Subj                                            VP:Pred
       │              ┌──────────────┬───────────────────────┐
       N           MV:past         NP:DO                PP:AdvP-place
       │              │         ┌─────┴───┐             ┌─────┴─────┐
      Prop           V_T        Det       N            Prep       NP:OP
       │           ┌──┴──┐       │        │             │       ┌───┴───┐
       │           V    Vprt     Art      Nc            │      Det      N
       │           │     │       │        │             │       │       │
       │           │     │       │        │             │      Art      Nc
       │           │     │       │        │             │       │       │
       We        looked  up     the    reference        in     the    book
```

Verb Particle or Preposition?

To do a sentence analysis, sometimes one must determine whether a word is a verb particle or whether the word is a preposition beginning a prepositional phrase. Consider the following examples.
- *The student copied down the assignment.*
- *He looked down the street.*

The word *down* could be either a verb particle or a preposition. To check for this, try putting the word with the NP which follows it and see if it could move as an adverbial prepositional phrase. This is the case in the second example above; *down the street* goes together as one unit, an AdvP-place. In the first example, *down* does not go with *the assignment* to answer any of the adverb questions. It goes with the verb (*copied down*) and *the assignment* is the DO.

Sometimes whether you are looking at a verb particle or a preposition is debatable.
- *The mayor boasted about the upcoming festival.*

Is the word *about* a verb particle or a preposition? I would like to call it a verb particle, making *boasted about* the verb with *the upcoming festival* the direct object. It seems to me that this captures the meaning of the

Verb Expansions and Variations 95

sentence better than trying to make *about the upcoming festival* into some sort of adverb phrase.

Conditional Verbs

Modals

Modals	
Present	**Past**
can	could
shall	should
will	would
may	might
	must

Conditional verbs have a modal. These somewhat alter the meaning carried by the verb, including carrying the meaning of future actions. The assignment of present and past for modals is a bit arbitrary, and grammarians sometimes disagree on the labels. My students made up a sentence to help them remember which of the modals on this list are present and which are past:

" Past forms '**must**' be '-**ould's**' or '-**ight**.' " (The rest are present.)

Thus, the verb cluster *might go* would be labeled past conditional; the verb cluster *shall conduct* would be labeled present conditional.

Quasi-modals

Quasi-modals	
Present	**Past**
seem to	seemed to
happen to	happened to
have to	had to
has to	used to
	ought to

Sometimes two words seem to be acting together as if they were a single modal. For example *"ought to"* seems like a replacement for the modal *should*. We can call these Quasi-modals.

Quasi-modals still would need a past or present label since they will be the first element in the verb cluster, so I would assign past or present as indicated in the box.

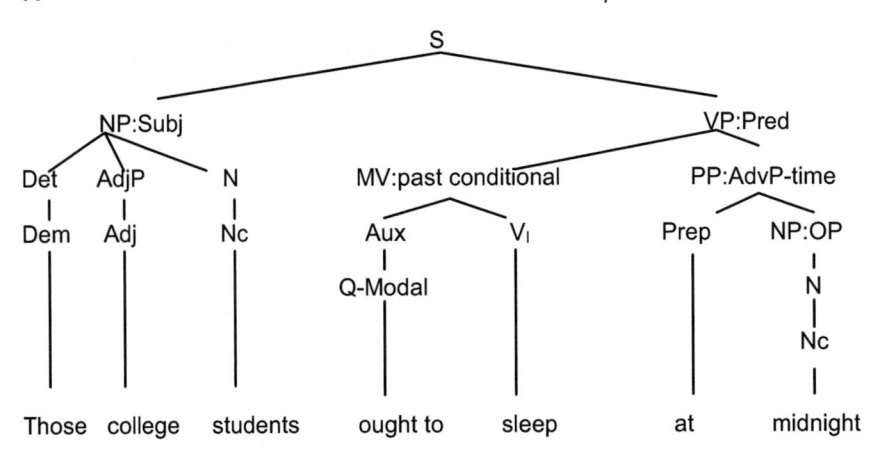

```
                              S
         ┌────────────────────┴──────────────────────┐
      NP:Subj                                     VP:Pred
   ┌────┼─────┐         ┌──────────────┐      ┌──────┴──────┐
  Det  AdjP   N      MV:past conditional    PP:AdvP-time
   │    │     │         ┌──────┴──┐         ┌────┴────┐
  Dem  Adj   Nc        Aux        V₁       Prep      NP:OP
   │    │     │         │         │         │         │
   │    │     │      Q-Modal      │         │         N
   │    │     │         │         │         │         │
   │    │     │         │         │         │        Nc
   │    │     │         │         │         │         │
 Those college students ought to sleep      at     midnight
```

Perfect Verbs

| Perfect ⟶ HAVE -en |

Verbs in perfect form include a form of HAVE (has, had, have) and the perfect form of a verb. This perfect form varies from verb to verb, but we designate it by writing *–en*. We write *HAVE* in all capital letters to indicate the general category and not the actual word, since that word could be *has, had,* or *have*.

For example, all of the following verbs are present perfect: *has written, have looked, has participated, have investigated, has regulated, have spoken, has given.* The same set of words with *had* instead of *has* or *have* would be past perfect. If all verbs in English were regular, the perfect form would theoretically always end in *–en*. However, notice that the perfect form in English more often ends in *–ed* instead of *–en.*

Perfect verbs can be combined with modals to produce perfect conditional. Notice that although the modal comes first in the verb cluster, the label *conditional* comes at the end of the verb label.

could have photographed	past perfect conditional
may have regulated	present perfect conditional
will have wrapped	present perfect conditional

Progressive Verbs

| Progressive ⟶ BE -ing |

Verbs in progressive form consist of a form of the verb *BE* and the *–ing*

Verb Expansions and Variations

form of the next verb in the cluster. For example, all of the following verbs are present progressive: *is holding, are cleaning, is twirling, am printing*. Past progressive examples would be *was chopping* and *were digging*. We write BE in all capital letters to indicate the general category of words, not the specific word. Forms of *BE* include *is, are, was, were, been, am,* and *be*.

Progressive verbs can be combined with modals and perfect forms as well.

may be jumping	present progressive conditional
had been babbling	past perfect progressive
could have been evaporating	past perfect progressive conditional
has been developing	present perfect progressive

The water *could have been evaporating* last week.

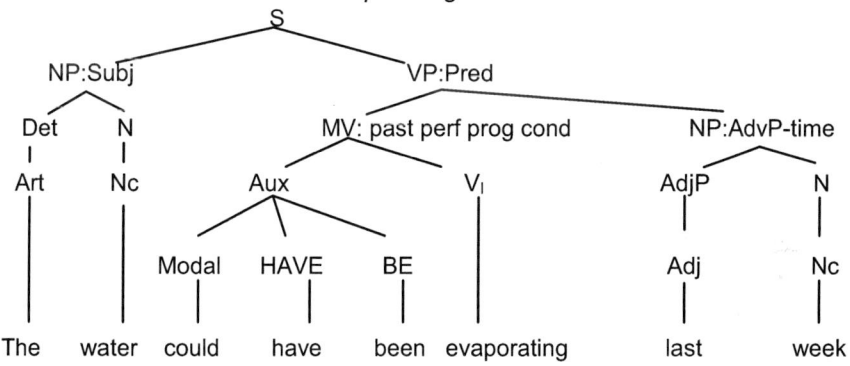

```
                          S
           _____
       NP:Subj                      VP:Pred
        /    \              _____
      Det     N          MV: past perf prog cond     NP:AdvP-time
       |      |          _____             /     \
      Art    Nc         Aux              V_I        AdjP      N
       |      |        __|__              |          |        |
       |      |    Modal HAVE BE           |         Adj       Nc
       |      |      |    |   |            |          |        |
      The   water  could have been    evaporating    last     week
```

Notice that in the MV label (past perfect progressive conditional), if all of those elements are in the verb cluster, the label is written in that order. The modal comes first in the verb cluster, but the word *conditional* comes at the end of the MV label. Also notice that the HAVE and BE are written in all capital letters.

Emphatic Verbs and Negatives

Emphatic

In the emphatic verb, we use a form of DO for emphasis (*I do respect you; she did try*). The past or present is indicated by the form of DO. Thus, the following are present emphatic: *does practice, do exercise.* The past emphatic uses *did*. The DO for the emphatic is indicated by **Emph-DO**. It appears in the Aux; <u>if there is an Emph-DO, there will NOT be any other verb form in the auxiliary.</u>

```
           VP:Pred
              |
         MV: past emphatic
          /        \
        Aux         V₁
         |          |
      Emph-DO       |
         |          |
        did        try
```

Negative

If the verb has been made negative, the word *not* or the contraction *n't* has been added. For the sake of clarity, we will add the negative **(Neg)** to the front of the Aux. Then we will show that it moves to a position after the first word of the "official" verb cluster.

If the verb does not have any element in the Aux before we make it negative, we might need to add a **supplementary form of the verb do (Supp-DO)**. For example, to make the verb *dances* into a negative, we say "*does not dance.*" We have added both the word *not* and the Supp-DO *does*. Other examples of negatives with Supp-DO include *didn't describe, doesn't include, don't participate.*

> Note: We use Supp-DO to supplement when there is a negative if there is no other Aux element. We use Emph-DO to emphasize a positively stated verb.

The addition of the negative (*not*) and Supp-DO does not add anything to the MV label. Notice in the tree which follows that the movement of the *not* is indicated with an arrow, and the formation of the contraction is indicated by ⌣.

If there is a BE-type linking verb (called a copula), then we simply add the Negative (Neg) to the Aux without a Supp-DO: *isn't, was not, were not,*

Verb Expansions and Variations

aren't. We will need to indicate that the *not* has been moved to a position after the V.

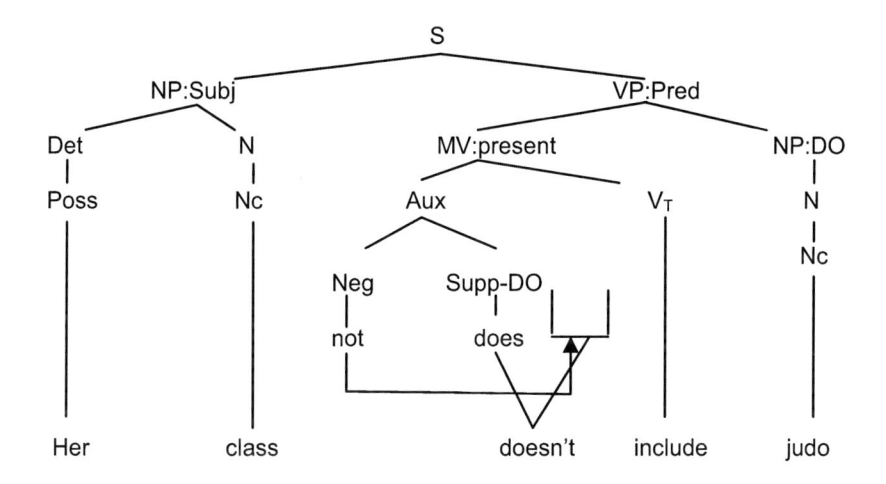

```
                                    S
                ┌───────────────────┴───────────────────┐
            NP:Subj                                  VP:Pred
          ┌─────┴─────┐                  ┌─────────────┼─────────────┐
        Det           N              MV:present                    NP:DO
         │            │             ┌─────┴─────┐                    │
        Poss          Nc           Aux          V_T                  N
                               ┌────┴────┐                           │
                              Neg     Supp-DO                        Nc
                               │         │
                              not       does

        Her         class              doesn't    include          judo
```

The negative may be added to any of the verb forms discussed above. Examples include *had not been babbling, couldn't have been evaporating, has not wrapped, might not go*. Since all of these verb clusters already have an element in the Aux, we do not need Supp-DO.

Passive Verbs

| Passive ⟶ BE -en |

The verbs we have looked at so far are **active**. **Passive** verb forms in English combine two of the elements we have seen in earlier forms: a form of BE plus the –en form of the verb.

Passive verbs can be formed from a transitive-type active verb. The original direct object (DO) becomes the subject. The original subject becomes the object of a prepositional phrase with the preposition *by*. This by-phrase becomes an adverb of agency (PP:AdvP-agency).

- *The dog chewed the bone.*
- *The bone was chewed by the dog.*

- *The first batter scored a run.*
- *A run was scored by the first batter.*

Since the original DO is now the subject, we label it the grammatical subject. It is in the subject position in the sentence. Since the original subject is now the OP, we label it as both the OP and logical subject (LogSubj).

> Note: Often in passive constructions, the by-phrase is dropped. An example would be the following: *A crime has been committed.* In this case, there is no logical subject.

Since V_c and V_g are both types of transitive verbs, we can also make a passive construction with them.

- *The administrators considered Hexaba a destructive influence.*
- *Hexaba was considered a destructive influence by the administrators.*

- *The panel of judges found her entry worthy of honorable mention.*
- *Her entry was found worthy of honorable mention. (Note that the logical subject has been dropped in this one.)*

- *The tyrant gave the department members a disgusting ultimatum.*
- *The department members were given a disgusting ultimatum by the tyrant.*

In the first example, the original verb was Vc. In the passive, I would argue that the V has become a V_L because *a destructive influence* renames *Hexaba*. Similarly, I would say that the V in the second example (*was found*) is also V_L because *worthy of honorable mention* describes the subject *her entry*. In the third sentence, the original verb was Vg. In the passive, it is a V_T.

You can also make a transitive verb passive if it has auxiliaries.

- *At the clinic, Becca was injecting the flighty thoroughbred.*
- *At the clinic, the flighty thoroughbred was being injected by Becca.*

- *Ivy could have been buying the commemorative coin.*
- *The commemorative coin could have been bought by Ivy.*

It is harder to see the passive when the verb cluster contains many elements, but the BE plus the –en form will be the last two elements. For

Verb Expansions and Variations 101

instance, the first example above shows past progressive passive. In the second example, the modal *could* makes the verb conditional; the *have been* makes the verb perfect (HAVE –en), and the *been bought* (BE -en) makes the verb passive. The verb *buy* is another irregular verb, and the *–en* form is *bought.* So, this is a past perfect passive conditional verb.

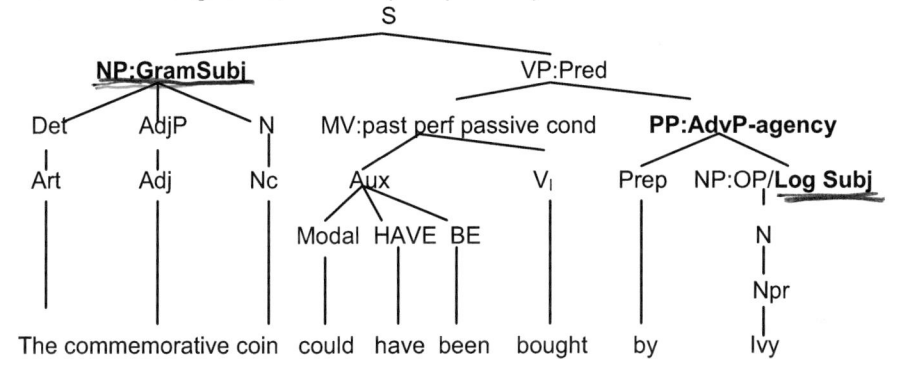

```
                              S
         ┌────────────────────┴────────────────────┐
    NP:GramSubj                                VP:Pred
  ┌──────┼──────┐         ┌──────────────────┬──────────────────┐
 Det   AdjP     N     MV:past perf passive cond         PP:AdvP-agency
  │     │       │       ┌──────┴──────┐              ┌──────┴──────┐
 Art   Adj     Nc      Aux            V₁            Prep    NP:OP/Log Subj
  │     │       │    ┌──┼──┐           │              │            │
  │     │       │  Modal HAVE BE       │              │            N
  │     │       │    │   │   │         │              │            │
  │     │       │    │   │   │         │              │           Npr
  │     │       │    │   │   │         │              │            │
The commemorative coin could have been bought        by           Ivy
```

Sometimes we use *got* or *get* to function as a BE Aux for passive in some slang expressions.

She got fired yesterday.

```
                          S
        ┌─────────────────┼─────────────────┐
   NP:GramSubj        VP:Pred
        │         ┌──────┴──────┐
        N     MV:past passive     NP: AdvP-time
        │       ┌────┴────┐              │
       Prop    Aux        V₁             N
        │      │           │             │
        │      BE          │             Nc
        │      │           │             │
       She   got         fired        yesterday
```

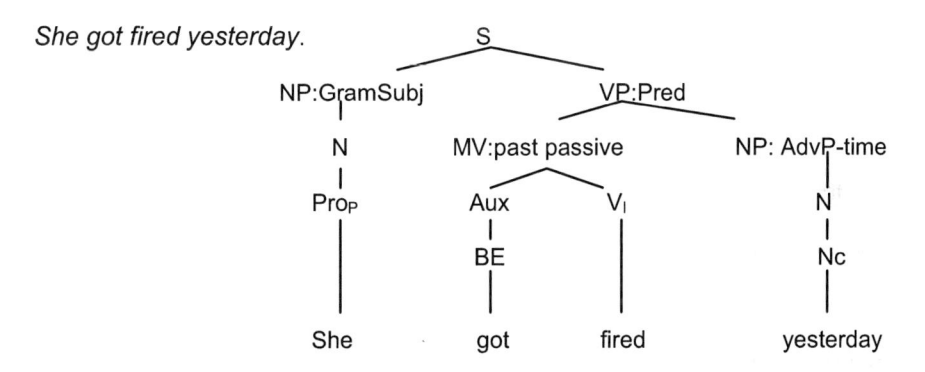

V Labels and Passive Verbs

Once a verb is made into the passive, the V label gets a bit difficult. In the example which follows, I am labeling it as V₁. I would say that this is the usual case with passive verbs. Only a type of transitive verb can be made into a passive. However, remember that Vc and Vg are both types of transitives. Consider the following examples.

1) *The quaking scientist handed the thief a new microscope.*

1a) *A new microscope was handed to the thief by the quaking scientist.*
1b) *The thief was handed a new microscope.*

2) *The press named Peter athlete of the week.*

2) *Peter was named athlete of the week by the press.*

3) *The royal family considered her worthy of respect.*

3) *She was considered worthy of respect by the royal family.*

In the first example (1a), we had a Vg verb made into a passive. In the true passive (*a new microscope was handed to the thief by the quaking scientist*), I would say that the new verb is V_I since it is followed by only adverbial prepositional phrases. In the second version (1b), the indirect object becomes the subject (*the thief was handed a new microscope*) and the V label changes from what was Vg to a V_T. In the second and third examples, the original verb is Vc. It is strange, but I think that making these into passives makes the V label into V_L because *athlete of the week* renames *Peter* and *worthy of respect* describes *she*.

Passive Verbs vs. Predicate Adjectives

Sometimes you might be wondering if a word that comes after a BE verb is a passive verb or an adjective functioning as a predicate adjective. To figure this out, try to <u>conjugate</u> the word. That is, try to put it in its "other" verb forms, such as putting it into these test frames: *Yesterday I _____ed. Today I am _____ing.* If you can't do that, the word is an adjective, not a passive verb. Another test is to look for a *by* phrase in the sentence or see if you could logically construct a *by* phrase. If so, the word is a passive verb.

- *The girl was despondent.* You can't say "*Today I am <u>despondenting</u>,*" so it is a predicate adjective.
- *The girl was considered for the job.* You can say, "*Today I am <u>considering</u>,*" so it is a passive verb. Also, you could insert a by phrase: The girl was considered for the job by the selection committee.

Compound Verb Phrases

As we have seen in the other structures, verb phrases may also be compound, joined by a Cjc (*and, or, but, nor*). Again, on the tree, we show a "Cjc triangle" with the points of the triangle connecting the same type of element.

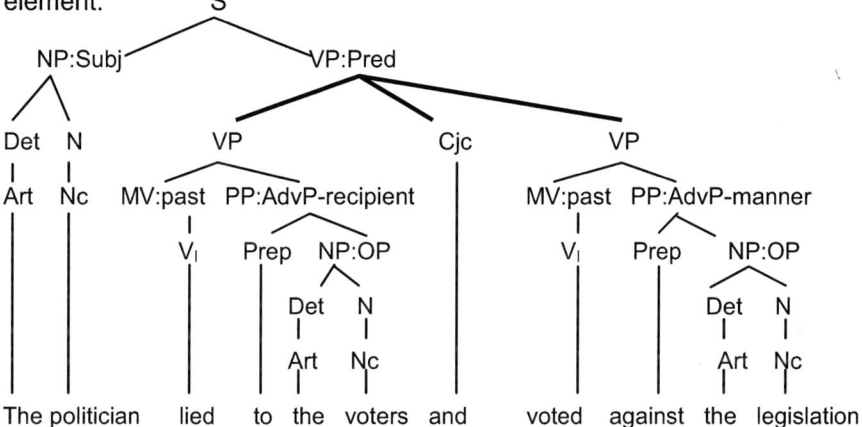

```
                                S
              ┌─────────────────┴──────────────────┐
           NP:Subj                              VP:Pred
          ┌───┴───┐          ┌──────────────┬───────┬──────────────┐
         Det     N          VP             Cjc                    VP
          │      │     ┌─────┴──────┐                      ┌───────┴────────┐
         Art    Nc  MV:past  PP:AdvP-recipient          MV:past    PP:AdvP-manner
          │      │     │     ┌──────┴──────┐              │        ┌────┴─────┐
          │      │    V_I  Prep         NP:OP            V_I     Prep       NP:OP
          │      │     │                ┌──┴──┐           │                 ┌──┴──┐
          │      │     │               Det    N           │                Det    N
          │      │     │                │     │           │                 │     │
          │      │     │               Art   Nc           │                Art   Nc
          │      │     │                │     │           │                 │     │
    The politician   lied    to       the  voters   and  voted  against   the  legislation
```

Notice that in the next example, the PP:AdvP-manner answers an adverb question for both of the VPs. Be sure to note how I treed this one to show that the adverb phrase refers to both VPs.

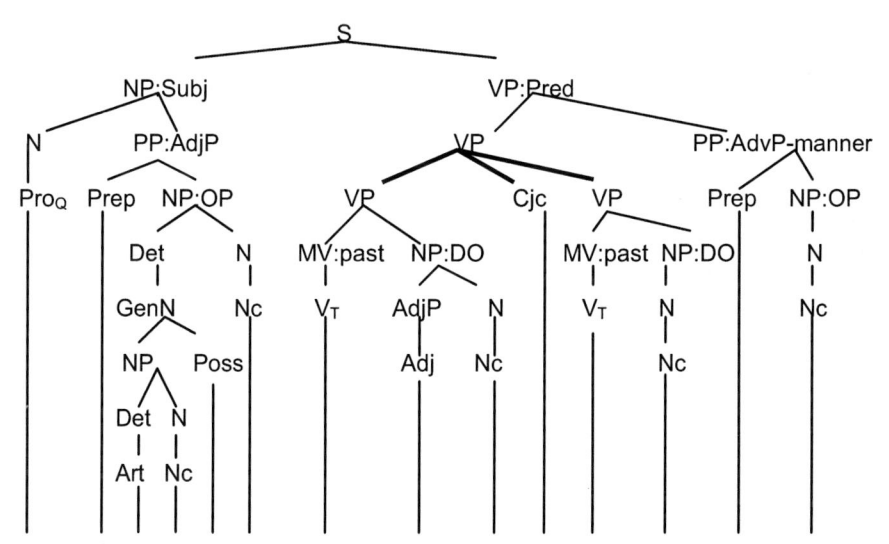

```
                                      S
                ┌─────────────────────┴──────────────────────┐
             NP:Subj                                      VP:Pred
       ┌────────┴────────┐                 ┌──────────────────┼──────────────────┐
       N              PP:AdjP             VP                                PP:AdvP-manner
       │         ┌──────┴──────┐     ┌─────┴─────┬─────┐                   ┌──────┴──────┐
      Pro_Q    Prep         NP:OP   VP          Cjc    VP                Prep          NP:OP
       │                ┌────┴───┐  ┌───┴────┐       ┌──┴───┐                           │
       │               Det       N MV:past NP:DO   MV:past NP:DO                        N
       │                │        │   │    ┌──┴──┐    │      │                           │
       │              GenN      Nc  V_T  AdjP   N   V_T     N                           Nc
       │          ┌─────┴───┐        │    │                 │
       │         NP        Poss      │   Adj   Nc          Nc
       │       ┌──┴──┐
       │      Det    N
       │       │     │
       │      Art   Nc
  Some   of   the guide's friends learned new  words  and took  pictures with enthusiasm
```

Sometimes the V elements share a common Aux, and sometimes with compound verb phrases, the auxiliary of the second VP is implied but not actually stated. In these cases, for grammatical analysis, we will add the Aux back in with a dotted line and parentheses. These situations are illustrated in the trees below.

They had been swimming and sunning at the beach.

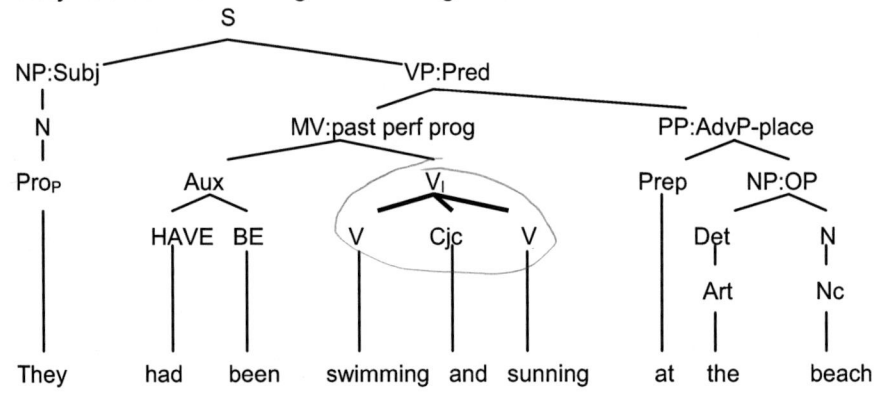

Many are dried and sold as curios or for traditional medicines.

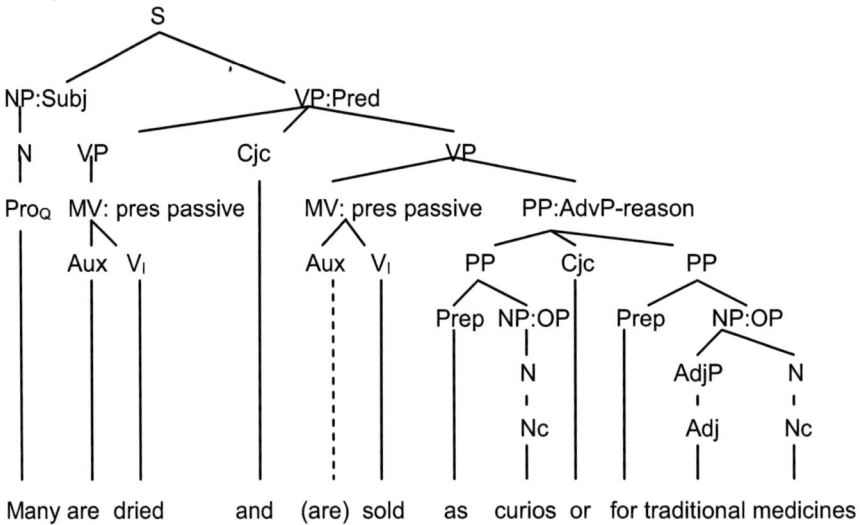

We can also combine verb phrases or even single verbs with Cjcorr.
- *The politician **not only** lied to the voters **but also** voted against the legislation.*
- *They had been **either** swimming **or** sunning at the beach.*

Verb Expansions and Variations

Verb Usage

Irregular Verb Forms and Particles

Some languages, such as oriental languages, do not have prepositions or verb particles. Therefore, speakers of these languages who learn English will have difficulty with verb particles.

Irregular verb forms also cause trouble if one is attempting to use Standard English. Irregular forms such as the ones below must simply be memorized.

swim	swam	(had) swum
rise	rose	(had) risen
swing	swung	(had) swung
sneak	sneaked	(had) sneaked
lie (to recline)	lay	(had) lain
lay (to place)	laid	(had) laid

The most troublesome verbs in English might be *lie* and *lay*. Remember that *lie* means "to recline" and *lay* means "to place or put something."

Lie is intransitive, and *lay* is a transitive verb with a direct object.

Verbs and Subjects

Another important usage rule is that verbs should agree with their subjects. This is not too much of a problem for native speakers of English, except in two cases.

- When the subject is compound, joined by the conjunction *or* or the Cjcorr *neither/nor* or *either/or,* then the verb agrees with the subject nearest to it.
    - Neither the boys nor the dog **knows** where the rabbit is.
    - Either the student or the archaeologists **give** the report at the conference.

- The verb agrees with the N element of the NP. For purposes of subject/verb agreement, any adjectival prepositional phrases that come after the N element are ignored.
    - *The messages of the candidate* **were** *confusing.* (The verb *were* goes with the N element *messages,* which is plural, not with the OP element *the candidate,* which is singular.)

- Each of the candidates **has** been selected with care. (The verb *has been selected* goes with the N element *each*, which is singular, not the OP element *the candidates*, which is plural.)
- One of the older travelers **is** lost again. (The verb *is* goes with the N element *one*, which is singular, not the OP element *the older travelers*, which is plural.)

Verbs and Writing Style

Strong Verbs

In general, writers should select verbs with care to strengthen their writing. More specific verbs often improve the image for the reader. For example, instead of writing "*The singer walked into the room,*" one could try "*ambled,*" "*shuffled,*" "*sashayed,*" "*pranced,*" or "*sauntered.*"

Another style rule often invoked is that one should not use passives. Passive constructions which drop the by-phrase are often used when the doer of the action is unknown or when the writer wants to hide the doer. For example, one can say "*A soldier was shot yesterday*" and not reveal that it was "friendly fire" by the soldier's own army.

Passive construction is also used if the receiver of the action is more important than the doer. For example, if the voters elected Roy Rabbit, but the person elected is more important than the people who elected him, then the passive construction (*Roy Rabbit was elected*) might be a better choice.

Finally, in science and social science, use of passive verbs is an established convention. So, a rule forbidding all use of the passive is not appropriate, but often sentence style can be improved by using active rather than passive verbs, particularly in fields such as journalism. Unless the doer is unknown or less important than the receiver, active verbs are a better choice than passives.

Parallelism

Verbs can also be used to make sentence elements parallel to each other.

Verb Expansions and Variations 107

Not Parallel	The Hawaiian students packed up the camp, greeted the day with a traditional chant, and the rest of the time was spent sailing to the next location.
Parallel	The Hawaiian students packed up the camp, greeted the day with a traditional chant, and spent the rest of the time sailing to the next location.

Not Parallel	The Owl Research Institute team gently untangled a female snowy owl from the trap, fitted her with a transmitter backpack, and finally she was released in Montana.
Parallel	The Owl Research Institute team gently untangled a female snowy owl from the trap, fitted her with a transmitter backpack, and released her in Montana.

Practice Sentences

I. Tree the following sentences.
1. Each candidate is positioning himself as a warm, friendly person.
2. People tune out the messages of candidates.
3. The doctor had given our assistant a small dose of laudanum.
4. Later, the president sat down at the desk, slid the sheaf of papers in front of her, and read the report over with careful consideration.
5. Gordon had adjusted his position on the chair and was clearing his throat.
6. The fish has been given a modified growth gene.
7. I used to nearly go crazy when the twins were little.
8. Penicillin was discovered in 1928 but largely ignored until WW II.
9. Members of the Taiwanese rock band were showing off their giant animal masks.
10. Inca rule was extending along the western edge of South America during the early sixteenth century.
11. The intruder's noiseless entrance did not give me any warning.
12. On a ridge in the Andes, archaeologists will study a newly discovered sacred center.
13. Scientists have raced to unearth mummies in a shantytown outside of Peru's capital of Lima.
14. The Inca must have created a functioning community without a written language, iron, or the wheel.

15. They had been calling it the Skeleton Coast.
16. The young male pup did have a thick new coat of fur.
17. Fantastic masks have long served double duty in the festival.
18. Each year, some camper had always left something on the beach.
19. The crown jewels of the automotive industry were becoming cheap imitators of themselves.
20. The biology student's miniature hedgehog was not found for days.
21. Several of the prisoners were terrified by their first glimpse of the sun in six years.
22. The moonlight was making me very morbid.
23. On Cheju Island, the women own the property and rule their households.
24. A 16-foot shark can instill terror into the heart of the toughest thrill seeker.
25. This shark's attack can be turned away by a hand.
26. The sharks won't be left out of this banquet.
27. The female elephant may have brought the herd a new baby during the night.
28. Queen Victoria did have a carrier gene for hemophilia.
29. Chimps were used for disease immunizations.
30. The stoneware spaniel would not become a great piece of American folk art.
31. I have always been curious.
32. The funds, food, and medicine for the hospital were donated.
33. The diver disarmed the bomb and gave up his life to protect our country.
34. All the chimps ought to have enjoyed their freedom.
35. Washington was becoming a legend even then.
36. In Java, an ancient art form is struggling for survival.
37. In ancient Indonesian culture, textile was endowed with magical properties by batik decoration.
38. This generation of seals has begun a new precarious journey into the sea.
39. The president had to carefully consider the ultimate goal of any military action.
40. Life could always be solved for them by peanut butter sandwiches and swim time.
41. She had to excuse herself and make a hasty departure.

Verb Expansions and Variations 109

42. The Jain Bird Hospital was founded by an Indian religious sect with a reverence for life.
43. I could never give up chocolate to be more fit.
44. The painstaking process of batik was revolutionized by the computer.
45. The slug could be producing one of nature's best lubricants.
46. My grandma used to preserve pickles in a huge stone jar.
47. Taiwan is witnessing the musical revolution of "mando-pop."
48. Scientists might harness the energy of a firefly and could learn the navigation system of the monarch butterfly.
49. The boy was not motivated last summer by his love of dolphins.
50. Dolphins were utilized as therapists for the boy with the rare genetic disease.

II. Write the following sentences to practice verb types.

1. Write one sentence for each of the seven basic sentence patterns.
2. Using the sentences you wrote for number 1, change the verbs to show the following verb types. Choose a different one of your sentences for each of the verbs listed. Underline the verb cluster.
    a. conditional   d. perfect progressive   g. perfect conditional
    b. perfect   e. progressive conditional
    c. progressive   f. perfect progressive conditional
3. Make two of your verbs emphatic.
4. Make two of your verbs negative.
5. Make the V_T sentence, Vg sentence, and Vc sentence into passives.

III. Practice verb usage.

1. Find 5 of the passive verbs in Section I. Rewrite the sentences to make them active. <u>In each case</u>, do you prefer the passive or the active? Why?
2. Use each of these irregular verb forms correctly in a sentence. Make sure that for "b," your sentence clearly indicates that it was in the past.
    a. lie   c. had lain   e. lay   g. had laid
    b. lay   d. lying   f. laid   h. laying
3. Reread the section on "Verbs and Subjects." Using the examples given, write 5 sentences showing challenging subject/verb agreement situations. Use <u>present tense</u> for your sentences.

Chapter 7
Nominal Phrase Choices

We have looked at nominal phrases (NP) that consist of a noun cluster with a required N element (either a noun or substitute pronoun). In English, we have other structures that assume the typical NP functions of subject (Subj), direct object (DO), indirect object (IO), predicate nominative (PredN), object of the preposition (OP), or object complement (OC). These structures substitute for a simple noun cluster. The nominal phrase substitutes are gerund phrases, noun clauses, and nominal infinitive phrases.

Gerund Phrases

Gerunds can function as subjects, direct objects, indirect objects, objects of preposition, and predicate nominatives. Gerund phrases can begin with a possessive pronouns (Poss) or genitive nouns (GenN). (See Chapter 4 if you need a review of these.) Unless it has a possessive determiner in front, gerunds begin with an "-ing word" followed by other elements of the VP. The –ing word is a form of a verb.

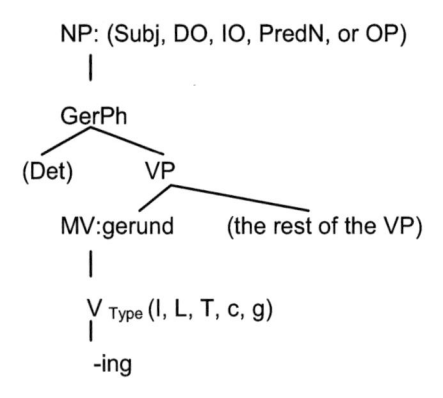

```
           NP: (Subj, DO, IO, PredN, or OP)
                        |
                      GerPh
                      /    \
                  (Det)     VP
                           /  \
                    MV:gerund   (the rest of the VP)
                        |
                     V Type (I, L, T, c, g)
                        |
                      -ing
```

As we saw in the adverbial infinitive phrase, the VP does not function as a predicate but can have any of the elements that we have been seeing in the VP:Pred. Since there is no subject element within the gerund phrase, there is no predicate function. The VP in the gerund is merely a part of the gerund phrase.

Nominal Phrase Choices

The veterinarian finished drawing blood samples from the caribou.

```
                             S
              ┌──────────────┴──────────────┐
          NP:Subj                       VP:Pred
         ┌───┴───┐              ┌──────────┴──────────┐
        Det      N           MV:Past                NP:DO
         │       │              │                     │
        Art      Nc             V_T                 GerPh
                                                      │
                                                      VP
                                       ┌──────────────┼──────────────┐
                                   MV:gerund        NP:DO         PP:AdvP-Source
                                       │         ┌────┴───┐       ┌────┴────┐
                                      V_T     NP:AdjP     N      Prep     NP:OP
                                                 │        │                ┌──┴──┐
                                                 N        Nc              Det    N
                                                 │                         │     │
                                                 Nc                        Art   Nc

         The  veterinarian  finished   drawing    blood   samples    from  the  caribou
```

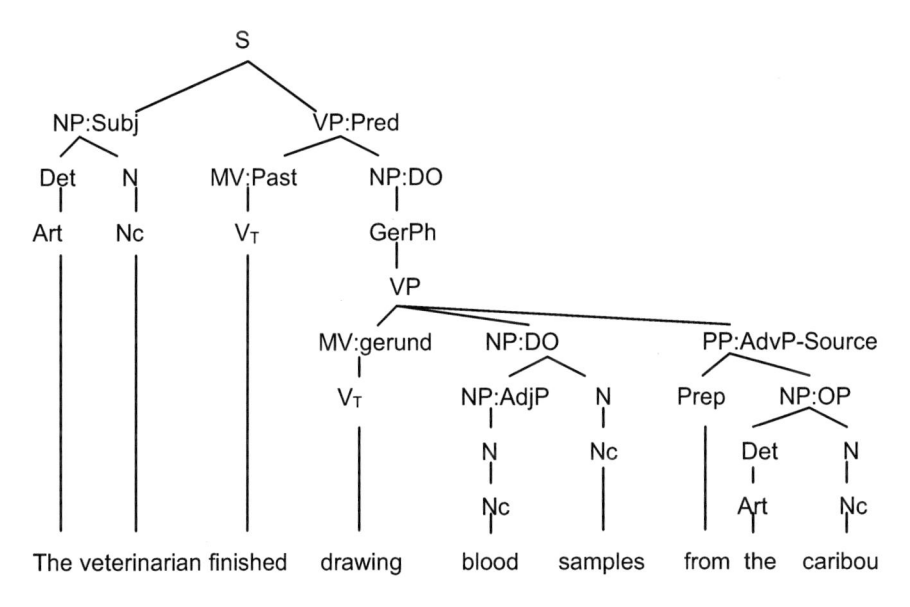

Next is an example of a gerund with a determiner in front.

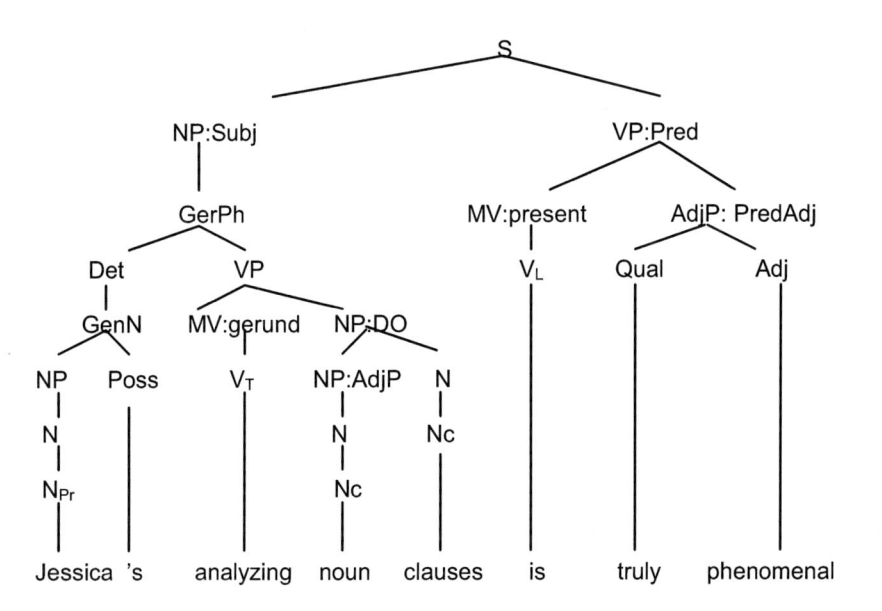

```
                                       S
                     ┌─────────────────┴─────────────────┐
                 NP:Subj                             VP:Pred
                    │                    ┌──────────────┴──────────────┐
                  GerPh              MV:present                  AdjP: PredAdj
            ┌───────┴───────┐            │                       ┌──────┴──────┐
           Det              VP           V_L                   Qual           Adj
            │          ┌────┴────┐
          GenN      MV:gerund  NP:DO
        ┌───┴──┐       │    ┌────┴───┐
       NP    Poss     V_T  NP:AdjP    N
        │                    │        │
        N                    N        Nc
        │                    │
       N_Pr                  Nc

     Jessica 's    analyzing   noun   clauses    is     truly    phenomenal
```

Notice that the gerund phrase is very versatile.

Gerund Phrase as NP:Subj	***Thanking her for her kindness*** *was his first priority of the day.*
Gerund Phrase as NP:DO	*The veterinarian finished* ***drawing blood samples from the caribou***.
Gerund Phrase as NP:IO	*The dentist should give* ***organizing his appointments each day*** *a chance.*
Gerund Phrase as NP:OP	*The accusation of* ***financing his re-election campaign with illegal foreign contributions*** *was uppermost in his mind.*
Gerund Phrases as PredN	*Her favorite activities in London are* ***visiting Westminster Abbey and touring the Tower of London***.

Noun Clauses

The *noun* part of the name of these structures comes because they function as typical NPs (subjects, direct objects, objects of prepositions, or predicate nominatives); the *clause* part of the name comes because they have **within them** both a subject and a predicate. Noun clauses begin with a subordinator and then have an NP:Subj and VP:Pred.

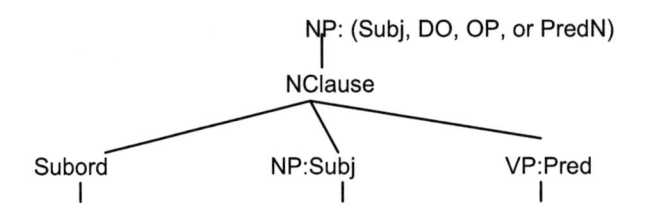

```
              NP: (Subj, DO, OP, or PredN)
                         |
                      NClause
              _____|_____
             |           |           |
           Subord     NP:Subj     VP:Pred
             |           |           |
```

There are two types of noun clauses, named for the type of subordinator that they have: *that/whether* noun clauses and *Wh* noun clauses.

That/Whether Noun Clauses

In this type of noun clause, the word *that* or *whether* begins the clause and acts as the subordinator.

That/whether Noun Clause as NP:Subj	***That we wanted to win the tournament*** *was no surprise to anyone.*
That/whether Noun Clause as NP:DO	*We wondered* ***whether the tiny dragon would be popular***.
That/whether Noun Clause as NP:PredN	*Our youngest brother's greatest talent is* ***that he could design landscapes for lawns***.

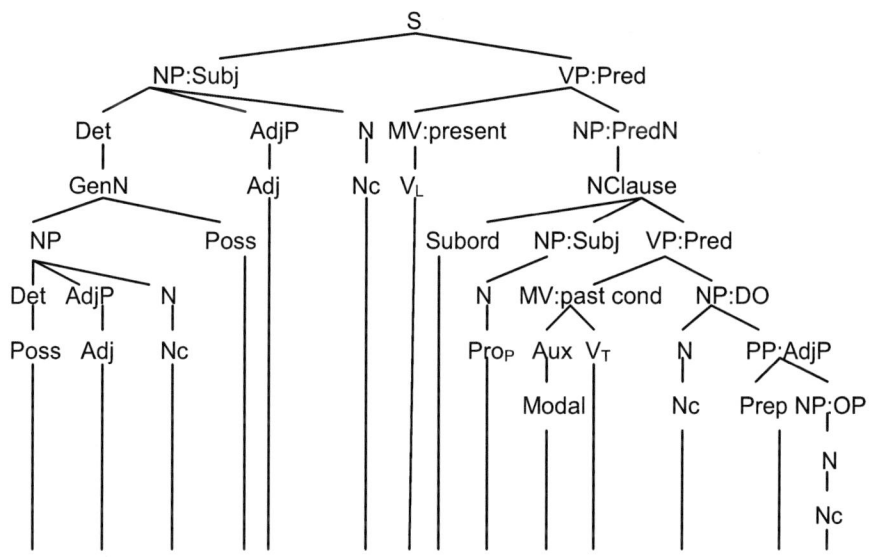

Nominal Phrase Choices

[Sentence diagram]

Our youngest brother's greatest talent is that he could design landscapes for lawns

Dropping the Subordinator

Sometimes if the noun clause is a direct object (DO) or predicate nominative (PredN), the word *that* is dropped. (The word *that* is not dropped if the noun clause is a subject.) However, the subordinator is still there grammatically, so add it with a dotted line and put parentheses around the word.

- The candidate claimed **he was experienced**. (NClause is the NP:DO.)
- Our concern was **the puppy would run away**. (NClause is NP:PredN.)

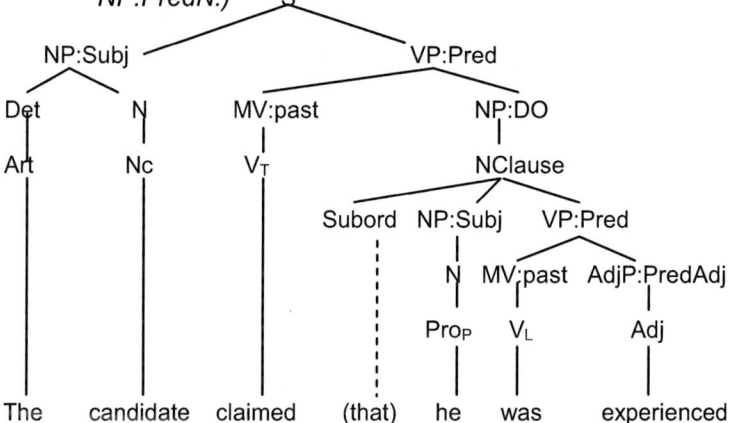

[Sentence diagram]

The candidate claimed (that) he was experienced

Wh Noun Clauses

The *Wh* is in the name of this type of noun clause because most (but not all) of the words that begin this type of noun clause begin with *wh: who, what, when, where, how, how often, why, which,* and *whose*. These noun clauses can function as subjects, direct objects, indirect objects, predicate nominatives, and objects of prepositions.

Wh Noun Clause as NP:Subj	***Whose plan for the budget would get accepted*** was a mystery for the legislators.
Wh Noun Clause as NP:DO	They decided ***who would represent the faculty on the board of trustees***.
Wh Noun Clause as NP:OP	The decision of ***what colors the flag should be*** was not made until Friday.
Wh Noun Clause as NP:IO	She gave ***when the meeting would end*** her utmost attention.
Wh Noun Clause as NP:PredN	The question remained ***whom they should replace***.

We will still tree the NClause with the three main divisions: Subord, NP:Subj, and VP:Pred.

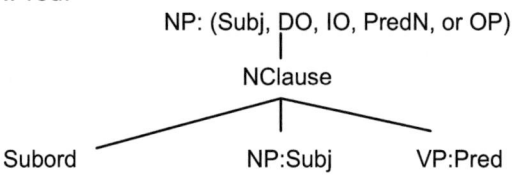

```
          NP: (Subj, DO, IO, PredN, or OP)
                       |
                    NClause
            _____|_____
           |           |           |
         Subord    NP:Subj     VP:Pred
```

However, these subordinators (*who, what, whom, when, where, how, how often, how well, why, which,* or *whose*) have a **dual function**, acting both as the subordinator for the noun clause and acting as a function within the noun clause itself. They are **both subordinators and pro-forms.**

Each of the noun clause examples in the right-hand column of the following chart could be inserted in the blank in the following sentence:

They discovered _____.

Nominal Phrase Choices   115

Wh Word	Replaces	Label	Examples
Who / What Whoever/ Whatever	NP:Subj	ProN	*who* would represent the faculty on the board of trustees / *what* made the sound
What	NP:DO NP:PredN	ProN	*what* the scientist found
Whom/ Whomever	NP:DO	ProN	*whom* they should replace
When	AdvP	ProAdv	*when* the meeting would end
Where	AdvP	ProAdv	*where* the reception would be
How	AdvP	ProAdv	*how* the petunias would grow by the walk
How often	AdvP	ProAdv	*how often* the bell would strike
How well	AdvP	ProAdv	*how well* the pump works
Why	AdvP	ProAdv	*why* the onion looked pink
Which (NP)	Det	ProDet	*which* suit he should wear
Whose (NP)	Det	ProDet	*whose* budget plan would get accepted
What (NP)	Det	ProDet	*what* colors the flag should be
How	PredAdj	ProAdj	*how* the daughter felt

Remember, noun clauses can function as a subject, direct object, predicate nominative, indirect object, or object of a preposition, but they most commonly function as the subject, direct object, or predicate nominative. For example, try each of the examples above in the following test frames.

- *They wondered _____.*   (Noun Clause as DO)
- *_____ was a mystery.*   (Noun Clause as Subj)
- *The issue is _____.*   (Noun Clause as PredN)
- *We gave _____ top priority.*   (Noun Clause as IO)
- *The question of _____ was complicated.* (Noun Clause as OP)

In the tree, we will label the pro-form in its correct position <u>within</u> the clause and then show that it has <u>been moved to the front</u> of the noun clause to act also as the subordinator of that clause. (In the example trees below, only the *Wh* noun clause is shown so that you can concentrate on the dual function of the *Wh* words.)

what made the sound

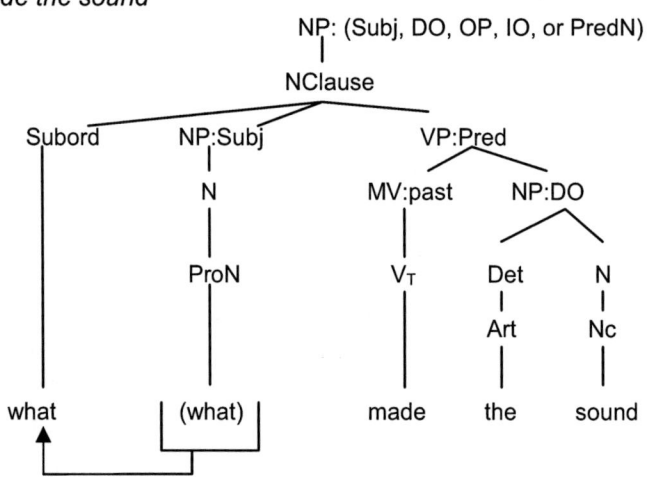

```
                    NP: (Subj, DO, OP, IO, or PredN)
                                  |
                              NClause
         ┌───────────────┬──────────────────┐
       Subord         NP:Subj            VP:Pred
         │               │            ┌─────┴─────┐
         │               N          MV:past     NP:DO
         │               │            │       ┌───┴───┐
         │              ProN          V_T     Det     N
         │               │            │        │      │
         │               │            │       Art    Nc
         │               │            │        │      │
       what            (what)        made     the   sound
```

The ProAdv *Wh* words (*when, where, how, how often, why*) are treed at the end with their appropriate AdvP label (AdvP-time, AdvP-place, AdvP-manner, AdvP-frequency, AdvP-reason). Then they are shown to be moved to the front to also act as the subordinator. They have a dual function and so appear twice in the noun clause.

how they figured out the sentence

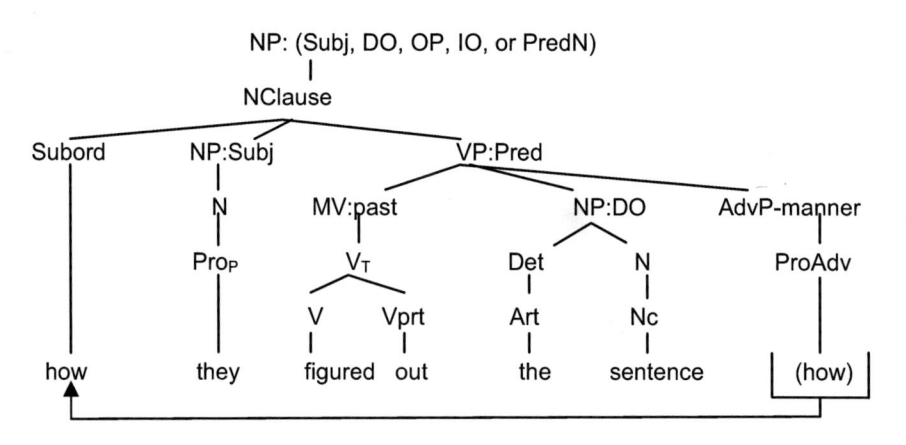

```
                      NP: (Subj, DO, OP, IO, or PredN)
                                    |
                                NClause
       ┌───────────┬────────────────────────────────┐
     Subord     NP:Subj                          VP:Pred
       │          │           ┌───────────┬──────────┬──────────┐
       │          N         MV:past     NP:DO              AdvP-manner
       │          │           │       ┌───┴───┐                │
       │         Prop         │      Det      N              ProAdv
       │          │        ┌──┴──┐    │       │                │
       │          │        V    Vprt Art     Nc                │
       │          │        │     │    │       │                │
      how        they   figured out  the   sentence          (how)
```

In the next tree, the word *what* has the dual function of acting as the NP:DO of the noun clause as well as the subordinator. It is shown in both the NP:DO place and in the subordinator place. In the NP:DO place, the

Nominal Phrase Choices

word is in parentheses to show that it is there grammatically but actually does not appear there.

what they wanted at the store

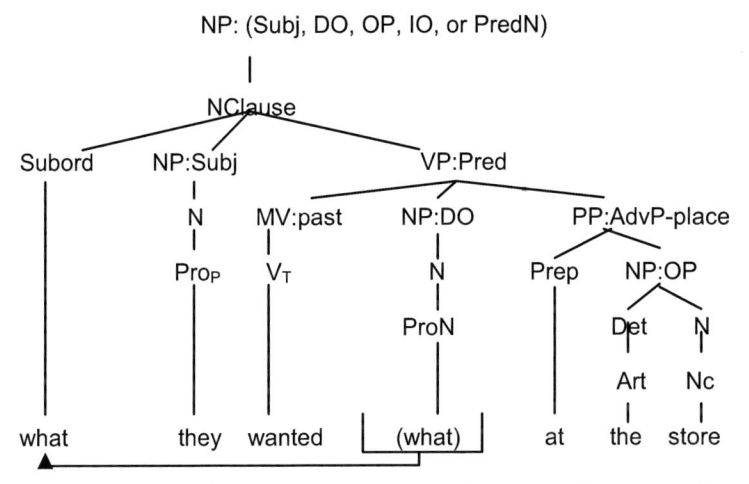

```
                    NP: (Subj, DO, OP, IO, or PredN)
                                  |
                              NClause
         ┌───────────┬─────────────────┴──────────────────┐
      Subord      NP:Subj                              VP:Pred
         |           |              ┌─────────┬───────────┴──────────┐
         |           N           MV:past    NP:DO              PP:AdvP-place
         |           |              |         |              ┌────────┴────────┐
         |          Prop           V_T        N             Prep            NP:OP
         |           |              |         |              |           ┌────┴────┐
         |           |              |        ProN            |          Det        N
         |           |              |         |              |           |         |
         |           |              |         |              |          Art        Nc
         |           |              |         |              |           |         |
       what         they         wanted     (what)           at         the      store
```

Remember, *Wh* subordinators in noun clauses will appear twice in the noun clause. They have a dual function.

The next example shows a ProDet: *which athlete would win the prize*

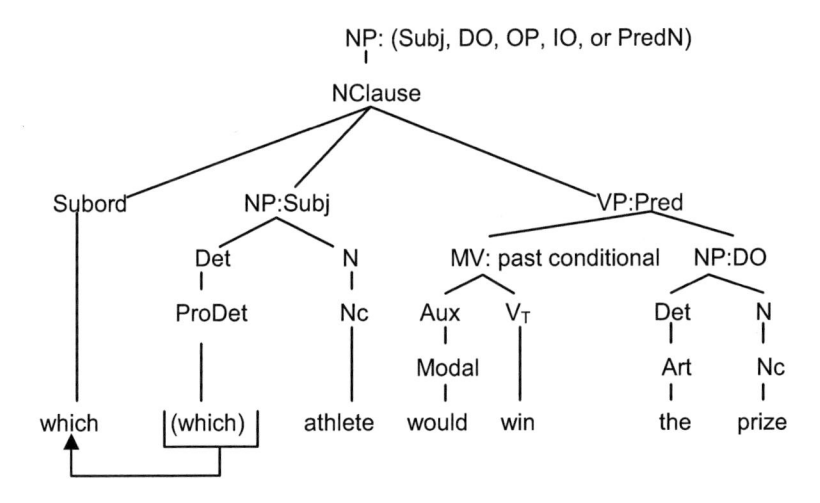

```
                         NP: (Subj, DO, OP, IO, or PredN)
                                        |
                                    NClause
         ┌───────────┬───────────────────┴────────────────────┐
      Subord      NP:Subj                                  VP:Pred
         |      ┌────┴────┐              ┌──────────────────┴──────────────┐
         |     Det         N         MV: past conditional               NP:DO
         |      |          |           ┌─────┴─────┐                 ┌─────┴─────┐
         |    ProDet       Nc         Aux         V_T               Det           N
         |      |          |           |           |                 |            |
         |      |          |         Modal         |                Art          Nc
         |      |          |           |           |                 |            |
       which  (which)   athlete      would        win               the         prize
```

If the ProDet is with the direct object, the noun cluster moves to the front of the noun clause with the subordinator, as in the next example: *which blue suit he should wear.*

Nominal Phrase Choices

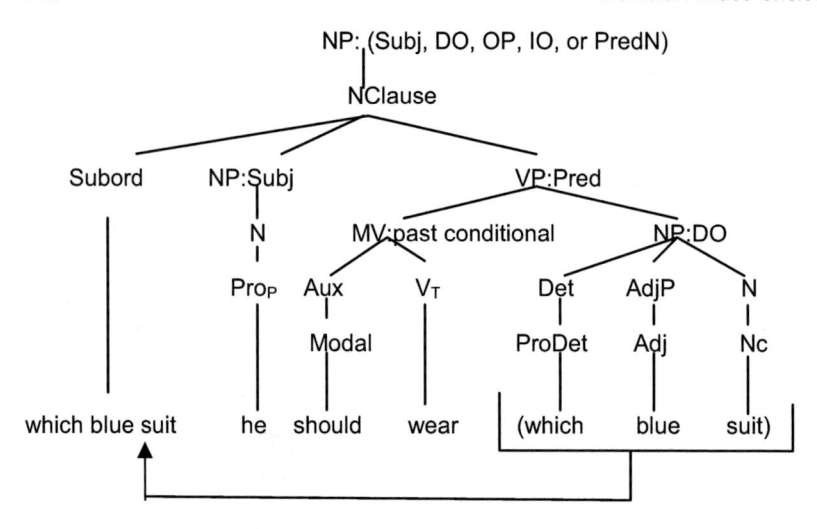

```
                    NP: (Subj, DO, OP, IO, or PredN)
                              |
                           NClause
         ┌──────────────┬────────────────┐
       Subord         NP:Subj          VP:Pred
         |              |         ┌──────┴──────┐
         |              N    MV:past conditional  NP:DO
         |              |      ┌─────┴─────┐   ┌───┼───┐
         |            Prop    Aux          V_T Det AdjP  N
         |              |      |            |   |    |   |
         |              |    Modal          |  ProDet Adj Nc
         |              |      |            |   |    |   |
    which blue suit    he   should        wear (which blue suit)
```

Next is an example of a *Wh* noun clause in a sentence. Notice that there is a ProAdj in this one. That is relatively unusual, but *felt* in this sentence is a linking verb.

The question remained how the daughter felt after the divorce.

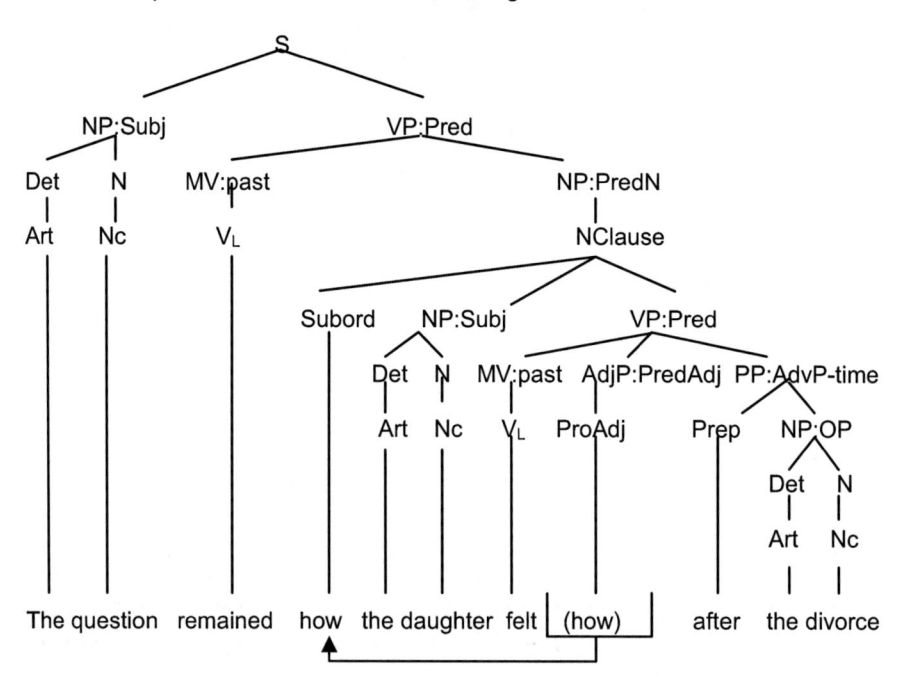

```
                              S
              ┌───────────────┴───────────────┐
           NP:Subj                         VP:Pred
          ┌───┴──┐            ┌──────────────┴──────┐
         Det     N          MV:past              NP:PredN
          |      |            |                     |
         Art    Nc           V_L                 NClause
          |      |            |         ┌──────────┼──────────┐
          |      |            |       Subord   NP:Subj     VP:Pred
          |      |            |         |      ┌──┴─┐   ┌────┼─────────┐
          |      |            |         |     Det   N  MV:past AdjP:PredAdj PP:AdvP-time
          |      |            |         |      |    |    |         |         ┌──┴──┐
          |      |            |         |     Art  Nc   V_L      ProAdj    Prep  NP:OP
          |      |            |         |      |    |    |         |         |   ┌─┴─┐
          |      |            |         |      |    |    |         |         |  Det  N
          |      |            |         |      |    |    |         |         |   |   |
          |      |            |         |      |    |    |         |         |  Art  Nc
          |      |            |         |      |    |    |         |         |   |   |
   The question remained    how   the daughter felt  (how)       after  the divorce
```

Nominal Infinitive Phrases

Nominal infinitive phrases (InfPh:Nom) have the same structure as adverbial infinitive phrases, but nominal infinitive phrases function as the subject, predicate nominative, object complement, or direct object.

Infinitive Phrase as NP:Subj	***To wait all day for the opportunity*** was difficult.
Infinitive Phrase as NP:PredN	The desire of our hearts is ***to master our study of grammar.***
Infinitive Phrase as NP:OC	The woman considered her hobby ***to be painting and collecting miniature figurines.***
Infinitive Phrase as NP:DO	I wanted ***to explore the cave that night.***

As we saw in an earlier chapter, an infinitive phrase consists of a subordinator and VP. It usually begins with the word *to* plus the infinitive form of a verb.

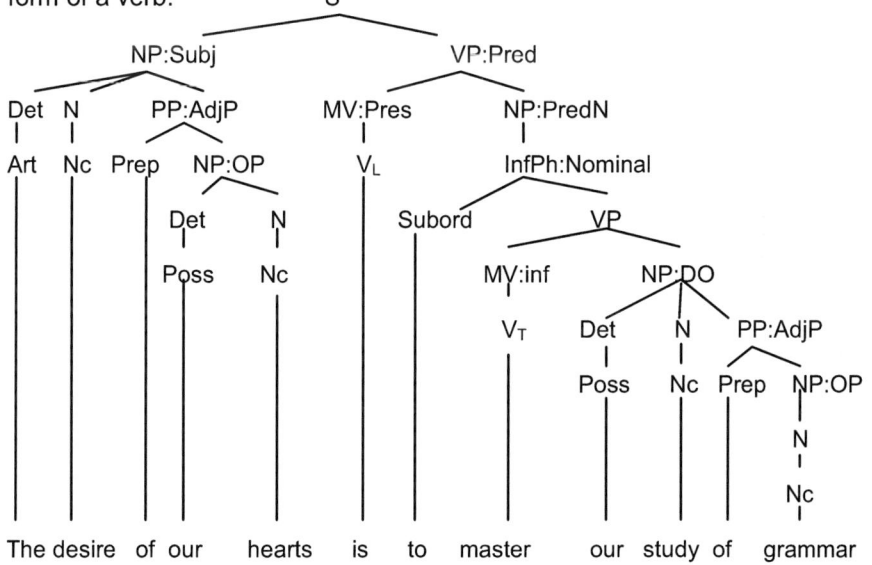

However, infinitive phrases can also begin with a *for* prepositional phrase. An example would be *for Hexaba to respond with respect*. We will call this a "*for/to* infinitive phrase" and will tree it as shown below.

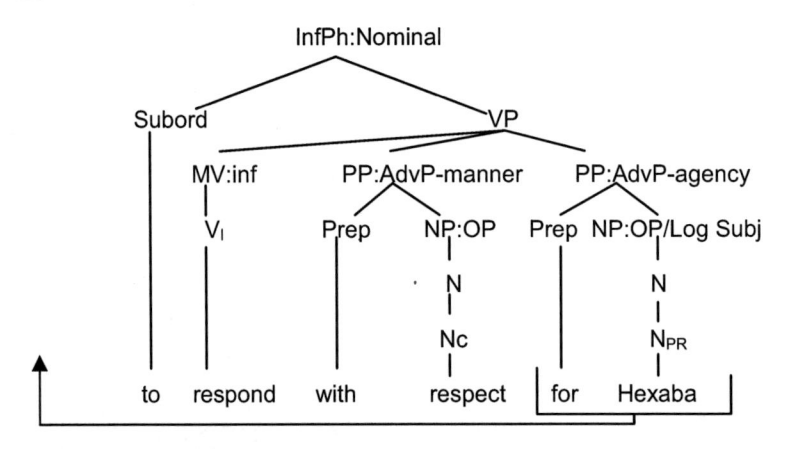

Nominal Phrase Choices

```
                    InfPh:Nominal
           ┌─────────────┴─────────────┐
        Subord                         VP
                    ┌──────────────┬──────────────┐
                  MV:inf      PP:AdvP-manner   PP:AdvP-agency
                    │         ┌─────┴─────┐    ┌─────┴─────┐
                   V_I       Prep       NP:OP  Prep   NP:OP/Log Subj
                    │         │           │     │           │
                    │         │           N     │           N
                    │         │           │     │           │
                    │         │           Nc    │          N_PR
                    │         │           │     │           │
                    to     respond       with  respect  for  Hexaba
```

The prepositional phrase *for Hexaba* is acting as an adverb of agency, telling by whom the action (to respond with respect) is being done. The label **Log Subj** denotes that in addition to functioning as the object of the preposition, the word *Hexaba* is functioning as a **logical subject.** If this infinitive phrase were a clause, *Hexaba* would be the NP:Subject and *responds with respect* would be the VP:Pred. So, in the infinitive phrase form, we label *Hexaba* as both the object of the preposition and the logical subject.

We can also have a passive infinitive. Notice that the MV label is **Inf Passive.**

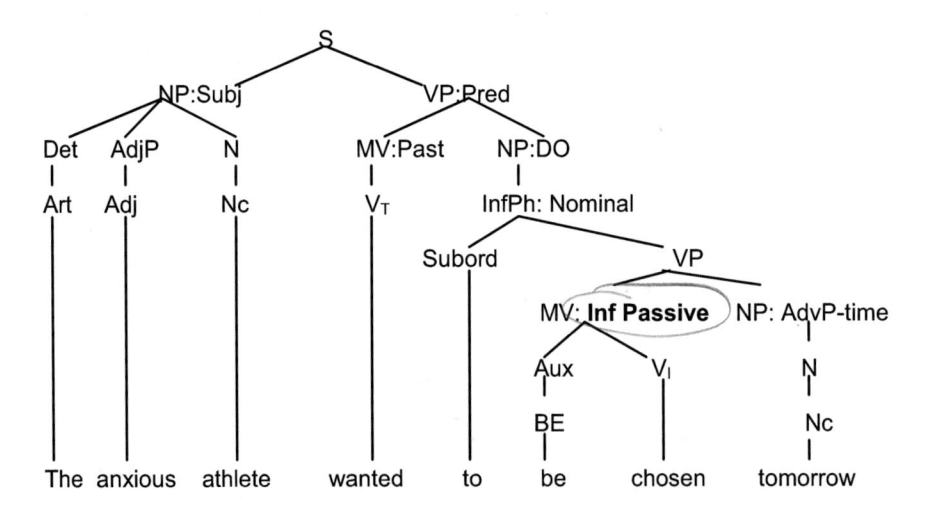

```
                                S
                ┌───────────────┴───────────────┐
              NP:Subj                         VP:Pred
        ┌───────┼───────┐               ┌───────┴───────┐
       Det    AdjP      N             MV:Past         NP:DO
        │      │        │               │               │
       Art    Adj       Nc             V_T          InfPh: Nominal
        │      │        │               │         ┌─────┴─────┐
        │      │        │               │       Subord        VP
        │      │        │               │         │     ┌─────┴─────┐
        │      │        │               │         │   MV: Inf Passive  NP: AdvP-time
        │      │        │               │         │    ┌────┴────┐      │
        │      │        │               │         │   Aux       V_I     N
        │      │        │               │         │    │         │      │
        │      │        │               │         │   BE         │      Nc
        │      │        │               │         │    │         │      │
       The  anxious  athlete          wanted      to   be      chosen  tomorrow
```

Nominal Phrase Choices   121

Differing Functions for Infinitive Phrases

At this point, we have looked at infinitive phrases that act as adverb phrases (Chapter 5) and infinitive phrases that act as subjects, predicate nominatives, object complements, and direct objects (this chapter). The structure of these infinitive phrases is the same; it is the function that differs. An InfPh:AdvP answers *why* (or sometimes *how*) and can often be moved to other locations in the sentence. An InfPh:Nom substitutes for a simple NP, most often as a subject or a predicate nominative.

Embedded Structures

Sometimes one of the NP choices is **embedded** within another one.

NClause embedded within GerPh	*The minister began* **explaining how Jesus' death can provide forgiveness for our sins.**
NClause embedded within InfPh:Nom	**To discover that the house Dickens lived in** *is open to the public was exciting.*
InfPh:Nom embedded within GerPh	*She insisted upon* **choosing to go to Stirling Castle.**
InfPh:Nom embedded within NClause	**That he wanted to visit the London Museum** *came as no surprise to the family.*
GerPh embedded within InfPh:Nom	*He wanted* **to begin taking pictures with his new digital camera.**
GerPh embedded within NClause	**Whether she would complete exploring The Royal Mile by evening** *was anyone's guess.*

Remember that the NP choices (gerund phrases, noun clauses, and nominal infinitive phrases) can appear anywhere in the sentence in a typical NP function spot:

      NP:Subj   NP:PredN   NP:DO
      NP:IO   NP:OC   NP:OP.

The first of the following examples has two gerund phrases embedded within an infinitive phrase. The gerund phrases are a compound NP:PredN. The second sentence has a noun clause within a nominal infinitive phrase. Notice that in this example, the subordinator in the noun clause has been dropped, but it is still grammatically in the structure, so we tree it with a dotted line and parentheses.

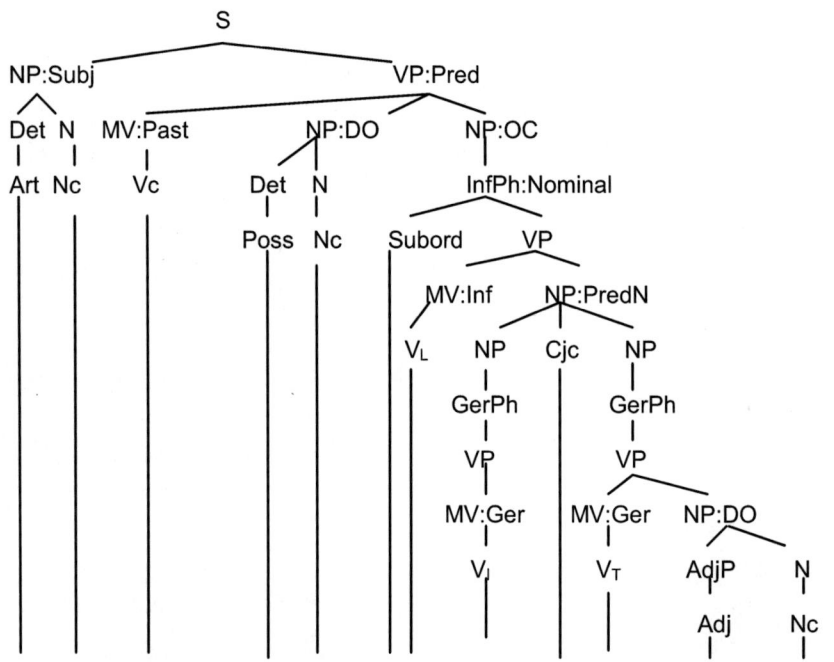

The woman considered her hobby to be painting and collecting miniature figurines

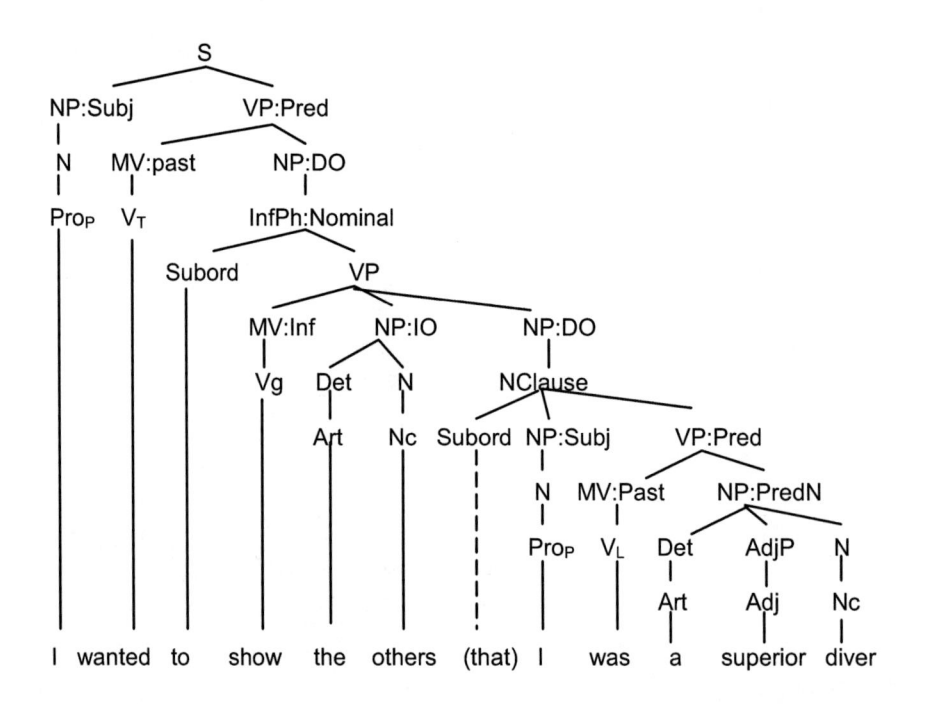

I wanted to show the others (that) I was a superior diver

Nominal Phrase Choices and Usage

Singular and Plural

Gerunds, noun clauses, and nominal infinitives are singular. Nominal phrase choices (gerunds, noun clauses, and infinitives) take a singular verb form.
- *What is needed at the moment **is** for all of the children to relax.*
- *Scrounging the bushes for ripe raspberries **was** a worthwhile experience in spite of the mosquitoes.*

Who and Whom

Formal English distinguishes between *who* and *whom*. In formal language situations, one should distinguish between the use of *who/whoever* (used for subjects <u>within noun clauses</u>) and *whom/whomever* (used <u>within noun clauses</u> most often as direct objects). In the following sentences, the noun clause is the object of the preposition.
- *The politician embraced the ideas of **whomever the voters supported**.*

Within the noun clause, the *whomever* is the subordinator. It also has the dual function as the DO. Since it is the direct object within the noun clause, one would use *whomever* rather than *whoever* in formal language situations.

- *The politician embraced the ideas of whoever spoke loudly and with conviction.*

In this sentence, the *whoever* is the subordinator, but this time the dual function is the subject within the noun clause. Therefore, one would use *whoever* rather than *whomever*.

Incorrect Nominal Usage

Gerunds are NP substitutes and so can be used as the subject of a sentence. However, don't use gerunds that are the object of a preposition (OP) as the subject of a sentence.

Nonstandard use of OP gerund as subject:	*By distributing diazinin on the yard is the way to remove ant populations.*
Standard use of gerund as subject:	*Distributing diazinin on the yard is the way to remove ant populations.*

Sometimes adverb clauses are used in a sentence when, in formal Standard English, a noun clause or gerund phrase should be used. These show up typically in the subject or predicate nominative position. In formal language situations, it is a misuse of an adverb clause to use it in the place of a noun clause. In the first two sentences in the chart, the adverb clause is being used as a predicate nominative, when a noun clause should be used. In the last example, the adverb clause is being used as a subject, when a noun clause should be used.

Nonstandard Use of Adverb Clause	Standard Use of a Noun Clause
The reason for the delay is **because the planes are grounded** at the Minneapolis/St. Paul Airport.	The reason for the delay is **that the planes are grounded** at the Minneapolis/St. Paul Airport.
The problems of the biologist's failing to get accurate results is **because she didn't clean the filters.**	The problems of the biologist's failing to get accurate results is **that she didn't clean the filters.**
When the books are returned late and damaged upsets the librarian.	**That the books are returned late and damaged** upsets the librarian.

Subjunctive Verb Form in Noun Clauses

In more formal language situations, we use the subjunctive in some noun clauses. Remember, with the subjunctive, the verb is a form that does not usually match the subject being used.

- We suggested that **the boy finish** his project before he began a new one.
- The resident hall advisor insisted that **the girls be** home before midnight.
- That **the graduate find** a job is advisable.

However, using the subjunctive in noun clauses may be disappearing in everyday English. A t-shirt I saw recently ignored the subjunctive in the noun clause of its message: "I wish I was skiing" (rather than "*I wish I were skiing*"). It is doubtful that very many people would notice the absence of a subjunctive form of the verb within a noun clause.

Nominal Phrase Choices and Punctuation

Fragments

Nominal phrase alternatives can end up as fragments. Now that you can identify the NP alternatives (gerunds, noun clauses, and infinitives), check your writing (or the writing of your students) to make sure that they are not punctuated as a sentence. Gerunds, noun clauses, and infinitives can end up as sentence fragments when they should be acting in an NP position within a sentence. If any of these three types of structures appears alone, it is a fragment.

One test for fragments is to use a test frame. If the structure is a full sentence, it should make sense in the blanks of a test frame such as the following: *I told them that _____.*

Try each of the following in the test frame. You will see the ones that "flunk" the test are merely gerund phrases, noun clauses, or infinitive phrases (a fragment by itself).

- *Expressing her opinion of the theatrical performance*
- *Expressing her opinion of the theatrical performance was a bad idea.*
- *Whose dirty dishes were sitting on the counter*
- *I did not know whose dirty dishes were sitting on the counter.*
- *For our basketball team to be able to win a game*
- *For our basketball team to be able to win a game would be a miracle.*

Nominal Phrase Choices and Style

Style Options

Varying the NP choices gives the writer more style options. You don't want to have these three NP choices appear as fragments, but you do want to use them for style variation within your sentences. Try substituting one type of NP structure for another to see which effect you like best, and vary your NP structures occasionally within your writing. You might need to practice writing these structures until they feel comfortable for you to use.

Parallelism

The NP choices can be used for parallelism. The stylistic rule of parallelism calls for the matching of structures in sentence elements with the corresponding elements that have the same function in the sentence. If you have elements that are joined by a coordinating conjunction (Cjc), those elements should all be in the same form, such as all gerund phrases, all noun clauses, all simple NPs, or all infinitive phrases.

Not Parallel	Parallel	Structure
The president enjoys seeing people, speaking at banquets, and meetings.	The president enjoys seeing people, speaking at banquets, and conducting meetings.	Gerund Phrases as DO
The opinion of the committee is that this computer equipment represents the best value and we should make the purchase.	The opinion of the committee is that this computer equipment represents the best value and that we should make the purchase.	Noun Clauses as PredN
What she wanted to do on her vacation was to see castles, visiting authors' homes and the Globe Theater.	What she wanted to do on her vacation was to see castles, to visit authors' homes and to tour the Globe Theater.	Infinitive Phrases as PredN

Practice Sentences

I. Tree the following sentences. Remember, the material from previous chapters is included within the sentences.
1. The scope of the operation suggests they had planned well.
2. The coaches ask for the public to join them in their protest.
3. The poet believes the tragedy of human life is being the victim of another's choices.
4. The novice camper was discovering how unattended stoves can burst into flames.
5. The idea very clearly is that the two college coeds could never perform such a feat.
6. The professor wanted to be kind yet frank.
7. He knew how she would be arriving that night.
8. We began to figure things out.

9. In his poetry, Robert Frost feels that nature is indifferent and unconcerned.
10. We want to anticipate what you are doing with the new product release.
11. This is what you have become.
12. What this quilt says is that the Civil War was everyone's battle.
13. Fires can show how destruction can occur in mere minutes.
14. Katrina wondered whether anyone in town spoke Swedish.
15. Many young boys do not understand females' painting their fingernails.
16. One glance at her face told him she was thinking the same thing.
17. She was beginning to feel the cold of the house on a winter's night.
18. Susan couldn't figure out whose handwriting stretched sloppily across her notebook.
19. Justin thought about his previous visit to the city and wondered whether Pastor Schwartz still shepherded the little congregation.
20. To prove his point without preaching a sermon, Stephen Crane incorporated his philosophy within the plot of his novels.
21. He explained to the officials what had happened to the vacationing couple and that he had sent a message to the office in America.
22. The pregnant tour guide had to excuse herself to whomever she was guiding and had to make a hasty departure.
23. Guaranteeing the safety of meats and produce has become an increasingly complex and uncertain proposition.
24. Whom the bandits raided became a concern to our family at home.
25. Wishful thinking is what carries many through life.
26. Laura's primary goal for the shopping trip was buying a green Nalgene bottle for her sister's birthday.
27. They examined how the buildings were laid out and how the fountains were designed.
28. What is different today is the type of food.
29. Scientists continue to find evidence of animal and plant DNA.
30. Inserting a pair of bacteria genes into corn DNA produces a certain kind of sugar.
31. Video games reward players for engaging in organized crime and murdering innocent people.
32. Utah hopes to lure visitors back to the site of the Olympic Games.
33. To see violent fits of drunken rage in an apartment without furniture is her only life.

34. The migrant worker's favorite spot is where the peaches are picked.
35. Why those girls liked to study beneath the branches of pine trees is a mystery.
36. They wondered whose idea of building sandcastles was illustrated on the beach below the cliff.
37. What is necessary may not always be convenient.
38. Everybody in the office has asked how often such acts occur.
39. Wondering whether the octopus has a rubbery feel distracted Laura and Tia from the danger.
40. They also analyzed what crops were grown on the steep terraces.
41. The gift for Tia should have been Laura's giving her a back rub.
42. To grasp Shakespeare's preoccupation with illusion and reality is to understand in part his popularity in different cultures and time periods.
43. To check an early opinion, the poll had asked who would suffer the most from the scandal.
44. The governor has said dealing with capitol politics is difficult.
45. Truman had pledged to fight for unconditional Japanese surrender to wipe out any future resistance.
46. What disturbed me most was admitting that my assessment of him had been wrong.
47. The seal became a beach master by defeating the previous master in combat.
48. The iguanas' eating brown algae in the warm water is fatal because they cannot digest it.
49. The nature photographers began their work by examining the healthy reef systems of Fiji.
50. Diving under the warm surface of the water was frustrating the Galapagos penguins because the fish went to the colder water.

II. Practice expanding your writing style repertoire. Write a sentence for each of the following. Make sure that the verb is singular if the nominal structure is a subject. All of these types of sentences are illustrated in this chapter.

1. Write a gerund phrase with a possessive determiner as the subject of a sentence.
2. Write a gerund phrase as the direct object (DO) or predicate nominative (PredN) of a sentence.

Nominal Phrase Choices   129

   3. Write a gerund phrase as the object of a preposition (OP) in a sentence.
   4. Write a *that/whether* noun clause as the subject of a sentence.
   5. Write a sentence with a *Wh* noun clause as the direct object (DO).
   6. Write a sentence with a noun clause using *which* as the subordinator.
   7. Write a sentence with a noun clause using *whom* as the subordinator.
   8. Write a sentence with a noun clause using *how often* as the subordinator.
   9. Write an infinitive phrase as the predicate nominative (PredN).
   10. Write an infinitive phrase as the direct object (DO).

III. Write examples.

   1. Reread the sections on nominal phrase choices and usage. Using the examples as models, write 2 original examples for each of the sections. Write nonstandard sentences and then change each of them to standard. If you are a future teacher, you can use these when you teach.

   2. Reread the section on parallelism. Write 3 sentences that are not parallel and then rewrite them to make them parallel. If you are a future teacher, you can use these when you teach.

IV. Examine your writing.

Reread some of your own academic prose. Examine your nominal phrase choices and usage as well as style. Can you find nonstandard usage in your college papers? If so, correct it and bring the sentences to class. Can you find parallelism violations in your formal writing? If so, correct them and bring them to class.

Chapter 8
Noun Cluster Expansions: Relative Clauses and Adjectival Infinitive Phrases

In addition to substituting for noun clusters with gerunds, noun clauses, or infinitives, we can also attach various structures to noun clusters which describe or rename. These attachment structures include relative clauses, adjectival infinitive phrases, adjectival participial phrases, appositives, and nominal complement infinitive phrases.

When we attach these structures, the NP becomes a **head**. The **NP:Head** can have any NP function: subject (Subj), direct object (DO), indirect object (IO), predicate nominative (PredN), object of the preposition (OP), or object complement (OC). When they describe the NP, they are called modifiers. We will look at two of these structures in this chapter: relative clauses and adjectival infinitive phrases. They both describe or give additional information about the NP head.

A note about the use of the word *head*:

This word is often used in grammar analysis to designate the chief word in a phrase, which identifies the type of phrase it is. Therefore, the N in an NP is often called the head. I am using the word *head* only to designate the word or group of words to which an attachment is made. Therefore, I am referring to a structure having a head only when that structure has an attachment. Using this definition, this chapter and the next three chapters discuss various structures that can have heads.

Relative Clauses

Relative Clauses have an adjectival function (**RelCl:AdjP**), giving more information about an NP. Relative clauses usually begin with a relative pronoun (ProRel) or with a prepositional phrase (PP) with the ProRel as the object of the preposition (OP). **The ProRel is a substitute within the relative clause for the head.**

> The ProRel will generally be *that, who, which, whose,* or *whom*.

Sentence	ProRel	Head
The senator **who made a ludicrous statement** was mocked by all.	Who	the senator
The sermon **which the pastor preached last week** was highly controversial.	Which	the sermon
The forceful blow shattered the chandelier **that was imported from Venice.**	That	the chandelier
The professors **whose classes are the hardest** are the ones **from which you learn the most.**	Whose Which	the professors' the ones
The senator **of whom we were speaking** was not able to be present at the meeting.	Whom	the senator

Like the subordinator of a noun clause, the relative pronoun (ProRel) begins the relative clause (unless it is an OP), but it also has a grammatical function within the relative clause.

Relative pronouns (ProRel) that can function as the subject of the relative clause	Relative pronouns (ProRel) that can function as the direct object of a relative clause	Relative pronouns (ProRel) that can function as the object of a preposition in a relative clause	Relative pronouns (ProRel) that can function as a determiner (relative pro-determiner) in a relative clause
who	whom	whom	whose
which	which	which	
that	that		

Head and Relative Clause	Function of ProRel
The archer **who shot the arrow at the target**	ProRel (**who**) is the Subj of the relative clause
This television **that we bought**	ProRel (**that**) is the DO of the relative clause
The act **in which Cassius dies**	ProRel (**which**) is the OP in a PP in the relative clause
The woman **whose reputation was tarnished by her actions**	ProRel (**whose**) is a Det in the relative clause

To tree relative clauses,
- Show the relative pronoun (ProRel) in a grammar tree in its grammatical position within the relative clause.
- Then draw a line to show that it has also been moved to act in its dual function as subordinator in the front of the relative clause.
- If the ProRel is the object of a preposition, <u>the preposition moves with the relative pronoun</u> to the subordinator position in front of the relative clause.
- With a ProRel, you will show <u>both</u> the location of the grammatical function within the relative clause and the location of the dual role as subordinator at the beginning of the relative clause.

Note in the diagram below that you draw two lines from the NP, one for the head and one for the relative clause. Then, from the relative clause, you always draw three lines: one for the subordinator (Subord), one for the NP:Subject and one for VP:Predicate.

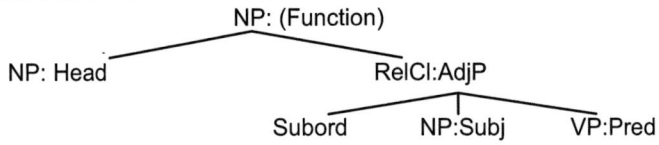

```
              NP: (Function)
             /            \
       NP: Head          RelCl:AdjP
                       /     |      \
                   Subord  NP:Subj  VP:Pred
```

In the following trees, only the NP:Head and the RelCl:AdjP are shown so that you can concentrate on the new material.

Since the ProRel in the following example is the subject of the relative clause, it does not have to be moved much to show its dual function as subordinator at the beginning of the relative clause.

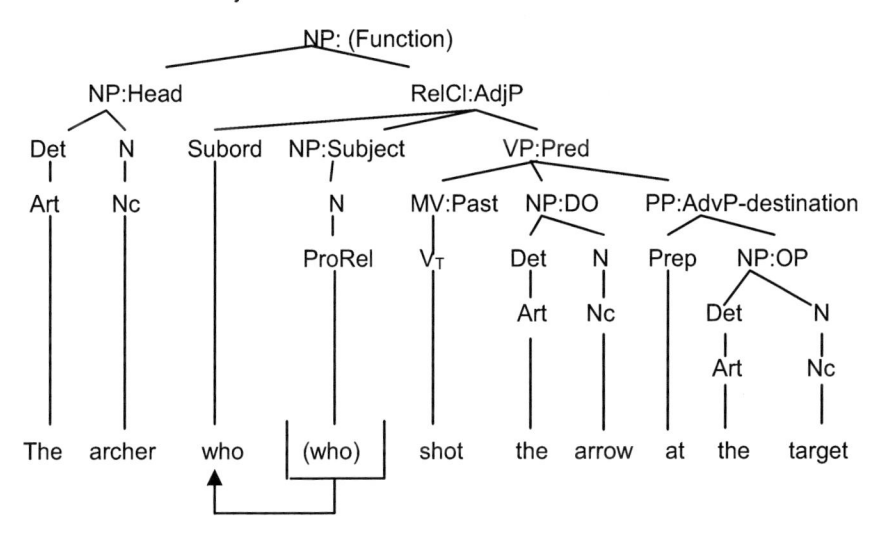

Relative Clauses and Adjectival Infinitive Phrases

[Tree diagram: "The archer who (who) shot the arrow at the target"
- NP: (Function)
  - NP:Head — Det (Art) "The", N (Nc) "archer"
  - RelCl:AdjP — Subord "who", NP:Subject N (ProRel) "(who)", VP:Pred — MV:Past V_T "shot", NP:DO Det (Art) "the" N (Nc) "arrow", PP:AdvP-destination Prep "at" NP:OP Det (Art) "the" N (Nc) "target"]

Notice that in this next example, the relative pronoun (ProRel) has been moved from its grammatical position as the direct object of the relative clause to its position at the beginning of the relative clause (to subordinate and introduce the dependent clause).

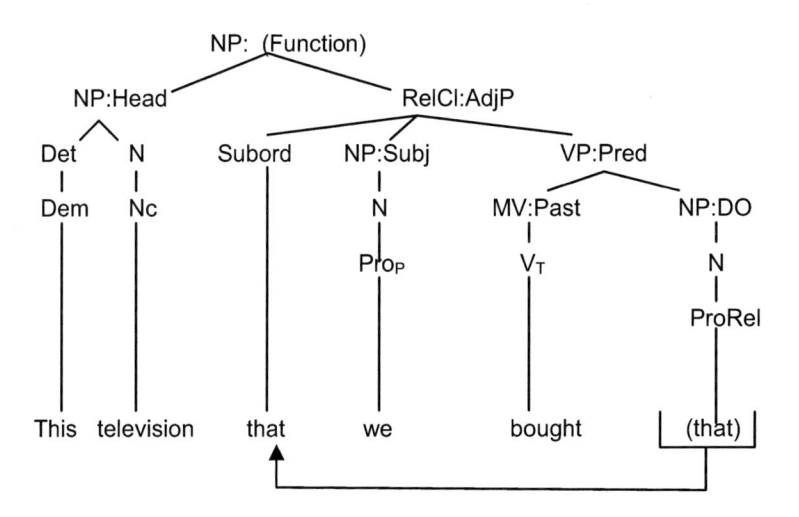

[Tree diagram: "This television that we bought (that)"
- NP: (Function)
  - NP:Head — Det (Dem) "This", N (Nc) "television"
  - RelCl:AdjP — Subord "that", NP:Subj N (Pro_P) "we", VP:Pred — MV:Past V_T "bought", NP:DO N (ProRel) "(that)"]

In the next example, the entire prepositional phrase moves to the front of the relative clause.

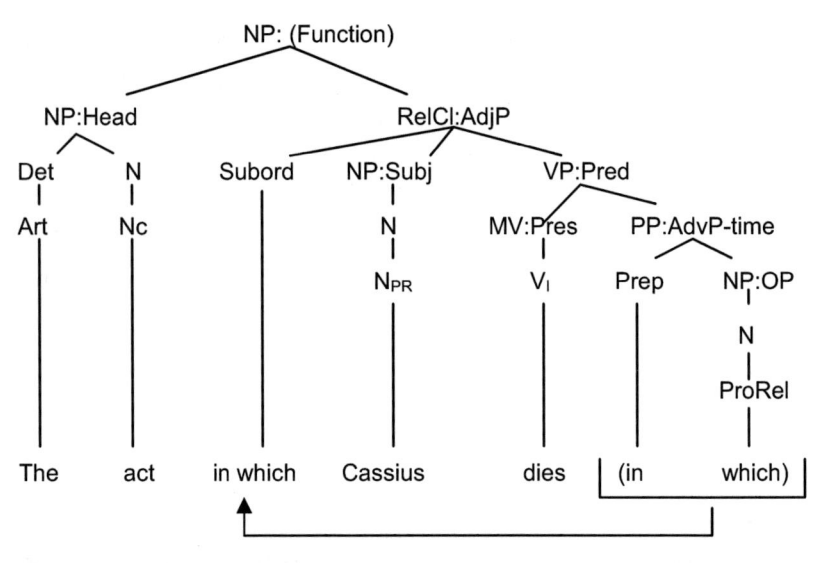

```
                          NP: (Function)
                    ┌───────────┴───────────┐
                NP:Head               RelCl:AdjP
              ┌────┴────┐         ┌────┬────────┴────┐
             Det        N       Subord  NP:Subj    VP:Pred
              │         │         │       │      ┌────┴────┐
             Art        Nc        │       N    MV:Pres  PP:AdvP-time
              │         │         │       │      │      ┌───┴───┐
              │         │         │      N_PR    V_I   Prep   NP:OP
              │         │         │       │      │      │      │
              │         │         │       │      │      │      N
              │         │         │       │      │      │      │
              │         │         │       │      │      │    ProRel
              │         │         │       │      │      │      │
             The       act    in which  Cassius  dies  (in   which)
                                 ▲                      │              │
                                 └──────────────────────┘
```

Tip: If you are having trouble finding the grammatical function of the ProRel within the relative clause, try mentally substituting the head for the relative pronoun. Then restructure the relative clause so that the elements are in their usual places. Tree the relative clause this way, except don't forget to put the ProRel back in instead of the head.

Let's try the tip above with the following sentence:

The senator made a ludicrous statement, which the newspapers quoted the next day.

- First, find the relative clause: *which the newspapers quoted the next day.*
- The ProRel is *which.*
- Try substituting the head (a ludicrous statement) for the ProRel (which). We now have "*a ludicrous statement the newspapers quoted the next day.*"
- Restructuring for a "normal order" in English, we get "*the newspapers quoted a ludicrous statement the next day.*"
- We can now more clearly see that "*a ludicrous statement*" is the direct object. Because the head would be a direct object in the

relative clause, the ProRel is a direct object, since the ProRel stands for the head.
- When you tree the relative clause, remember to put the ProRel in its grammatical position as well as show it has been moved to the front of the relative clause. Therefore, what you tree is "*The senator made a ludicrous statement which the newspapers quoted (which) the next day.*"

This sentence is illustrated in a tree on the next page.

Below is an example in which the ProRel is a determiner. Notice the NP:GramSubj and passive verb in the relative clause. It also has a *by-*phrase (PP:AdvP-Agency) with an NP:OP/LogSubj.

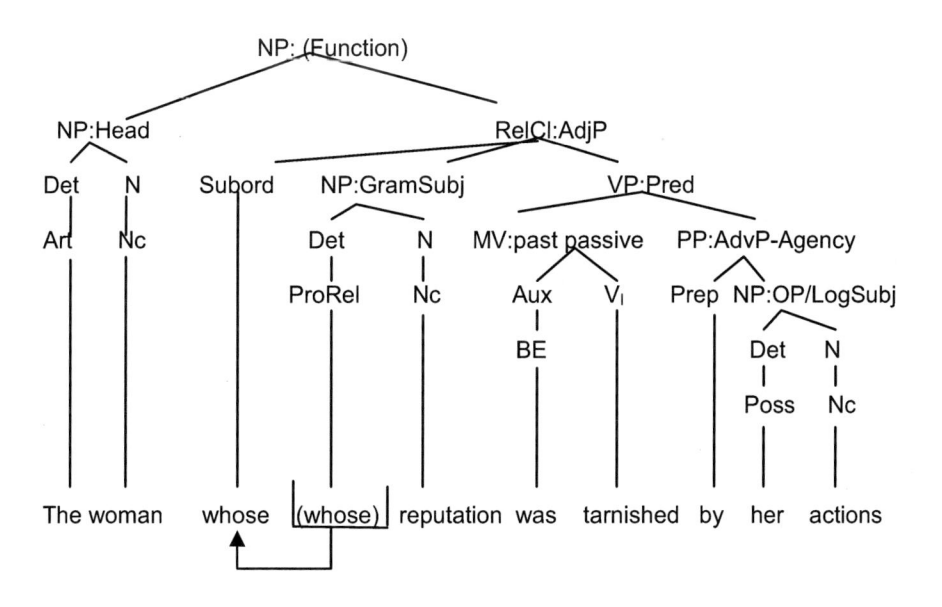

```
                        NP: (Function)
              ┌──────────────┴──────────────┐
           NP:Head                      RelCl:AdjP
           ┌──┴──┐         ┌──────────────┼──────────────┐
          Det    N      Subord      NP:GramSubj        VP:Pred
           │     │         │         ┌────┴────┐    ┌─────┴─────┐
          Art   Nc                  Det       N   MV:past passive  PP:AdvP-Agency
           │     │         │         │         │    ┌──┴──┐       ┌─────┴─────┐
           │     │         │       ProRel     Nc  Aux    V₁     Prep  NP:OP/LogSubj
           │     │         │         │         │    │     │       │    ┌────┴────┐
           │     │         │         │         │   BE     │       │   Det        N
           │     │         │         │         │    │     │       │    │         │
           │     │         │         │         │    │     │       │   Poss       Nc
           │     │         │         │         │    │     │       │    │         │
       The woman       whose     (whose)  reputation was tarnished  by  her    actions
```

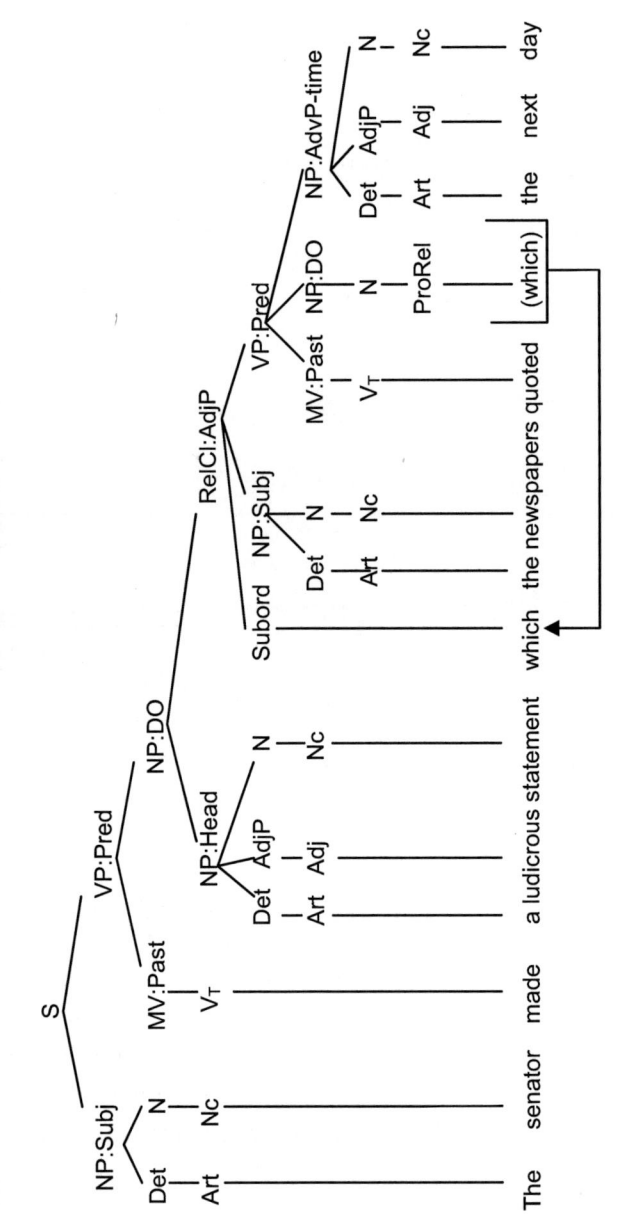

Relative Clauses and Adjectival Infinitive Phrases

Relative Clauses and Adjectival Infinitive Phrases 137

> Remember, relative clauses can be attached to any NP in the sentence.
> All relatives have a head.

Examples of relative clauses (in bold) attached to various NPs within sentences are shown on the table which follows. The NP:Heads are underlined.

Relative clause attached to subject of sentence	*The Civil War,* **which was everyone's battle,** *devastated families.*
Relative clause attached to direct object of sentence	*Scientists discovered* <u>mummies</u> **that showed evidence of an advanced civilization.**
Relative clause attached to indirect object of sentence	*The kind husband bought* <u>his wife</u>, **who was completely surprised,** *an opal ring.*
Relative clause attached to predicate nominative of sentence	*The nasty woman is* <u>an evil presence</u>, **which oppresses everyone around her.**
Relative clause attached to object of preposition within sentence	*The trip package included the luxury of* <u>maid service</u>, **which the mother particularly appreciated.**

Relative Clauses with a Missing Relative Pronoun

Sometimes, the relative pronoun has been dropped from the spoken or written sentence. However, the relative pronoun is still there grammatically, so we will tree it with a dotted line and put the missing relative pronoun word in parentheses.

Watch for these missing relative pronouns when the relative pronoun (ProRel) is functioning as the direct object of the relative clause. For example, in the sentence *The government abandoned the public relations doctrine they had been developing for years,* the word *that* has been dropped. It should be treed as *the public relations doctrine **that** they had been developing for years*. The relative pronoun *that* is grammatically functioning as the direct object of the relative clause: *they had been developing **that** (the public relations doctrine) for years.*

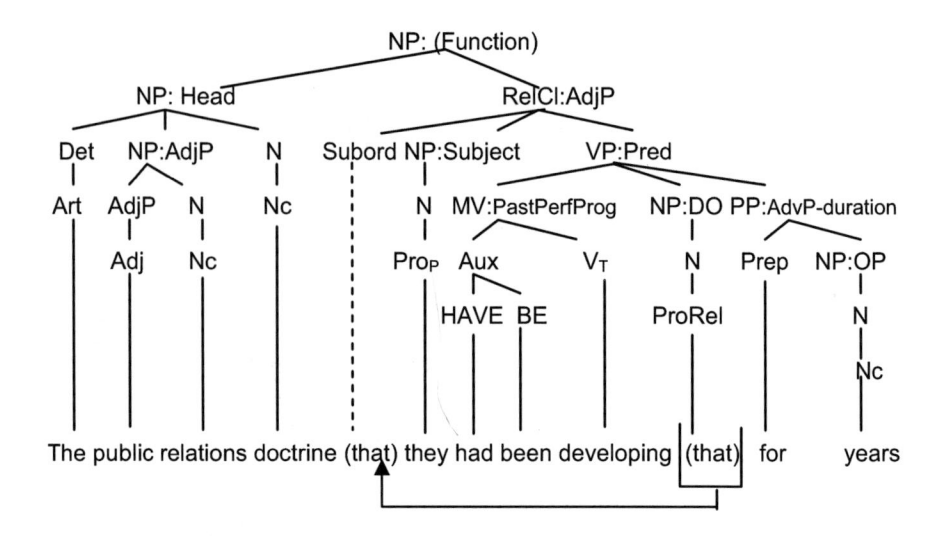

```
                         NP: (Function)
            _____|_____
       NP: Head                              RelCl:AdjP
    _____|_____                    _____|_____
  Det   NP:AdjP   N          Subord NP:Subject           VP:Pred
   |    __|__    |                |      |                 |
  Art  AdjP  N   Nc               N   MV:PastPerfProg  NP:DO   PP:AdvP-duration
        |   |                     |      __|__          |         __|__
       Adj  Nc                  Prop   Aux    Vₜ        N       Prep  NP:OP
                                       _|_              |              |
                                      HAVE BE        ProRel            N
                                                                       |
                                                                       Nc
The public relations doctrine (that) they had been developing (that)  for      years
```

Sometimes both the preposition and the ProRel seem to have been dropped.

- *That was the moment I knew what career I wanted.*
- *That was the moment **in which** I knew what career I wanted.*

Restrictive and Nonrestrictive Relative Clauses

Relative clauses can be either restrictive or nonrestrictive, depending upon the sentence. Both types modify, but <u>restrictive modifiers restrict (limit) the definition of the NP:Head</u>. Restrictive modifiers are needed to correctly determine the NP:Head. Nonrestrictive modifiers merely add more information to the NP:Head. Try the following tests to determine if the relative clause is restrictive or nonrestrictive.

Restrictive	*Which Test*
For this test, ask *"Which?"* before the NP:Head. If the relative clause answers this question, then it is restrictive. The purpose of the relative clause is to clarify *which one*.	
Nonrestrictive	*By-the-Way Test*
For this test, insert the phrase *by the way* after the relative pronoun in the relative clause. If this fits with the meaning, then the clause is nonrestrictive.	

Relative Clauses and Adjectival Infinitive Phrases 139

Nonrestrictive	*Pause Test*
Try pausing both before and after you say the relative clause. This can also be combined with the *by-the-way* test. If the meaning in the sentence fits with the pauses, it is nonrestrictive.	

These tests are not "foolproof," but they can help you decide whether the relative clause is restrictive or nonrestrictive.

Sentence	Test	Type
The wild turkey whose tail feathers were missing landed on our bird feeder.	**which wild turkey?** the one whose tail feathers were missing	Restrictive
His pet hedgehog, which was five years old, developed a tumor.	*which* **by the way** *was five years old*	Non-restrictive
The large ant mound interested the scientists, who had been in the country for years.	*who* **by the way** *had been in the country for years*	Non-restrictive
The students whom she had been tutoring passed the test easily.	**which students?** The ones she had been tutoring	Restrictive

Sometimes only the writer can say whether a relative clause is restrictive or nonrestrictive.

Consider the sentence *My son **who ran in the Twin Cities Marathon** is a veterinarian*. If I have only one son, then the clause is nonrestrictive: *My son, who, by the way, ran in the Twin Cities Marathon, is a veterinarian*. The relative clause in this scenario merely adds additional information to the head. If, however, I have two sons and only one son ran in the marathon, then the clause is restrictive because I need it to tell <u>which</u> of the sons I mean: *which son? The one who ran in the Twin Cities Marathon*.

We will label our relative clauses in grammar trees as either restrictive or nonrestrictive.

```
              NP: (Function)
             ╱            ╲
       NP: Head      RelCl:AdjP- Restrictive
                      ╱    |    ╲
                  Subord NP:Subject VP:Pred
```

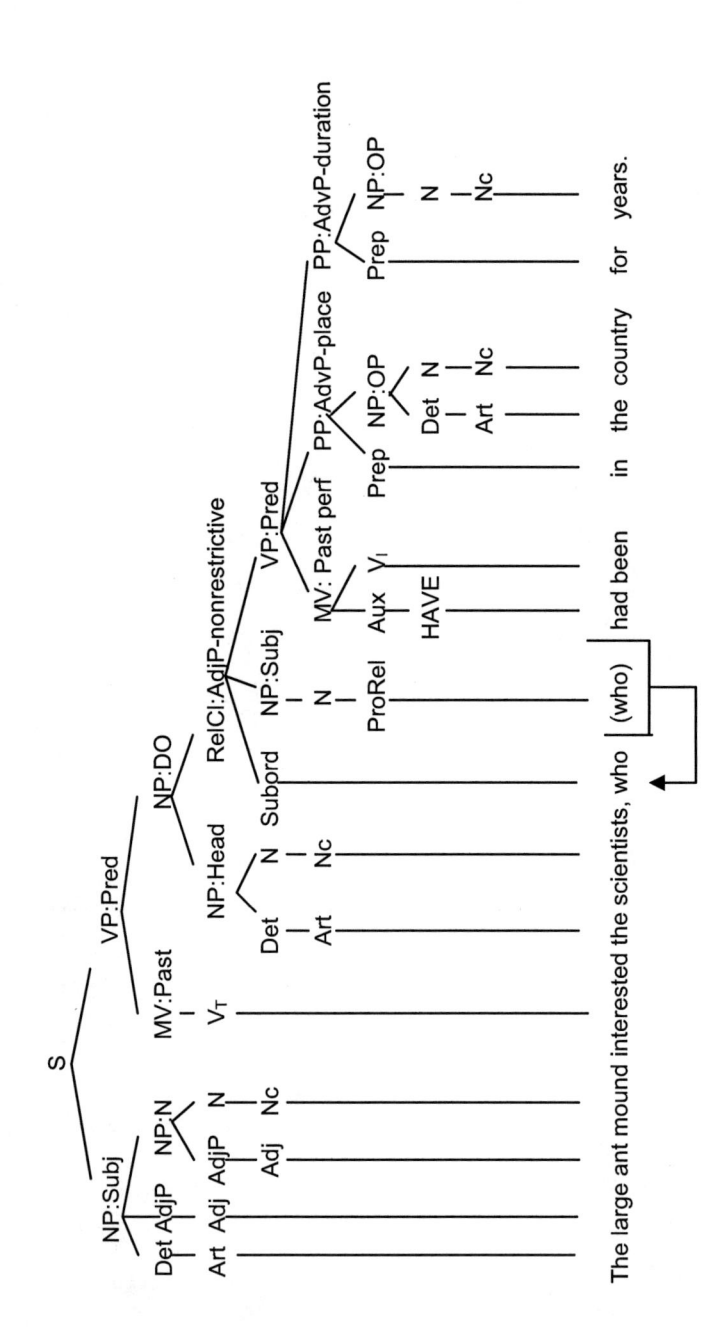

Relative Clauses and Adjectival Infinitive Phrases

The large ant mound interested the scientists, who (who) had been in the country for years.

Relative Clauses and Adjectival Infinitive Phrases 141

Compound Heads

Sometimes the head to which an adjectival structure is attached is compound, such as in the sentence below.

- *Kiel, Hall, and Sluis, who were the top three candidates, gave impressive speeches.*

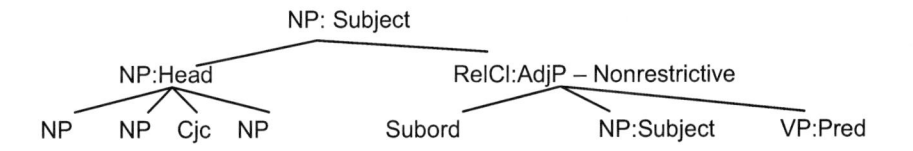

```
                         NP: Subject
              _____|_____
         NP:Head                RelCl:AdjP – Nonrestrictive
       ___|___                   _____|_____
   NP   NP  Cjc  NP          Subord    NP:Subject   VP:Pred
```

Adjectival Infinitive Phrases

Adjectival infinitive phrases (**InfPh:AdjP**) can be formed by changing some relative clauses into infinitive phrases. Adjectival infinitive phrases are <u>restrictive</u>. Like relative clauses, they are attached to NP:Heads and are used to restrict the NP:Head by the information they provide.

Below are some examples with adjectival infinitive phrases that have been formed from relative clauses.

Sentence has Relative Clause	Sentence has Adj Infinitive Phrase
Hexaba is the person **whom we must avoid**.	Hexaba is the person **for us to avoid**.
The material **which you must learn for the exam** is in this textbook.	The material **for you to learn for the exam** is in this textbook.
The coed has a paper **that she should write**.	The coed has a paper **to write**.
The mother bought a book **that her son could read**.	The mother bought a book **for her son to read**.

If you are having trouble identifying adjectival infinitive phrases, it might be helpful to mentally convert the infinitive phrase into the corresponding relative clause to show yourself that it has an adjectival function as the relative clause does. Notice that the corresponding relative clause generally has a modal auxiliary in the verb cluster (*must, should, could, would, can, will, may, might, must*) and that the verb is active, not passive or linking.

Sentence has Adj Infinitive Phrase	Sentence with Relative Clause
The secretary **to replace Dianne** is Jack.	The secretary **who will replace Dianne** is Jack.
Heather is the very person **to organize this meeting.**	Heather is the very person **who can organize this meeting**.
Someone **for us to admire** is the janitor of the church.	Someone **whom we should admire** is the janitor of the church.

This type of infinitive phrase has an adjectival function, providing more information about the NP:Head, and is restrictive. Therefore, we will tree it as indicated below. Take a minute to review how to tree infinitives.

In this tree, I am showing the NP:Subj of the last example above. This is a partial tree so that you can better see the adjectival infinitive phrase.

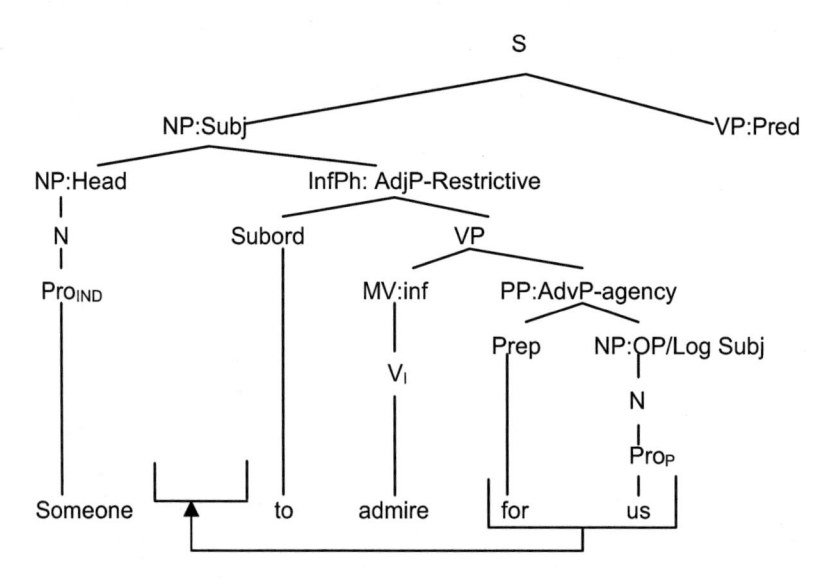

```
                                    S
                    _____|_____
                NP:Subj                           VP:Pred
         _____|_____
     NP:Head          InfPh: AdjP-Restrictive
        |             _____|_____
        N          Subord              VP
        |                         _____|_____
     Pro_IND                    MV:inf    PP:AdvP-agency
                                  |        ____|____
                                  V_I    Prep   NP:OP/Log Subj
                                                     |
                                                     N
                                                     |
                                                   Pro_P
        |              |           |        |         |
     Someone          to        admire     for        us
```

Similar Structures with Different Functions

Difference between Noun Clauses and Relative Clauses

The same structure could be either a *Wh* noun clause or a relative clause. It is not the structure that determines which it is; it is the function.

- The relative clause is attached to an NP and functions as an AdjP, whereas the noun clause functions as an NP.
- The relative clause has a head; the noun clause is the NP.
- It might help you to think a bit more about the names of these structures. The noun clause is called noun clause because it functions as an NP. The relative clause has a relationship with the NP (it is a "relative" to the NP).

Sentence with Noun Clause	Sentence with Relative Clause
The modern philosophers wondered **who believed in universal truth.**	Tolkien, **who believed in universal truth**, wrote fantasy to show his philosophy.
Wheret hey had camped the night before was now a smoldering ruin.	The sheriff of Nottingham looked for Robin Hood's gang in Sherwood Forest, **where they had camped the night before.**
At the banquet, Gwenhyvar announced **whom Arthur would name as his heir to the throne.**	Galahad, **whom Arthur would name as his heir to the throne,** was knighted in an impressive ceremony.

Differences among the Types of Infinitive Phrases

- The **adverbial infinitive phrase** generally answers the adverb question why. As an adverb phrase, it can often be moved to another part of the sentence without destroying the meaning of the sentence.
- **Nominal infinitive phrases** function as an NP in the sentence. They can be subjects, predicate nominatives, object complements, or direct objects.
- **Adjectival infinitive phrases** have a restrictive adjectival function. They follow NP:Heads and provide information that restricts the NP:Head.

They are all treed the same way, except for the function notation. Remember, in the *for/to* infinitive phrases, the *for*-phrase is an adverb phrase of agency, and the OP of the for-phrase is also the logical subject.

Relative Clauses and Usage

There are two main usage issues that involve relative clauses.

Ending a Sentence with a Preposition

This situation can arise when the relative pronoun (ProRel) should be the object of the preposition (OP). Remember, in Standard English, the entire prepositional phrase is moved to the front of the relative clause along with the ProRel. When just the ProRel is moved, the sentence might end with a preposition, violating this usage rule. However, this is important only in formal language situations; in informal language situations, ending a sentence with a preposition is generally accepted.

Sentence ending in a Preposition	Sentence in Standard English
That book is the one that they made reference to.	*That book is the one **to which** they made reference.*
The scholarship committee selected the writer whom they will give the prize to.	*The scholarship committee selected the writer **to whom** they will give the prize.*

Who and Whom

In formal language situations, one should distinguish between the use of *who* and the use of *whom*. *Who* is used for subjects, and *whom* is used for direct objects, indirect objects, and objects of prepositions.

- *The president's wife, **whom** the psychologist identified as an enabler, wrote an autobiography.* (*Whom* is the direct object of the relative clause.)
- *The prize will go to the person **who** sells the most boxes of cookies.* (*Who* is the subject of the relative clause.)
- *Peter, in **whom** we have great confidence, was chosen to do the research on kudu breeding.* (*Whom* is the OP of the preposition of the relative clause.)

Adjectival Structures and Punctuation

Punctuation with Nonrestrictive Modifiers

In general, nonrestrictive modifiers are set off by punctuation marks, usually commas. They could also be set off by dashes or parentheses. We do not use punctuation marks around restrictive modifiers. Remember that relative clauses may be either restrictive or nonrestrictive. Adjectival infinitive phrases are not set off by marks of punctuation because they are restrictive.

Fragments

If the relative clause is punctuated as a separate sentence, it is a fragment. Remember, <u>relative clauses must be attached to their heads.</u>

- *The British intelligence agency claimed that their efforts were more successful at finding weapons.* **Which could be used for mass destruction during terrorist attacks**.

This relative clause has been detached from its head (weapons) and so is a fragment. In fact, the relative clause is restrictive and should not be set off from its head by even a comma, much less a period: *The British intelligence agency claimed that their efforts were more successful at finding weapons* **which could be used for mass destruction during terrorist attacks** (**which** weapons? *weapons which could be used for mass destruction during terrorist attacks*).

A relative clause fragment will fail the "complete sentence test," as do other types of fragments. If it is a sentence and not a fragment, it should make sense if you insert it into a test frame such as the following:

    I told them that _____.

Our relative clause fragment does not make sense in the test frame, and so we would conclude that it is a fragment.

- *I told them that* <u>Which could be used for mass destruction during terrorist attacks.</u>

The full sentence would make sense in the test frame.

- I told them that <u>The British intelligence agency claimed that their efforts were more successful at finding weapons **which could be used for mass destruction during terrorist attacks.**</u>

Relative Clauses and Style

In writing, it is important that the head of the relative clause is clear to your reader. For example, consider a sentence such as the following.
- Italy, Germany, and France, which voted against the European constitution, caused the fall in the price of Eurostocks.

The relative clause here is confusing. Does the relative clause (*which voted against the European constitution*) refer to France or to all three of the countries? If it refers to just France, a writer would be well advised to put *France* first or second in the list to make the head clear.
- Italy, France (which voted against the European constitution), and Germany caused the fall in the price of Eurostocks.

If the relative clause refers to all three, then the relative clause could be modified to show that.
- Italy, Germany, and France, all of which voted against the European constitution, caused the fall in the price of Eurostocks.

Practice Sentences

I. Restrictive or Nonrestrictive? The following sentences have had all commas removed. <u>Label</u> the relative clause in each as either restrictive or nonrestrictive, and <u>put commas back in</u> as required. If the relative clause could be either restrictive or nonrestrictive, depending upon the meaning, explain that.
1. The sermon that the pastor preached last week was highly controversial.
2. The mother whose daughter won the spelling bee was the most excited.
3. Matt whose birthday is on Christmas celebrates it in July instead.
4. The boys whom I am teaching to cook covered me in flour while we were baking a German chocolate cake.

Relative Clauses and Adjectival Infinitive Phrases

5. The wedding that I will be attending next week is in Wisconsin.
6. Early American Literature, which will only meet next fall, is being taught by an adjunct professor.
7. The contractors whose bids are the lowest are the ones that we should contact to do the repairs.
8. The senator of whom we were speaking was not able to be present at the meeting.
9. The woman whose flower won a blue ribbon at the state fair attributes her success to a little bit of patience and a lot of Miracle Grow.
10. Julia, whose scores on the test were the highest, skipped class for the entire next week.
11. The nanny reprimanded the children, over whom she usually had impeccable control.
12. The forceful blow shattered the chandelier that was imported from Venice.
13. The senator made a ludicrous statement that was mocked by all who heard it.
14. The means by which I go to and from work is the city bus.
15. The basketball team won their most important game of the season, which was against our rival.
16. The swooning girls enjoyed the cake the desperate boys made for them.
17. The celebrity about whom the biography was written issued a statement of disapproval.
18. My boyfriend, whom I will marry, will be proposing in New York City in Times Square next weekend.
19. The person whom she trusts the most should be her spouse.
20. The zookeeper handed the loris that we got from the Saint Louis Zoo a bit of fruit.

II. Tree the following sentences. As you tree these sentences, remember that in addition to relative clauses and adjectival infinitive phrases, you will also be seeing the structures that you learned in previous chapters. Some sentences are included for review. If the sentence does have a relative clause or adjectival infinitive phrase, you might find it helpful to circle the head and underline the "attachment" before you begin to tree.

1. Individuals who had mental illnesses were being treated inhumanely in many societies in the past.
2. A hedgehog is the animal for you to choose as your mascot.
3. The glorious pink and orange sunset was mesmerizing both the tourists, whom the guide had brought to the canyon for the first time.
4. That is becoming the difficulty of mapping a place that is unknown.
5. That was the year to which the mad scientist hoped to return with his time machine.
6. We were told that the dining room table was made with professional products.
7. A crucial fact to remember is that the Japanese had instigated America's entrance into World War II.
8. The successful testing of the atomic bomb on July 16, 1945, presented the possibility of Japanese surrender without the deaths of thousands of Americans that an invasion would entail.
9. Swimming in the ocean has been a fitness technique for the mermaid to try after splashing around all day.
10. Painting pictures to sell for charity is a nice idea.
11. A person whose record of accidents, traffic violations, and tickets is extensive will find car insurance expensive.
12. Photo albums and picture frames should be very popular gifts to give as wedding presents.
13. Tory must be bringing home a new lotion for me to use.
14. Mary had gone to the store to buy bread and eggs, which she needed for a brownie recipe.
15. The commander could have an interesting assignment for us to do.
16. Activating the cell phone would be the most difficult task for the elderly woman to do.
17. She realized that her enemy was the man she had met on the Internet.
18. She was intending to buy the Pontiac that resembled her grandfather's jalopy.
19. The Romans might have brought the Celts, whom they considered savages, horses for war.
20. The lawyers, who, by constant manipulation, deceived the clients, were fired.

Relative Clauses and Adjectival Infinitive Phrases 149

21. Keith's wedding is the one I will be attending next week in Indiana.
22. The religious sect had created sanctuaries that we visited on our tour of Asia.
23. The professors whose classes are the hardest are the ones from whom you will learn the most.
24. The proud father enjoyed the card his daughter had made for him with her picture scanner.
25. The zookeeper handed the loris a bit of fruit to tempt him.
26. The woman in the blue sweater is the mother whose daughter is winning the spelling bee.
27. We have much to say.
28. I am strengthened for the moments in which I am not this calm, cool, and collected.
29. One of the first to arrive will be Donavan.
30. She handed the groupings separately to Jake, who, in turn, arranged them on the peg board wall in the new "stocking stuffer" section behind the aisles in the rear of the store.
31. The important fact for us to remember is that God is always with us.
32. Photographs that are too dark or too light might be altered for better quality.
33. My best friend will be mailing me a package that contains various peculiar and unrelated items.
34. These are the dishes for somebody to wash.
35. The boy who should call my roommate plays for the college tennis team, which will be going to Chicago this weekend.
36. The only student to apply for the internship might be Kristin.
37. Soon the others in the band reached the spot at which Douglas waited.
38. She is crocheting a sweater for her granddaughter to wear outside.
39. The disciplined equestrian will be training for the next Olympic Games, which will be held in his hometown.
40. The Tiffany yellow diamond pendant we found is quite rare.
41. This armadillo, which originally lived in South America and Central America, migrated into the United States around 1850.
42. Kamitlietian is president of TechnoSoft, which she founded last year.

150   *Relative Clauses and Adjectival Infinitive Phrases*

43. The copyright owners who helped to push the law say that these products will destroy the industry.
44. Hester Prynne wore a scarlet letter, which the townspeople had meant as a symbol of shame.
45. Paying attention to people who are not the faintest risk as a security threat will eventually defuse the charge of profiling.
46. Interested parties, of whom she spoke highly, might also wonder whether his outspoken opposition to the plan was a cover for the sort of clandestine activities for which he was particularly suited.
47. Peter gave Heidi, whose smile was evident, a look that expressed his opinion of this sentiment.
48. The greatest scandal to engulf the church had previously been the arrest of the priest.
49. The young man has been writing a sonnet to melt the heart of his girlfriend.
50. For the next month, which Parliament dubbed Coronation Month, Buckingham Palace was host to several concerts and grand dinners.

III. Practice writing relative clauses. (Be sure to use *who* and *whom* in Standard English for these sentences.) Decide in each case if the relative clause is restrictive or nonrestrictive and punctuate it appropriately.

1. Use the following sentence as a base sentence:
   After the test, the teacher gave the child a sticker.

   a. Add a relative clause to the subject in which the ProRel is the Subj.
   b. Add a relative clause to the subject in which the ProRel is the DO.
   c. Add a relative clause to the subject in which the ProRel an OP.
   d. Add a relative clause to the subject in which the ProRel is a Det.
   e. Add a relative clause to the direct object in which the ProRel is the Subj.
   f. Add a relative clause to the direct object in which the ProRel is the DO.
   g. Add a relative clause to the direct object in which the ProRel is an OP.
   h. Add a relative clause to the direct object in which the ProRel is a Det.

Relative Clauses and Adjectival Infinitive Phrases 151

    i. Add a relative clause to the indirect object in which the ProRel is the Subj.
    j. Add a relative clause to the indirect object in which the ProRel is the DO.
    k. Add a relative clause to the indirect object in which the ProRel is an OP.
    l. Add a relative clause to the indirect object in which the ProRel is a Det.
    m. Add a relative clause to the object of the preposition in which the ProRel is the Subj.
    n. Add a relative clause to the object of the preposition in which the ProRel is the DO.
    o. Add a relative clause to the object of the preposition in which the ProRel is an OP.
    p. Add a relative clause to the object of the preposition in which the ProRel is a Det.

2. Use the following sentence as a base sentence: *Deb became a psychologist.*
    a. Add a relative clause to the subject in which the ProRel is the Subj.
    b. Add a relative clause to the subject in which the ProRel is the DO.
    c. Add a relative clause to the subject in which the ProRel is an OP.
    d. Add a relative clause to the subject in which the ProRel is a Det.
    e. Add a relative clause to the predicate nominative in which the ProRel is the Subj.
    f. Add a relative clause to the predicate nominative in which the ProRel is the DO.
    g. Add a relative clause to the predicate nominative in which the ProRel is an OP.
    h. Add a relative clause to the predicate nominative in which the ProRel is a Det.

Chapter 9
Noun Cluster Expansions: Adjectival Participial Phrases and Adjectival Appositives

In English, we have a choice of types of adjectival structures that can be attached to NP:Heads. In this chapter, we will study two more modifier structures with adjectival functions. Like relative clauses and adjectival infinitive phrases, these structures describe and add more information to the nominal phrases that they follow (their heads).

Active Participial Phrases

Active participial phrases (**ActPartPh:AdjP**) consist of a VP beginning with an *–ing* word. Participial phrases can be formed from certain relative clauses. For example, from the relative clause *who is bursting with energy*, we can form the active participial phrase *bursting with energy*. To make the active participial phrase here, we drop the relative pronoun and the BE Aux (*is*).

- Addie, **who is bursting with energy**, *sorted the filing cabinets.*
- Addie, **bursting with energy**, *sorted the filing cabinets.*

Tree active participial phrases under an NP. (The following tree does not have the VP:Pred completed so you can focus on the new structure.)

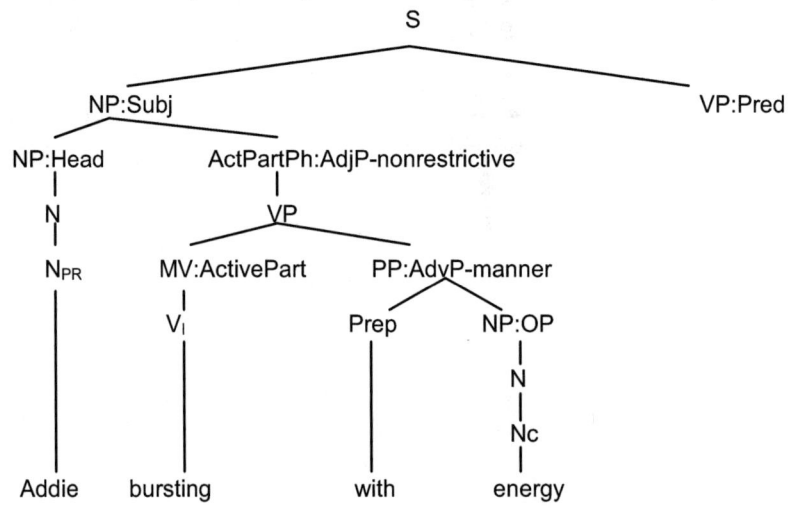

```
                                S
                 ┌──────────────┴──────────────┐
              NP:Subj                        VP:Pred
        ┌────────┴────────┐
     NP:Head        ActPartPh:AdjP-nonrestrictive
        │                   │
        N                   VP
        │           ┌───────┴────────┐
       N_PR     MV:ActivePart    PP:AdvP-manner
        │           │           ┌─────┴─────┐
        │           V_I        Prep       NP:OP
        │           │           │           │
        │           │           │           N
        │           │           │           │
        │           │           │          Nc
        │           │           │           │
      Addie      bursting      with      energy
```

Adjectival Participial Phrases and Adjectival Appositives 153

Passive Participial Phrases

Passive participial phrases consist of a VP beginning with the passive form of a verb (*-en* form). Remember that the *–en* form of verbs in English is often written as *–ed,* and there are other irregular verb forms as well. Like active participial phrases, passive participial phrases can be formed from certain relative clauses. In the following example, we drop the relative pronoun and the BE Aux (*was*) from the relative clause to get the passive participial phrase.

- Danika, **who was selected as top assistant by the committee**, organized the workload efficiently.
- Danika, **selected as top assistant by the committee**, organized the workload efficiently.

Adjectival passive participial phrases (**PassPartPh:AdjP**) are also attached to NP:Heads and are treed under an NP, similarly to active participial phrases. Notice the MV label and adjectival function.

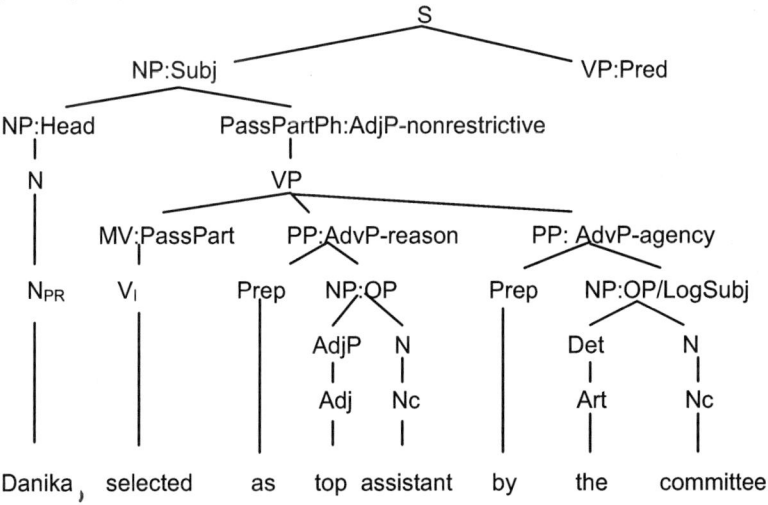

```
                              S
              ┌───────────────┴──────────────┐
           NP:Subj                        VP:Pred
      ┌──────┴──────┐
  NP:Head    PassPartPh:AdjP-nonrestrictive
     │                 │
     N                VP
     │       ┌─────────┼─────────────┐
    NPR   MV:PassPart  PP:AdvP-reason  PP: AdvP-agency
     │      │       ┌───┴───┐      ┌────┴────┐
     │      Vı     Prep   NP:OP   Prep   NP:OP/LogSubj
     │      │      │     ┌─┴─┐    │      ┌──┴──┐
     │      │      │   AdjP  N    │     Det    N
     │      │      │     │   │    │      │     │
     │      │      │    Adj  Nc   │     Art    Nc
     │      │      │     │   │    │      │     │
  Danika  selected  as  top assistant  by  the committee
```

> Notice that within both the active participial phrase and the passive participial phrase, the VP does <u>not</u> function as a predicate (because there is no subject in the phrase), but it can have any of the elements that we have been seeing in the VP:Pred. The participial phrase has a VP structure but not a predicate function.

Restrictive and Nonrestrictive Participial Phrases

As we saw with relative clauses, participial phrases can be either restrictive or nonrestrictive, depending upon meaning. Also, the same punctuation guidelines apply to nonrestrictive participial phrases. Remember, restrictive modifiers restrict (limit) the definition of the NP:Head. Restrictive modifiers are needed to correctly determine the NP:Head. Nonrestrictive modifiers merely add more information to the NP:Head. As you did with relative clauses, try the following tests to help you decide whether the participial phrase is restrictive or nonrestrictive.

Restrictive	Which Test
For this test, ask *"Which?"* before the NP:Head. If the participial phrase answers this question, then it is restrictive. The purpose of the participial phrase is to clarify *which one*.	
Nonrestrictive	*Pause Test*
Try pausing both before and after you say the participial phrase. If the meaning in the sentence fits with the pauses, it is nonrestrictive.	

Sentence	Test	Type
The evening approached like a woman **trailing long gray veils**.	**Which woman?** The one trailing long gray veils	Restrictive Active Participial Phrase
The island, **settled originally by Britons**, was invaded later by Roman troops.	Pause where the commas are. These pauses fit with the meaning of the sentence.	Nonrestrictive Passive Participial Phrase
The doctor, **trembling at the pounding on the door**, was hidden by the CIA.	Pause where the commas are. These pauses fit with the meaning of the sentence.	Nonrestrictive Active Participial Phrase
Victims **targeted for the terrorist attacks** were educated and productive citizens.	**Which victims?** The ones targeted for the terrorist attacks	Restrictive Passive Participial Phrase

Adjectival Participial Phrases and Adjectival Appositives

Moving Nonrestrictive Participial Phrases

Unlike relative clauses, adjectival participial phrases that are nonrestrictive may be moved to a position directly in front of the head. If this move has taken place, tree the participial phrase after the head as usual and then show that it has been moved. This movement of the participial phrase to a position in front of the NP:Head can take place if the NP is functioning as the subject.

Resolving to continue making good decisions, the young man boarded the train.

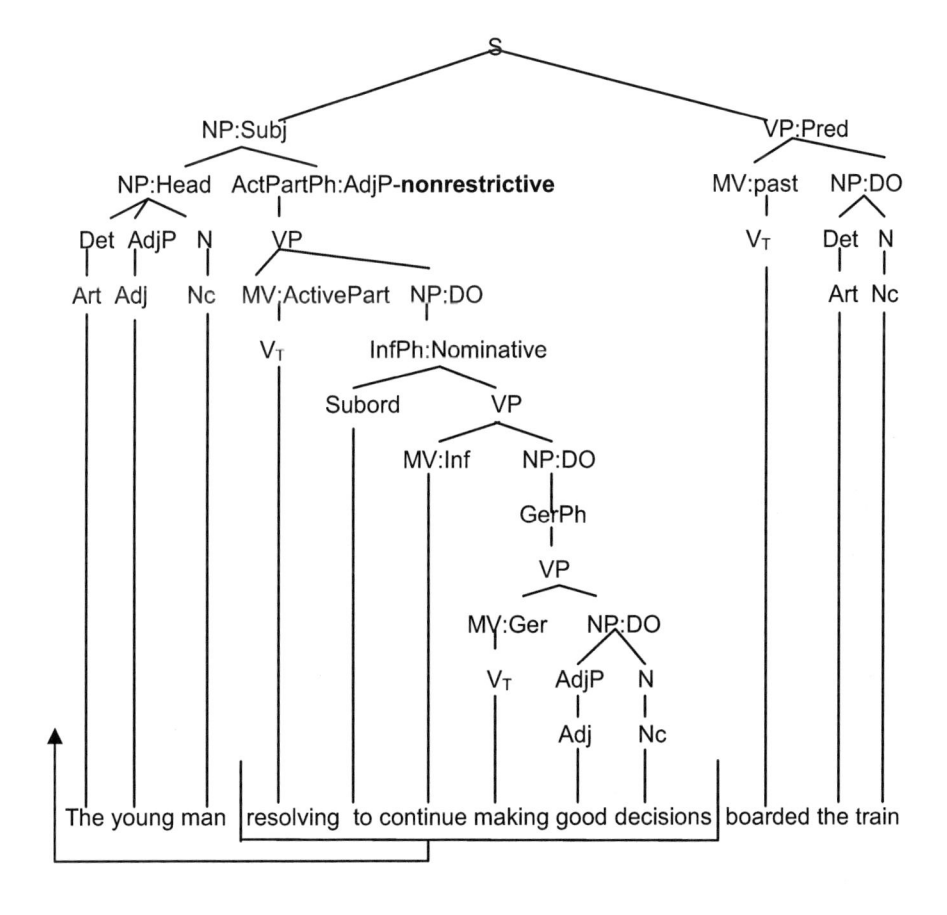

Adjectival Appositives with Adjectival Complements

Adjectival appositives (**AdjP:App**) are adjective phrases that follow an NP:Head and describe it. Their function is similar to that of participial phrases, but they do not have a VP as the structure.

An adjectival appositive consists of a required adjective and an optional adjectival complement. An **adjectival complement** follows the adjective and completes the idea expressed by the adjective. The adjectival complement often takes the form of a prepositional phrase.
- *The child, **wild with anticipation**, ran to the front of the line.*

As we saw with participial phrases, nonrestrictive adjectival appositives can be moved to a position directly in front of the head.
- ***Wild with anticipation**, the child ran to the front of the line.*

An adjectival appositive is shown in a grammar tree following its NP:Head and under an NP functioning as a Subj, DO, IO, OP, OC, or PredN. If it has been moved to a position in front of the head, tree it following the NP:Head and then show that it has been moved.

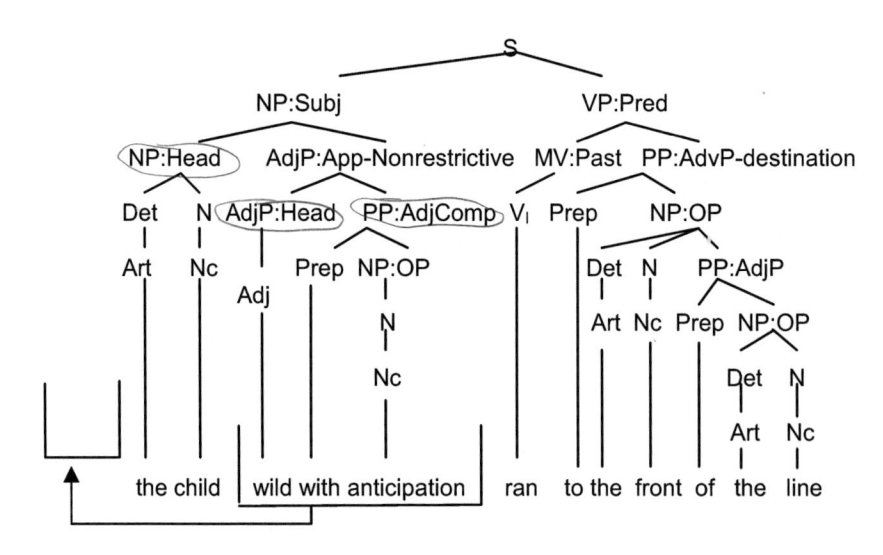

Adjectival Participial Phrases and Adjectival Appositives 157

Restrictive or Nonrestrictive Appositives

Adjective phrases functioning as appositives are almost always nonrestrictive, merely adding descriptive details to a nominal phrase. They are generally set off by commas or dashes. Occasionally, the adjective phrase functioning as an appositive could be restrictive. An example would be the following sentence: *The young man adept at carving is the one we want.* In this sentence, the adjectival appositive *adept at carving* shows us *which* young man we want. Therefore, in this case, the adjectival appositive is restrictive, and we do not use any commas.

Other Places for Adjectival Complements (AdjComp)

Besides adjectival appositives, adjectives followed by a prepositional phrase adjectival complement can be functioning as a predicate adjective (PredAdj) or an adjective object complement (AdjP:OC) with a Vc verb.

Adjective Complement as part of Pred Adj	The child was **wild with anticipation**.
Adjective Complement as part of AdjP:OC	The adults considered the child **unruly beyond control**.

Compound Structures

Compound Heads

Remember, as we saw in Chapter 8, heads can be compound. Even one adjectival prepositional phrase can be attached to a compound N as shown below. (The triangle on the tree indicates a section that is not completely treed.)

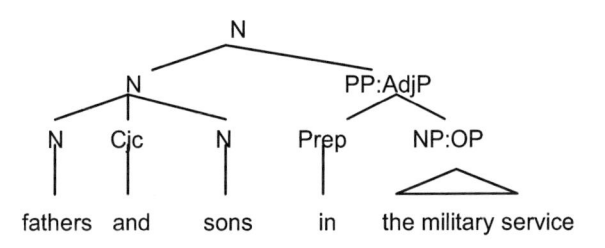

```
                    N
           ┌────────┴────────┐
           N                 PP:AdjP
       ┌───┼───┐           ┌───┴───┐
       N   Cjc  N          Prep   NP:OP
       │   │    │           │      △
    fathers and sons         in   the military service
```

Compound Appositives and Participial Phrases

We can also have compound adjectival appositives or compound participial phrases with a coordinating conjunction (Cjc) or correlating conjunction (Cjcorr) between the elements.

- *Many versions of the Grail story, both medieval and modern, exist in literature.*
- *In 313, Constantine passed legislation enforcing tolerance and restoring property to Christians.*

When we have compound adjectival structures in English, we frequently mix adjectival appositives with active or passive participial phrases. These are all <u>adjectival modifiers</u>.

- *Dejected and filled with remorse, the psychiatrist packed his belongings.*

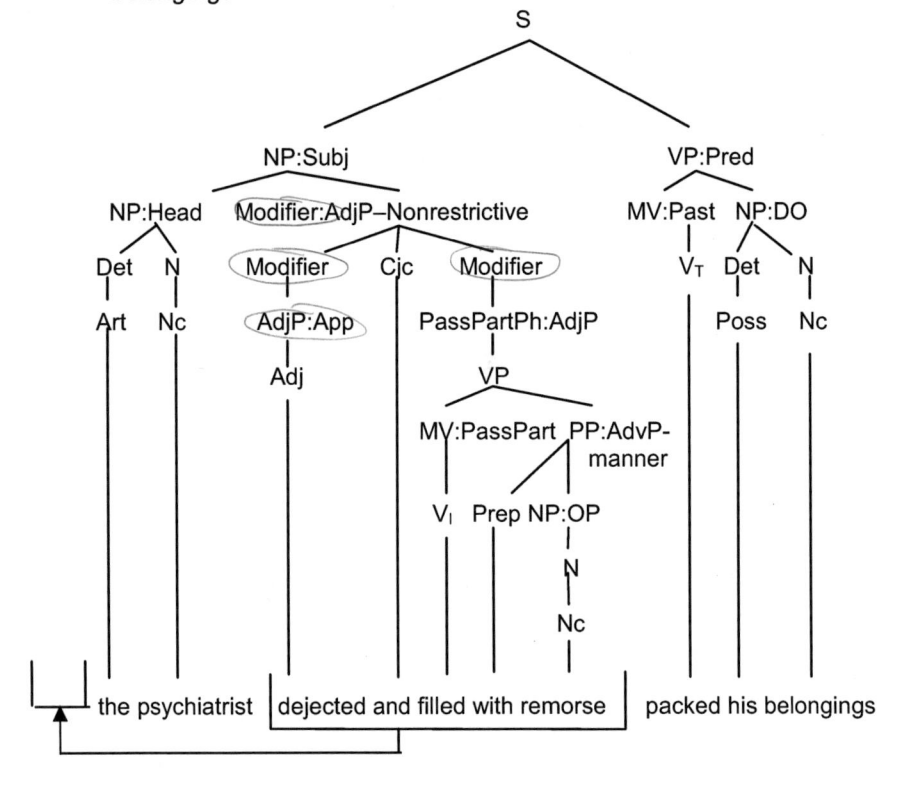

```
                              S
           ┌──────────────────┴──────────────┐
         NP:Subj                           VP:Pred
    ┌──────┴──────────────┐              ┌────┴────┐
 NP:Head   Modifier:AdjP–Nonrestrictive  MV:Past  NP:DO
  ┌─┴─┐    ┌────────┬────┬────────┐       │      ┌──┴──┐
 Det  N  Modifier  Cjc  Modifier         V_T    Det    N
  │   │    │              │               │      │     │
 Art  Nc  AdjP:App    PassPartPh:AdjP           Poss   Nc
           │              │
          Adj             VP
                    ┌─────┴─────┐
              MV:PassPart   PP:AdvP-manner
                   │        ┌────┴────┐
                  V_I      Prep    NP:OP
                                     │
                                     N
                                     │
                                     Nc
```

the psychiatrist | dejected and filled with remorse | packed his belongings

Adjectival Participial Phrases and Adjectival Appositives 159

Sometimes we have two or more adjectival modifiers with the same NP:Head that do not have a coordinating conjunction (Cjc) connecting them. All of the modifiers may come after the head, or one modifier may come in front of the head and one may come after. In this case, I would argue that grammatically this is a compound in which the Cjc has been dropped. So, I would tree this with a dotted line under the Cjc and the conjunction *and* in parentheses.

Military invasions—Roman, Anglo-Saxon, Viking, Norman—dominate the written histories of Britain.

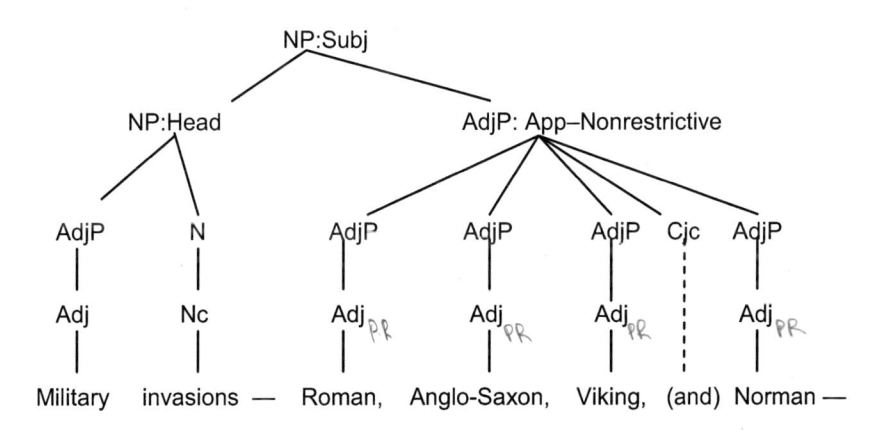

```
                           NP:Subj
                          /        \
                  NP:Head            AdjP: App–Nonrestrictive
                  /    \            /    |    |    |    \
               AdjP     N        AdjP  AdjP  AdjP  Cjc  AdjP
                |       |          |    |     |    :    |
               Adj     Nc        Adj   Adj   Adj   :   Adj
                |       |        PR     PR    PR   :    PR
                |       |          |    |     |    :    |
             Military invasions — Roman, Anglo-Saxon, Viking, (and) Norman —
```

On the next page is another example. Notice that one modifier comes after the head, but one modifier has been moved in front of the head.

Encompassing history, literature, art and politics, the Arthurian myth, idyllic and idealistic, is diverse and pluralistic.

Adjectival Participial Phrases and Adjectival Appositives

The following tree has only the subject shown so that you can concentrate on the compound.

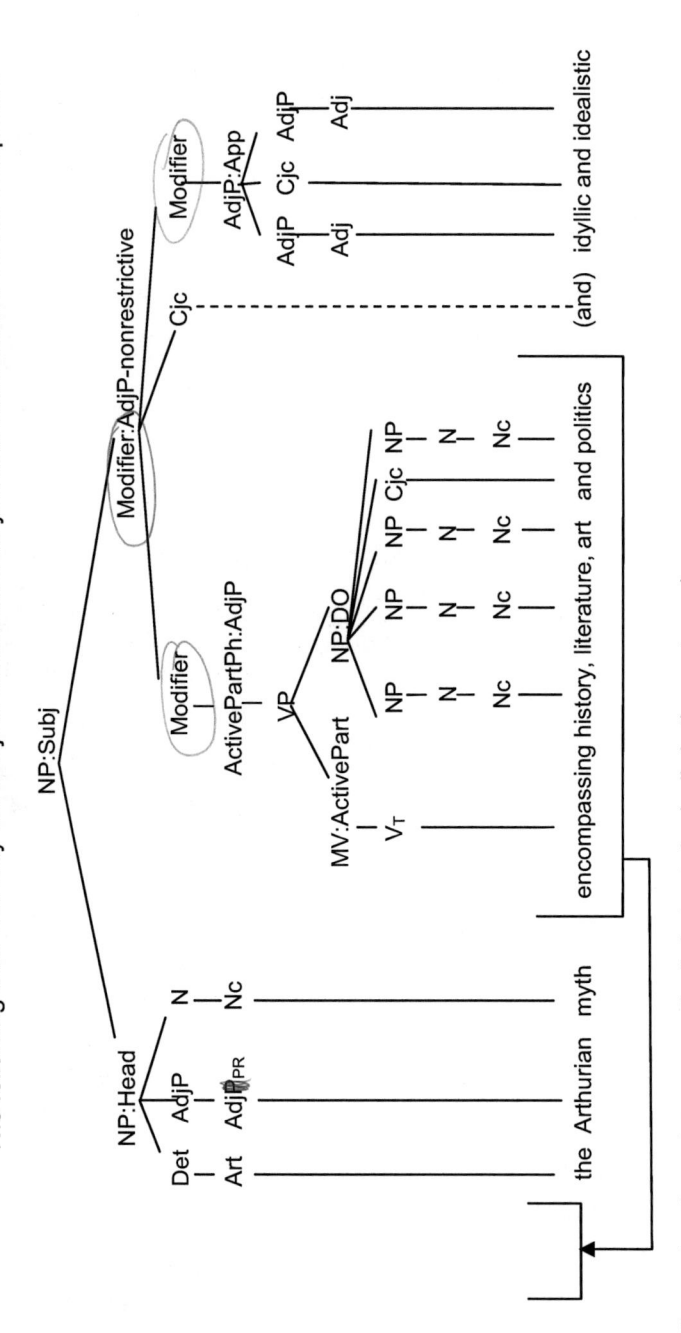

(The conjunction exists grammatically but not physically in the sentence.)

Distinguishing between Active Participial Phrases and Gerund Phrases

- Active participial phrases and gerund phrases are identical in structure; they differ only in function.
- The **active participial phrase** is attached to an NP and functions as an AdjP; the **gerund phrase** functions as an NP.
- The active participial phrase has an NP:Head. The gerund phrase is the NP.

Sentence with GerPh	Sentence with ActPartPh
Protecting the weak and serving the king and his lady became hallmarks of a knight of the Round Table.	*Protecting the weak and serving the king and his lady,* Bedwyr is the most frequently mentioned knight in early Welsh poems.
The land became a wasteland brought on by his **suffering from a weapon wound that would not heal**.	The Fisher King, **suffering from a weapon wound that would not heal**, was finally healed by Galahad and the Holy Grail.
Being courteous and well mannered made Gawaine a favorite with the ladies.	Tristan, **being courteous and well mannered,** drank the wine that contained a love potion.

Noun Cluster Expansions and Punctuation

- Nonrestrictive modifiers are generally set off by punctuation marks, usually commas. They could also be set off by dashes or parentheses. We do not use punctuation marks around restrictive modifiers.

- Also, make sure that participial phrases do not end up as fragments. Review the use of test frames to check for fragments (Chapter 7).

Noun Cluster Expansions and Sentence Style

Using the structures we have been studying in the last two chapters can add to the style of your writing in two ways. First, these structures can add vital or even merely interesting detail to your sentences. Second, using these four structures (relative clauses, adjectival infinitive phrases, participial phrases, and adjectival appositives) can add variety to your sentences and keep them from being choppy.

Examples using NP Expansion Structures		
Specialized kilns once produced high-quality black pottery. A dozen of these small kilns were found among the objects.	Combine using a **relative clause.**	A dozen small, specialized kilns, **which once produced high-quality black pottery,** were found among the objects.
Conservationists have imported sheep to Florida. These are sheep that will eat kudzu and stop the weed's spread.	Combine using an **adjectival infinitive phrase.**	Conservationists have imported sheep **to eat kudzu and to stop the weed's spread in Florida.**
The nonhibernating wolverine scours its icy range for small prey. It is designed for the demanding northern winter.	Combine using a **passive participial phrase.**	The nonhibernating wolverine, **designed for the demanding northern winter,** scours its icy range for small prey.
Only 1,500 breeding pairs of thick-billed parrots nest in the old-growth conifers. These trees are falling increasingly to chain saws.	Combine using an **active participial phrase.**	In these old-growth conifer trees, **falling increasingly to chain saws,** only 1,500 breeding pairs of thick-billed parrots nest.
The aerial view shows the Tower of London in 1597. It is outstanding in its accuracy.	Combine using an **adjectival appositive.**	The aerial view, **outstanding in its accuracy,** shows the Tower of London in 1597.

Adjectival Participial Phrases and Adjectival Appositives 163

When you are revising your prose, consider doing the following:
- Add some of these structures into your existing sentences.
- Combine two existing sentences. Reconstruct one of the sentences into one of these structures (a relative clause, adjectival infinitive phrase, participial phrase, or adjectival appositive). Then insert the rewritten portion into the other sentence by attaching it to an NP:Head.

Noun Cluster Expansions and Usage

Make sure that all modifiers are placed in the sentence next to the nominative structure that they modify. The following are examples of misplaced passive participle phrases.
- *Covered with a special glaze, she put the ham in the oven.* (The ham is covered with glaze, not the woman.)
- *Held every year in a local coffee shop, the college students participating in The Spoken Word have a chance to read their poetry to an appreciative audience.* (The Spoken Word is held every year in a local coffee shop, not the college students.)

Practice Sentences

I. Tree the following sentences. Be sure to label the participial phrases as either restrictive or nonrestrictive. Also, remember that structures from previous chapters are included. Not all of the sentences have new structures.

1. Stranded by the side of the road, Sarah and Steve were picked up by a trucker.
2. The mail carrier had seen the pair of children sitting near the door on the veranda of the mansion.
3. Dabbing at her eyes with the hankie again, Petunia was giving her governess a watery smile.
4. The massive sandstone monolith looming over the flat Australian desert is a sacred site to the indigenous population.
5. Signaled by the electronic ding that gave voice to the full-glass door, Edith sauntered down the stairs to greet the first customer.
6. The light streamed through the half circle window nested in the peak of the attic bedroom.

7. The two men were setting up lights, glowing over another winter landscape and shining on a white sheet.
8. At one of Cornell University's massive greenhouses, the researcher examines rice plants engineered to tolerate conditions that would kill ordinary rice.
9. Chicks born and raised in captivity are the best hope for this prairie chicken.
10. The dog, hot and sweaty, began to wag his tail with exuberance previously unseen.
11. After a further glass of champagne urged on her by Cyrus, the musician burst into a particularly rollicking polka.
12. The hair of bright auburn, artistically dulled by gray, was a wig.
13. Each morning brought new stories of young children victimized by the men they had been raised to trust.
14. A driver chased by police had been threatening the neighborhood.
15. The sword, heavy and massive in size, was an exact replica of the one belonging to Wallace.
16. Old maps that illustrate mythical islands based on legends told by monks in Portugal are priceless.
17. Firebombing raids, effective in destroying Japanese cites, were now unsuccessful in pushing Japan to the point of surrender.
18. American soldiers, still hungry for revenge, fought against German forces in Europe and Japanese forces in Asia and the Philippines.
19. Roosevelt initially funded the atomic program, code-named the Manhattan Project, to use against Germany.
20. Harry Truman, stunned but vowing to continue Roosevelt's foreign policies, took over the presidency.
21. Scientists chose a site at Alamogordo, close to Los Alamos, to test the plutonium bomb to destroy the enemy forces.
22. The man jumping up and down was trying to get my attention.
23. Tired and hungry, the baby cried all night.
24. Amy, intelligent yet inexperienced as a mother, smiled longingly at the thought of having a baby.
25. Crowned in glory, the girls carrying armloads of flowers had stepped back from the podium.
26. I am staring at the afternoon sun spreading rays onto Flathead Lake.

Adjectival Participial Phrases and Adjectival Appositives 165

27. I want to take pictures of a long leather couch with only one small girl sitting on the end, bobbing her doll from knee to knee.
28. Last night we had ended up at Mich's house, clogged with dirt and piles of mail and two 3-D puzzles in the shape of castles.
29. Couches that have exhausted their springs were shoved against the wall in front of a TV surrounded by DVDs.
30. They will get that thud of restlessness pounding in their chests and look around for room to feel independent, to decide things, to stretch, to make sharp edges on their lives.
31. The seal pup must have been oblivious to the approaching danger.
32. The book given to me is a best seller and has 500 pages.
33. Temples at the base of the pyramid, connected by a long causeway, and three smaller pyramids designated for the burial of queens were also built by Khufu.
34. The woman's biting of her fingernails was extremely annoying to the man sitting beside her at the airport.
35. Seeing no other possibility, Jane took the steep path to reach the top of the mountain.
36. Looking out the window and barking, the dog was having the time of its life during the car ride.
37. The castle, tall and majestic, deteriorated over the years under the leadership of the haphazard knight.
38. Beautiful and skinny, Krissy had become the most popular girl who attended Jefferson High.
39. The water leaking from the hole in the pipe needs to be cleaned up.
40. The student running for vice president claimed that he could do a much better job.
41. Fearing for their lives, the rabbits of Watership Down decided to run away to avoid their master who kept them in small cages.
42. My son-in-law's sister ate an apple dripping with juice to maintain her health and keep away from doctors.
43. The teacher sporting the gold sweatshirt missed the play that everyone is talking about.
44. A basketball game that lasted for three hours was played by the group coming from Dallas.
45. Hurt and fearful, Juan clutched his wound and ran for help.

46. The wall decorated by my little sister's crayons made me depressed.
47. The Al-Qaeda terrorists, responsible for the September 11 attacks, had first engaged U.S. troops in 1993.
48. Collected over the years by countless unremembered bards, most early Welsh poetry remains anonymous.
49. The earliest poems attributed to Myrddin seem to place him in the northern Britain of the late sixth century.
50. Some foods that are low in protein or vitamins might be enhanced to increase their nutritional value.

II. **Write a sentence for each of the following**. Make sure that your modifiers are not misplaced.

1. Use the following (or one like it) as a base sentence: *The boss sent the engineer a new assignment.*
   a. Add an active participial phrase to the subject of the sentence.
   b. Add an active participial phrase to the indirect object of the sentence.
   c. Add an active participial phrase to the direct object of the sentence.
   d. Add a passive participial phrase to the subject of the sentence.
   e. Add a passive participial phrase to the indirect object of the sentence.
   f. Add a passive participial phrase to the direct object of the sentence.
   g. Add an adjectival appositive to the subject of the sentence.
   h. Add an adjectival appositive to the indirect object of the sentence.
   i. Add an adjectival appositive to the direct object of the sentence.

2. Use the following (or one like it) as a base sentence: *That software is a wonder.*
   a. Add an active participial phrase to the subject of the sentence.
   b. Add a passive participial phrase to the subject of the sentence.
   c. Add an adjectival appositive to the subject of the sentence.
   d. Add an active participial phrase to the predicate nominative.
   e. Add a passive participial phrase to the predicate nominative.
   f. Add an adjectival appositive to the predicate nominative.

Chapter 10
Adjectival and Adverbial Choices and Expansions

We studied adverbs in Chapter 5, and in the last two chapters, we have been looking at various adjectival structures. Now it is time to look at other structures that can function as adjectives and adverbs and at ways that both adjectival and adverbial phrases can expand.

Adjectival Complement Infinitive Phrases

We have seen infinitive phrases function in three ways so far:
- As an adverb (InfPh:AdvP)
- As an NP (InfPh:Nom)
- As an adjective phrase (InfPh:AdjP)

Infinitive phrases can also be used to complete an adjective. We call these adjectival complement infinitive phrases (**InfPh: AdjComp**). They follow adjectives. Remember, a **complement** follows a structure of some sort and completes the idea of that structure. Therefore, adjectival complements follow and **complete** adjectives.
- *She is happy **to examine the pottery for any defects**.*
- *The clown was eager **to dye his hair**.*

> Look for this type of infinitive phrase especially when the sentence has a linking verb followed by a predicate adjective. The adjectival complement infinitive will follow the adjective.

Although this is a bit more uncommon, we can also find adjectival complement infinitive phrases completing an adjective phrase that is functioning as an object complement. Remember, an object complement comes after the direct object in a sentence with a Vc. If the object complement (OC) is an AdjP, then it can have an infinitive phrase (InfPh: AdjComp) attached to complete it.
- *The nervous groom found it impossible **to sleep that night**.*

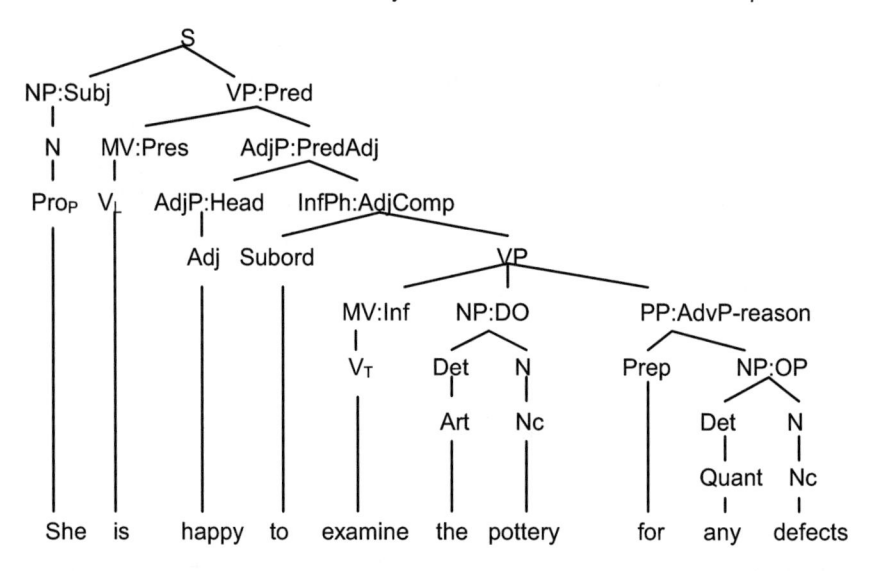

```
                          S
          ┌───────────────┴───────────┐
       NP:Subj                    VP:Pred
          │              ┌───────────┴──────────┐
          N           MV:Pres              AdjP:PredAdj
          │              │          ┌───────────┴──────────┐
         Prop           V_L     AdjP:Head            InfPh:AdjComp
                                    │         ┌────────────┴─────────┐
                                   Adj      Subord                   VP
                                                        ┌─────────────┼──────────────┐
                                                      MV:Inf        NP:DO        PP:AdvP-reason
                                                        │         ┌───┴───┐      ┌─────┴─────┐
                                                       V_T       Det      N    Prep        NP:OP
                                                                  │       │              ┌───┴───┐
                                                                 Art      Nc            Det      N
                                                                                         │       │
                                                                                       Quant    Nc
                                                                                         │       │
          She           is       happy       to     examine     the    pottery   for    any    defects
```

Adjectival Complement or Adverbial?

You may have some trouble deciding whether an infinitive phrase has an adjectival complement function or an adverbial function. To solve this, try the following:

- Look to see if the sentence has a linking verb and predicate adjective pattern. If it does and an infinitive phrase follows the predicate adjective, it is likely to be an adjectival complement infinitive. Assume that an infinitive phrase following an adjective is an adjectival complement unless you have very good reasons for labeling it with a different function.

- Try inserting *in order to* or try moving the infinitive phrase to the front of the sentence to see if it changes the meaning of the sentence at all. Adverbial infinitive phrases can usually be moved; adjectival complement infinitive phrases stay with the adjective. For example, in the sentence above, we would not generally say, "*In order to examine the pottery for any defects, she is happy.*" This makes the sentence awkward and changes the original meaning of the sentence.

Adjectival and Adverbial Choices and Expansions 169

Pseudo-Adjectival-Complement Infinitive Phrases

A slight variation of the adjectival complement infinitive phrase is the pseudo-adjectival-complement infinitive phrase. In this situation, the complement infinitive has a closer connection to the adjective. If you were to remove the complement infinitive phrase, you would substantially alter the original meaning.

- *The yard was **fun to mow**.* (The yard is not *fun*; it is fun *to mow*.)

In the true adjectival complement infinitive phrase, you can remove the infinitive phrase without altering the original meaning. (You would certainly know less, but the meaning that remains would be the same.)

- *She is **thrilled to receive the Nobel prize**.*

Try removing the infinitive phrase. What you have left is *"She is thrilled."* With or without the infinitive phrase, she is thrilled. We just know more about her thrill with the adjectival complement infinitive phrase added.

A pseudo-adjectival-complement infinitive phrase is much less common than the true adjectival complement infinitive phrase. To show a closer connection between the adjective and the infinitive phrase in the InfPh:PseudoAdjComp, we could make some slight changes in our treeing method.

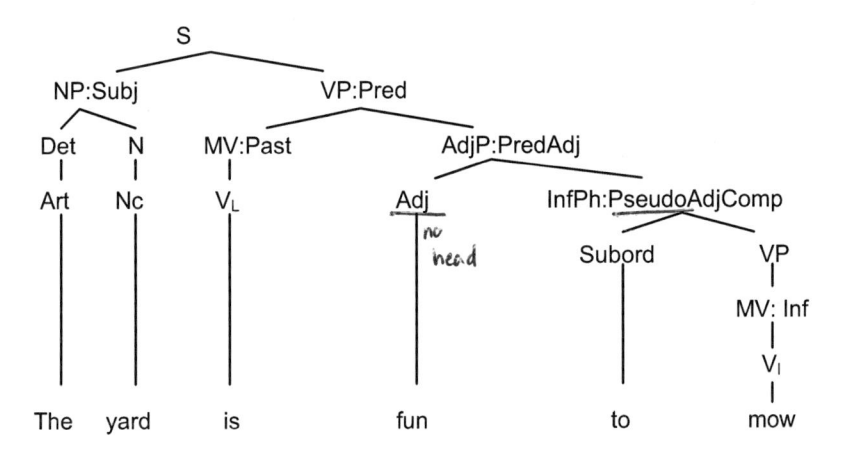

```
                              S
                    ┌─────────┴─────────┐
                 NP:Subj              VP:Pred
                 ┌──┴──┐       ┌────────┴────────┐
                Det    N    MV:Past         AdjP:PredAdj
                 │     │       │          ┌──────┴──────┐
                Art    Nc      V_L        Adj      InfPh:PseudoAdjComp
                 │     │       │           │         ┌────┴────┐
                 │     │       │          no       Subord      VP
                 │     │       │         head         │         │
                 │     │       │           │          │       MV: Inf
                 │     │       │           │          │         │
                 │     │       │           │          │        V_I
                 │     │       │           │          │         │
                The  yard     is          fun         to       mow
```

Review of Infinitive Phrase Structure

Remember, an infinitive phrase consists of a subordinator and a VP structure. The VP structure does not function as a predicate since there is no subject, but it can have any of the VP elements in it.

Also, remember that an infinitive phrase can begin with a *for* prepositional phrase as in the example *The professor will be thrilled **for you to write sentences for the book***. The prepositional phrase *for you* functions as an adverb of agency, telling by whom the action (*write sentences for the book*) is being done. We also label the OP (*you*) as the logical subject because if this infinitive phrase were a clause, *you* would be the NP:Subject and *write sentences for the book* would be the VP:Predicate. So, in the infinitive phrase form, we label *you* as both the object of the preposition and the logical subject.

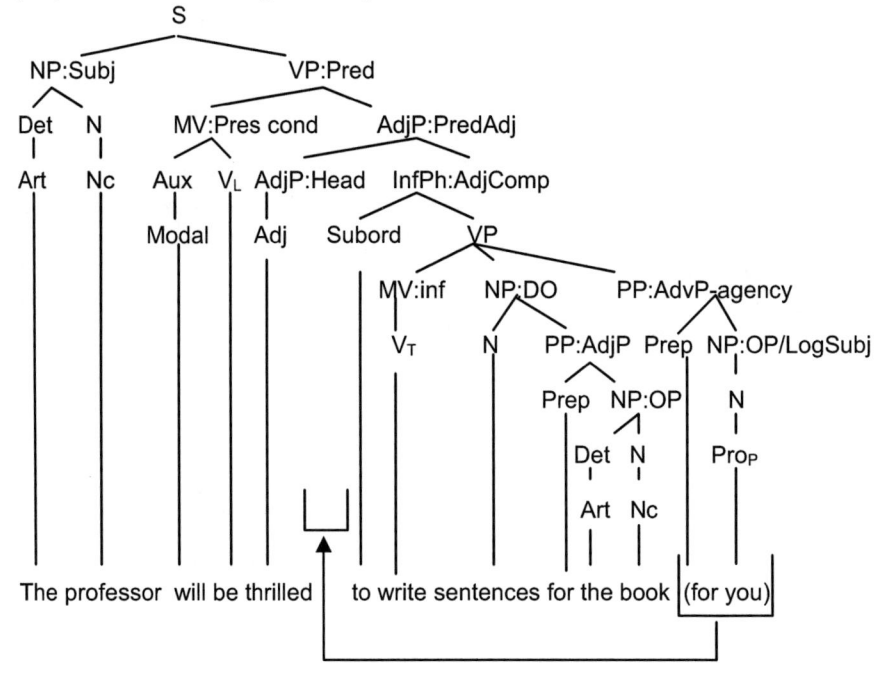

```
                    S
        ┌───────────┴───────────┐
     NP:Subj                 VP:Pred
      ╱╲              ┌─────────┴──────────┐
    Det  N        MV:Pres cond        AdjP:PredAdj
     │    │          ╱╲              ┌──────┴──────┐
    Art  Nc       Aux  V_L      AdjP:Head   InfPh:AdjComp
                   │    │           │        ┌────┴────┐
                 Modal  Adj       Subord     VP
                                          ┌───┼────────────┐
                                       MV:inf NP:DO    PP:AdvP:agency
                                          │    ╱╲       ┌────┴─────┐
                                         V_T   N     PP:AdjP     Prep  NP:OP/LogSubj
                                                      ╱╲                  │
                                                   Prep NP:OP              N
                                                         ╱╲                │
                                                       Det  N             Prop
                                                        │    │
                                                       Art  Nc

The professor will be thrilled   to write sentences for the book  (for you)
```

Notice that the adjectival complement infinitive phrase is part of the predicate adjective. It comes after the adjective and completes it.

Adjectival and Adverbial Choices and Expansions 171

Adjectival Complement Clauses

Another type of adjectival complement is used when we make adjectival comparisons. Like adjectival complement infinitive phrases, this type of adjectival complement follows and completes an adjective phrase. However, in this case, the adjectival complement does not have an infinitive structure; grammatically, it has a dependent clause structure, with a subordinator, NP:Subject, and VP:Predicate. We call it an adjectival complement clause (**Cl:AdjComp**). It is a clause that <u>completes</u> the adjective.

Ellipsis

Most of the time when we make comparisons, we have dropped part of the grammatical structure. This is known as **ellipsis** (deleting words), a fairly common procedure in construction of English sentences. For example, when we say, "*Michael is shorter than Steven,*" we are really saying, "*Michael is shorter than Steven is short.*"

Sentence	Sentence with deleted words added
Heidi is more talented than Jenny.	Heidi is more talented than Jenny **is talented.**
Roy is less articulate than a penguin.	Roy is less articulate than a penguin **is articulate.**
Tony is as athletic as a rock.	Tony is as athletic as a rock **is athletic.**

Notice that sometimes the comparison form of an adjective is a single word like *shorter* and sometimes it is a two-word form such as *more talented*. If <u>it is a two-word comparison, the first word is a qualifier.</u> The word *than* in the first two example sentences above is the <u>subordinator</u> to the clause.

Treeing Adjectival Complement Clauses

When we tree adjectival complement clauses, we show the missing elements with a dotted line on the tree and the missing words in parentheses.

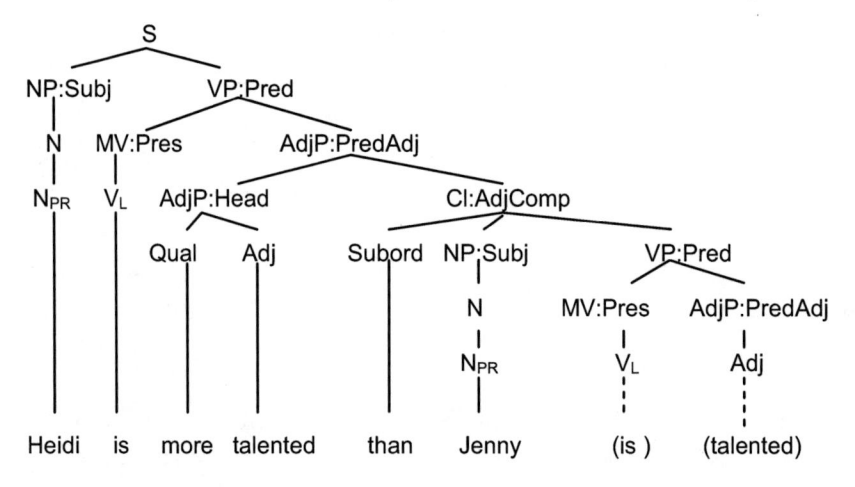

172 — Adjectival and Adverbial Choices and Expansions

```
                    S
         _____|_____
      NP:Subj                VP:Pred
        |           _____|_____
        N        MV:Pres              AdjP:PredAdj
        |           |           _____|_____
       N_PR        V_L       AdjP:Head              Cl:AdjComp
        |           |         ___|___        _____|_____
        |           |       Qual    Adj   Subord  NP:Subj      VP:Pred
        |           |        |       |      |        |       ____|____
        |           |        |       |      |        N    MV:Pres  AdjP:PredAdj
        |           |        |       |      |        |       |          |
        |           |        |       |      |      N_PR     V_L        Adj
        |           |        |       |      |        |       |          |
      Heidi        is      more  talented  than    Jenny    (is)    (talented)
```

In this next example tree (*Tony is as athletic as a rock*), notice that the first *as* is the qualifier under the AdjP:Head and *athletic* is the Adj. The second *as* is the subordinator.

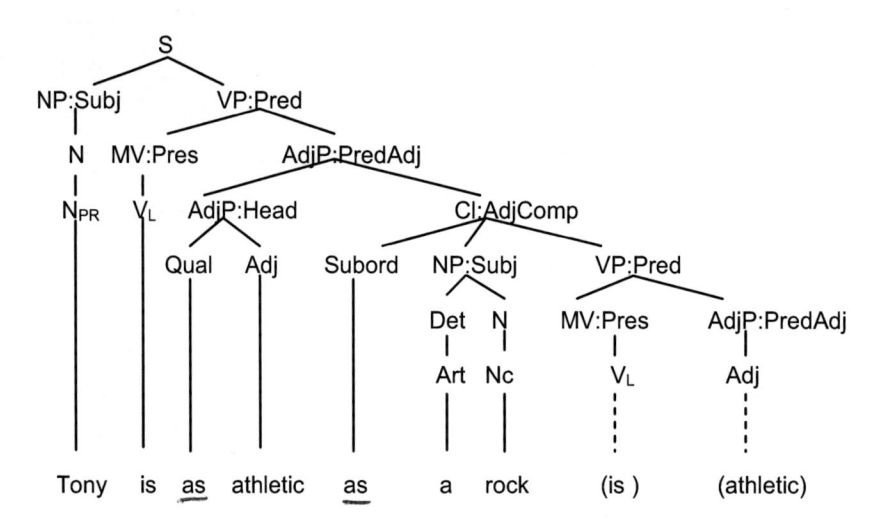

```
                    S
         _____|_____
      NP:Subj                VP:Pred
        |           _____|_____
        N        MV:Pres              AdjP:PredAdj
        |           |           _____|_____
       N_PR        V_L       AdjP:Head              Cl:AdjComp
        |           |         ___|___        _____|_____
        |           |       Qual    Adj   Subord  NP:Subj      VP:Pred
        |           |        |       |      |     ___|___    ____|____
        |           |        |       |      |    Det     N  MV:Pres  AdjP:PredAdj
        |           |        |       |      |     |      |     |          |
        |           |        |       |      |    Art    Nc    V_L        Adj
        |           |        |       |      |     |      |     |          |
       Tony        is       as   athletic   as    a     rock  (is)    (athletic)
```

Notice that the next sentence has <u>a head within a head</u>.

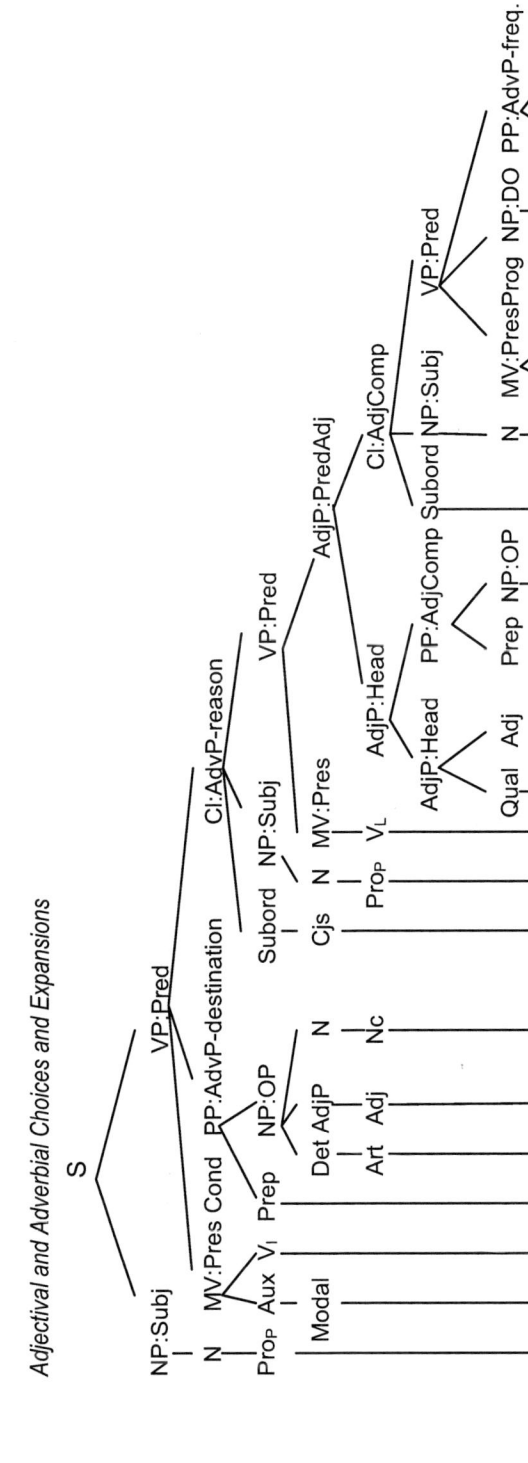

Adjectival and Adverbial Choices and Expansions

I will go to the grocery store because we are so desperate for food that we are eating oatmeal for every meal

174 *Adjectival and Adverbial Choices and Expansions*

In addition to completing predicate adjectives, clauses can also function to complete an adjectival appositive. We looked at adjectival appositives in Chapter 9. There we saw adjectival appositives with a prepositional phrase as the adjectival complement (*The child,* **wild with anticipation***, ran ahead of her parents)*. We also saw that nonrestrictive adjectival appositives can be moved to a position directly in front of the NP:Head (***Wild with anticipation***, *the child ran ahead of her parents.)*. The situation is similar when a clause completes the adjectival appositive except that we often see ellipsis in the clause.

- **Faster than a speeding bullet***, Superman was able to leap tall buildings in a single bound.*
- **As mysterious as the Bermuda Triangle***, the energy fields in that area baffled the investigators.*
- *The technical writer,* **more articulate than the boss***, gave the report for the department.*

Adjectival Complement Clauses in Adjectival Appositives

Notice the following in the example tree on the next page.

- It has an adjectival appositive (AdjP:App) attached to an NP:Head that is the subject of the sentence.
- The adjectival appositive is nonrestrictive and has been moved to a position in front of the NP:Head. We tree it after its head and show that it has been moved.
- <u>Within</u> the adjectival appositive, there is an AdjP:Head and a clause functioning as an adjectival complement (Cl:AdjComp).
- The predicate adjective of the sentence also has an AdjP:Head and an adjectival complement.
- The adjectival complement that is part of the predicate adjective is an infinitive phrase (InfPh:AdjComp).

Adjectival and Adverbial Choices and Expansions 175

Faster than a speeding bullet, Superman was able to leap tall buildings in a single bound.

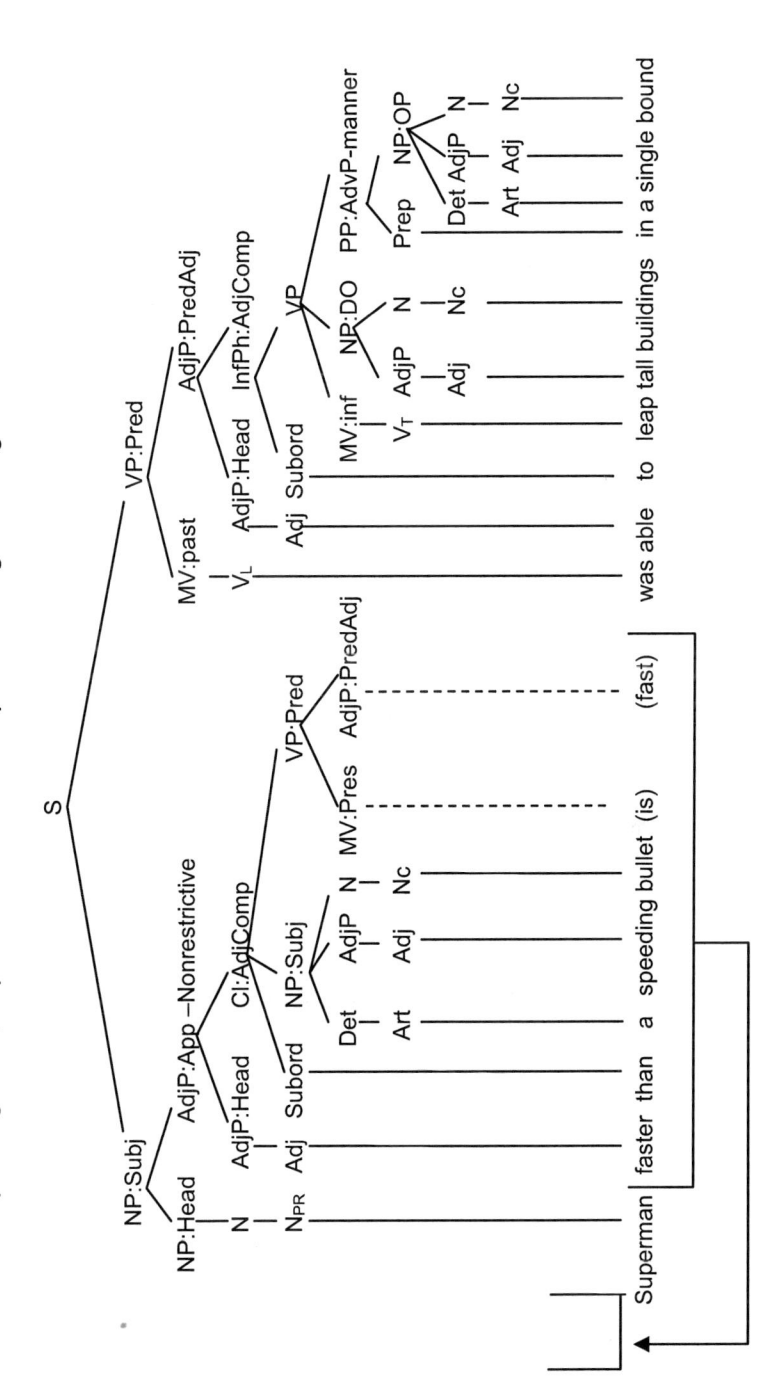

Prepositional Phrases as Predicate Adjectives

In most cases, a predicate adjective is a single-word adjective, an adjective with a qualifier in front, or a single-word adjective with an adjective complement attached. However, we can also occasionally see sentences in which the predicate adjective structure is a prepositional phrase.

*He is **like a wolverine** in his approach to business.*

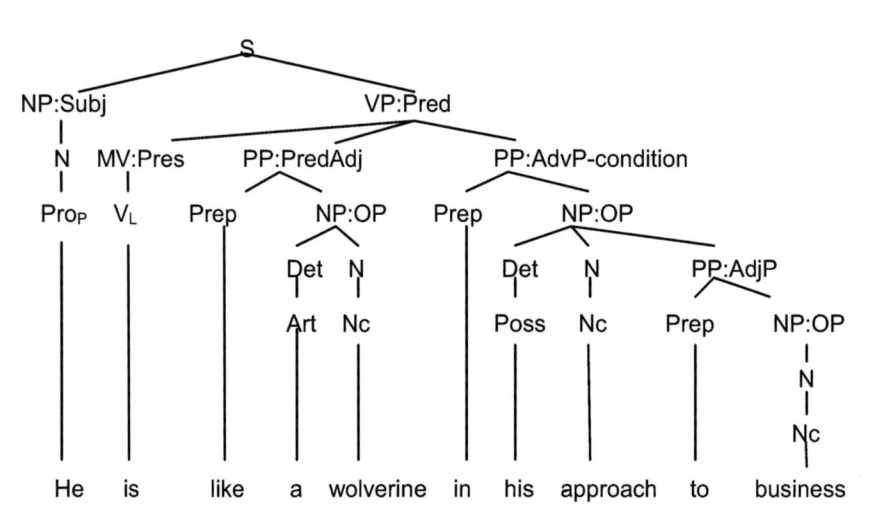

```
                              S
                ┌─────────────┴──────────────┐
            NP:Subj                       VP:Pred
              │              ┌──────────────┼──────────────┐
              N   MV:Pres  PP:PredAdj            PP:AdvP-condition
              │      │       ┌──┴──┐              ┌────────┴────────┐
             Prop   V_L     Prep  NP:OP          Prep             NP:OP
              │     │        │   ┌──┴──┐          │        ┌────────┼────────┐
              │     │        │  Det    N         │       Det       N       PP:AdjP
              │     │        │   │     │          │        │        │       ┌──┴──┐
              │     │        │  Art   Nc          │       Poss     Nc     Prep  NP:OP
              │     │        │   │     │          │        │        │       │     │
              │     │        │   │     │          │        │        │       │     N
              │     │        │   │     │          │        │        │       │     │
              │     │        │   │     │          │        │        │       │     Nc
              │     │        │   │     │          │        │        │       │     │
              He    is      like  a  wolverine    in      his   approach    to  business
```

Infinitive Phrases as Adjectival Object Complements

Most of the time, an adjectival infinitive phrase is attached to an NP:Head. On rare occasions, an adjectival infinitive phrase can function as a "stand-alone" adjective phrase such as an adjectival object complement.

- The lawyers have shown themselves to be deceitful.

The example sentence above has a Vc verb (*have shown*) with an NP:DO (*themselves*) and AdjP:OC (*to be deceitful*).

Adjectival and Adverbial Choices and Expansions 177

Review of Adjectival Structures

As you can see from the chart that follows, we have options for the type of adjectival structures we can use.

Adjectival Structures PredAdj, AdjP:App, or AdjP:OC	
Single-word adjective (with optional qualifier)	The student was **very nervous**. (Used as PredAdj)
Single-word adjective with PP complement added (PP:AdjComp)	The student was **aghast at her scheming**. (Used as PredAdj)
Single-word adjective with InfPh complement added (InfPh:AdjComp)	The student was **thrilled to be chosen as class representative**. (Used as PredAdj)
Single-word adjective with clause complement added (Cl:AdjComp)	The student was **smarter than the others around her**. (Used as PredAdj)
Prepositional phrase (PP)	The student was **like an exotic plant**. (Used as PredAdj)
Adjectival Infinitive phrase (InfPh:AdjP)	The voters considered her **to be well-informed and wise**. (Used as AdjP:OC)

In nonstandard English, in addition to the list in the chart above, an infinitive phrase can even be a predicate adjective: *that coat is **to die for**.*

Adverbial Complement Phrases and Clauses

Remember, a complement of any kind completes the idea expressed in the structure that it follows. <u>The type of complement is named for the structure that it follows</u>. Thus, an adjectival complement follows an adjective phrase. In the same way, a structure following and completing an adverb phrase would be an adverbial complement. For example, prepositional phrases can complete an adverb.

- *The espionage expert crouched **close to the building**.*

Also, a clause can be an **adverbial complement (Cl:AdvComp)**, following an adverb phrase and completing the idea expressed in that adverb. When we make an adverbial comparison, the adverb phrase consists of an AdvP:Head and an adverbial complement clause (Cl:AdvComp).

- Like adjectival complement clauses, this type of adverbial complement grammatically has a dependent clause structure, with a subordinator, NP:Subject, and VP:Predicate.
- Like adjectival comparisons, adverbial comparisons have complement clauses that almost always have **ellipsis** of part of the grammatical structure.

Sentence	Deleted Words Added
Heidi dribbles and shoots the ball better than Jenny.	*Heidi dribbles and shoots the ball better than Jenny **dribbles and shoots the ball**.*
Raymond plays the trumpet more expertly than the tuba.	*Raymond plays the trumpet more expertly than **he plays** the tuba.*
Spencer will try harder than Marlowe.	*Spencer will try harder than Marlowe **will try**.*

Notice that sometimes the comparison form of an adverb is a single word like *better* and sometimes it is a two-word form such as *more expertly*. If it is a two-word comparison, the first word is a qualifier.

As we did with adjectival complement clauses, when we tree adverbial complement clauses, we show the missing elements with a dotted line on the tree and the words in parentheses.

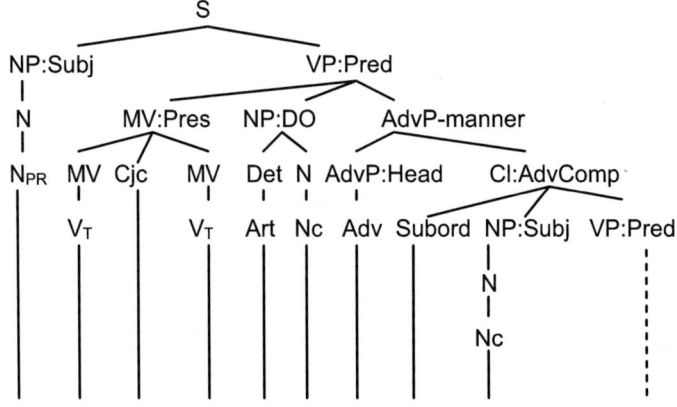

```
                              S
                ┌─────────────┴─────────────┐
            NP:Subj                      VP:Pred
              │          ┌──────────┬──────────┐
              N        MV:Pres    NP:DO     AdvP-manner
              │       ┌───┴──┐    ┌─┴─┐    ┌─────┴──────┐
             N_PR    MV    Cjc   MV  Det N  AdvP:Head  Cl:AdvComp
              │      │      │    │   │  │      │      ┌────┴────┐
              │     V_T     │   V_T Art Nc    Adv  Subord NP:Subj VP:Pred
              │      │      │    │   │  │      │      │      │       ⋮
              │      │      │    │   │  │      │      │      N       ⋮
              │      │      │    │   │  │      │      │      │       ⋮
              │      │      │    │   │  │      │      │      Nc      ⋮
              │      │      │    │   │  │      │      │      │       ⋮
           Heidi dribbles and shoots the ball better than  Jenny (dribbles and shoots the ball)
```

Notice that in the previous example tree, the MV is compound (joined by a Cjc), and the entire VP of the adverbial complement clause has been ellipted. In the next example, the subject and verb have been dropped, but the direct object is still there.

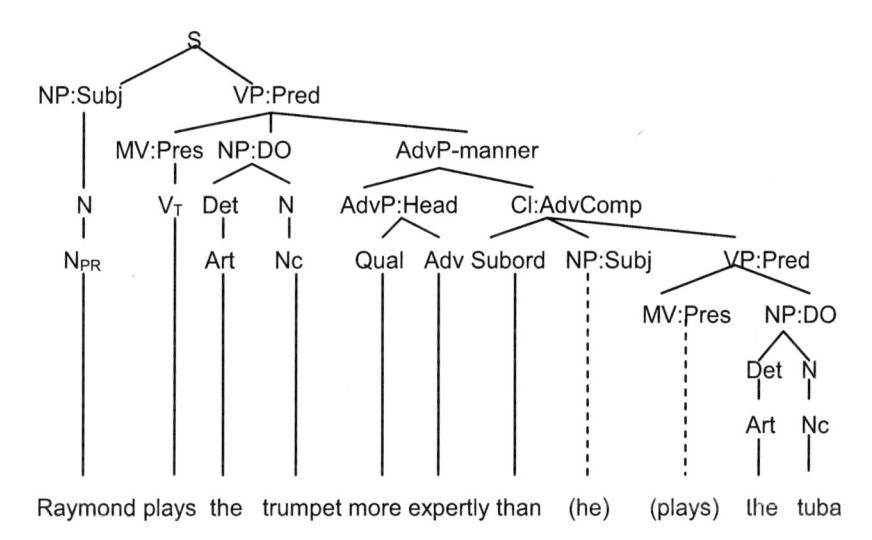

```
                              S
             ┌────────────────┴──────────────────┐
          NP:Subj                             VP:Pred
             │              ┌──────────┬─────────┴──────────┐
             │           MV:Pres     NP:DO              AdvP-manner
             │              │         ┌┴┐          ┌────────┴────────┐
             N              V_T      Det N      AdvP:Head        Cl:AdvComp
             │              │        │   │       ┌──┴──┐    ┌────┬───┴────┐
            N_PR            │        │   │      Qual  Adv  Subord NP:Subj  VP:Pred
                                                                          ┌───┴───┐
                                                                       MV:Pres  NP:DO
                                                                                 ┌┴┐
                                                                                Det N
                                                                                │  │
                                                                                Art Nc

        Raymond plays the  trumpet  more expertly than  (he)  (plays) the tuba
```

Structures That Have Become Adverbial

Participial phrases (both active and passive) that are restrictive definitely function as AdjP. We looked at these in Chapter 9. I would argue that participial phrases that are nonrestrictive but <u>are located either right after their NP:Head or right before the NP:Head</u> are usually still adjectival in function.

However, sometimes nonrestrictive participial phrases (both active and passive) have been <u>moved to a position away from the NP:Head.</u> When this has occurred (unless the phrase is misplaced), the participial phrase can function as an adverb phrase (AdvP), often an <u>adverb phrase of condition.</u>

- *Julie weaseled out of a post-dinner game of pool,* ***blaming jet lag for making it an early night.*** (This is an active participial phrase functioning as an adverb of condition: ActPartPh:AdvP-condition.)

- *To save paper, the grammar students were doing their homework on their hands, **using nontoxic pens that washed off easily.*** (This is an active participial phrase functioning as an adverb of instrument: ActPartPh:AdvP-instrument.)

- *The nun packed up the papers and headed for the door, **driven to distraction by the constant phone calls and other interruptions.*** (This is a passive participial phrase functioning as an adverb of condition: PassPartPh:AdvP-condition.)

Look for these adverbial participial phrases especially at the end of a sentence, set off by a comma. If a participial phrase is not right next to an NP:Head (either right after the head or right before the head), it is adverbial.

Here are some things to remember about participial phrases:

- If the participial phrase is immediately after an NP or immediately in front of an NP, it is probably adjectival in function.

- If a participial phrase is somewhere else in the sentence, especially at the end of a sentence, it is adverbial (or misplaced).

- Participial phrases that have an adverbial function are often an adverb phrase of condition, but notice in the tree on the next page that the participial phrase is an adverb phrase of instrument.

- Notice that the structure of the participial phrase is the same whether its function is adjectival or adverbial.

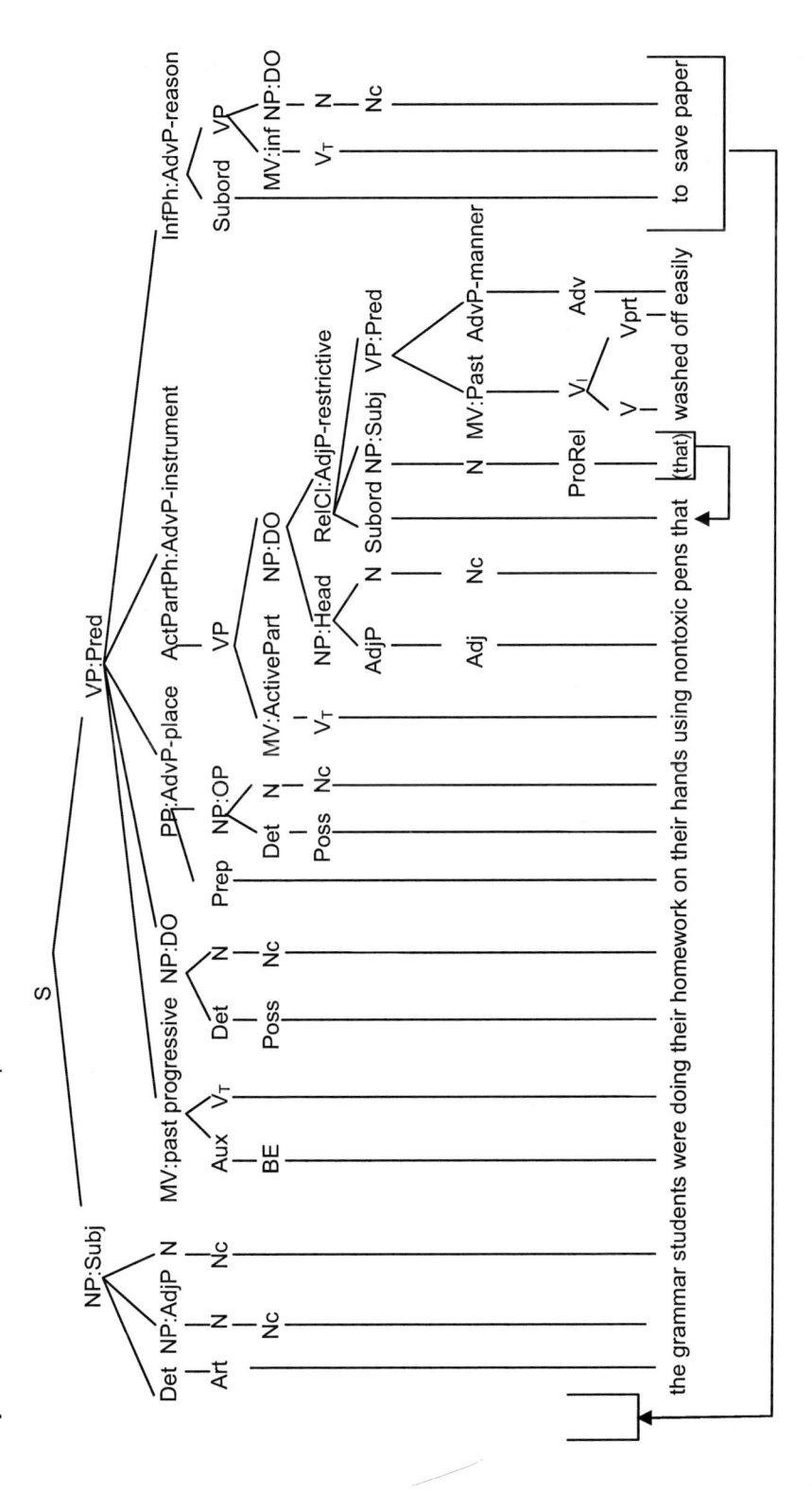

Adjectival and Adverbial Choices and Expansions 181

Misplaced or Dangling Modifiers

Misplacing Participial Phrases

Sometimes a participial phrase that was supposed to be adjectival has either "wandered" from its head, maybe even "attached" to the wrong NP (misplaced modifier), or else the sentence does not even contain the NP:Head to which the participial phrase was supposed to be attached (dangling modifier). Unlike the adverbial participial phrases we just looked at, these modifiers were supposed to be adjectival in function and were supposed to be attached to an NP:Head. So, a misplaced modifier has been moved away from its head, and a dangling modifier does not have a head in the sentence. These sentences need to be rewritten.

Misplaced or Dangling Modifier	Rewritten Sentence
While swimming in the pool, the appetizers were served. (The appetizers were not swimming.)	While I was swimming in the pool, the appetizers were served.
She kicked the dog hurrying to get away from the house. (The dog was not hurrying to get away from the house.)	Hurrying to get away from the house, she kicked the dog.

Misplacing Adverbs

An adverb can become misplaced if it is attached to the wrong VP in the sentence. In the example below, one adverb phrase is clearly misplaced.
- *She waved while she was marching at the crowd.*

The adverb clause *while she was marching* is an AdvP-time, and the phrase *at the crowd* is an AdvP-destination. The adverbial prepositional phrase (*at the crowd*) should be attached to the verb *waved*, not the verb *was marching*:
- *She waved at the crowd while she was marching.*

In the following example, we can't tell to which verb the adverb should be attached because of its placement.
- *The child who had been practicing **energetically** jumped in the pool.* (Had the child been practicing energetically or did the child jump in the pool energetically?)

A writer should watch for and correct misplaced or confusing modifiers.

Adverb Structures and Punctuation

The longer, more complex adverb structures are often set off from the rest of the sentence by commas. Also, participial phrases acting as adverbs usually come at the end of a sentence and are set off with a comma before them.
- *Julie weaseled out of a post-dinner game of pool, blaming jet lag for making it an early night.*

Usage in Adjectival and Adverbial Complement Clauses

As you saw earlier in the chapter, most of the time when we make comparisons, we drop part of the comparison. However, this ellipsis can cause problems in Standard English when pronouns are used. The subject form of the pronoun is used even when the rest of the comparison has been dropped. See the examples that follow.
- *Dr. Simonson is a more accomplished pianist than* **he.**
- *Her lawyers can find the legal loopholes better than* **they.**

Using the subject form in comparisons such as these is fairly formal usage. It would be considered even more formal language use to complete the comparisons.

Practice Sentences

I. Tree the following sentences. As always, review structures are included.
1. Roy is more athletic than Buddy.
2. The space shuttle completed what it was designed to do.
3. The taxi driver should have been able to find the British Museum.
4. The cheesemonger was dismayed to find out that the dairymaid had decided to get married.
5. Kurt felt like slamming his hand on the table until the cups and saucers bounced.
6. I know I used to almost go nuts when I couldn't pour my heart and soul into my work. (The *go* is slang usage.)
7. Diane held the handle with both hands, pausing as she rotated the lever, as her thoughts returned to the accident.

8. Caraway seeds with ginger and salt were used to prevent hysterics more often than chamomile with white vinegar.
9. The tour group leader was so perplexed that she merely collapsed on a chair in one of the reception rooms of Kensington Palace.
10. These altered organisms might become harder to manage than the original ones.
11. The reporter filed his story with Associated Press, giving the names of the seventeen people who had been washed overboard in the storm.
12. Spot will fetch the paper quicker than Bitsy.
13. While Cissie sat on the floor with Ophelia, playing one of their little games with her, the puppy entered the room.
14. The nurse survived the accident, kept from major injury because she was wearing a seat belt.
15. Staple foods that are high in protein or vitamins might be offered in place of junk foods.
16. The sea is full of bioluminescent single-cell life forms known as dinoflagellates.
17. This light creates auras around the fish, betraying them to predators.
18. Julie weaseled out of a post-dinner game of pool, blaming jet lag for making it an early night.
19. Getting close to the funnel clouds to collect data without getting killed is the goal for a team of daredevil researchers. (*Getting* is slang in this sentence for *being*.)
20. With the coming of cell phones, mockingbirds, mynahs, and other mimics are likely to get into the act.
21. Visitors have been eager to climb Ayers Rock, now known by its aboriginal name, since the first road reached it in 1948.
22. Stumbling to her feet, Alice searched for her overalls, finding them between the living room and bedroom in a heap on the heavily urethaned pine floor.
23. Alice sat on the concrete floor, sorting through the new shipment of Philips screwdrivers, monkey wrenches, hammers, and levels.
24. Whether people are getting sicker from food today than they were fifty years ago is a matter of debate.
25. Armadillos are susceptible to leprosy, which is difficult for veterinarians to detect.

Adjectival and Adverbial Choices and Expansions   185

26. The seal pup would be in a playful mood.
27. Someone must be willing to clean the bathtub.
28. The anger of the terrorist group is immune to negotiation.
29. Kris is as good as his word.
30. The young soldier had become ready to commit a suicide bombing.
31. Without control, we will not be able to monitor spending.
32. In excruciating pain yet determined to hit a grand slam, Number 32 bore the pain and tried again.
33. His adrenaline must have taken over because he hit the ball so hard that it flew over the fence, making it a grand slam.
34. Lonna was excited to take the spotlight job despite her fear of heights.
35. Reading that book is like having a grand adventure.
36. Her mother's eyes were so filled with disappointment that the teen turned away.
37. The students were excited to see that their team was playing better than their rivals.
38. We all felt like peaches from a jar whose seal has been finally broken after a winter of collecting dust.
39. My chair is black and red to match my curtains that Mom had bought for me.
40. Neither the left nor the right has been particularly inclined to consider this issue judiciously.
41. She told him that she was not available to go to the game.
42. Her driving makes me scared to ride with her.
43. Chris hopes the treasure will be enough to pay for his retirement.
44. His laughing was annoying for the rest of us to listen to.
45. Nobility, fine and pure as light, radiated from her presence.
46. Their laughter during the performance was considered boorish.
47. Anthony went to sleep, crying his eyes out, disturbed by the book he had read.
48. Mobile Masterpiece Theater is proud to present tonight's special feature.
49. Walking away isn't as easy as running.
50. Helen returns graded papers back within a week more consistently than Lisa.

II. Write sentences as directed below.

1. Write a sentence in which the PredAdj, Appositive, or AdjP:OC is a qualifier and single-word adjective.
2. Write a sentence in which the PredAdj, Appositive, or AdjP:OC is a single-word adjective with a prepositional phrase complement.
3. Write a sentence in which the PredAdj, Appositive, or AdjP:OC is a single-word adjective with an infinitive phrase complement.
4. Write a sentence in which the PredAdj, Appositive, or AdjP:OC is a comparison adjective with a clause complement.
5. Write a sentence in which the PredAdj, Appositive, or AdjP:OC is a prepositional phrase.
6. Write two sentences with an adverbial comparison, using an adverb complement clause attached to the adverb.
7. Write a sentence with an active participial phrase at the end position, making it adverbial. Make sure it is not misplaced or dangling. Make sure that you punctuate it correctly.
8. Write a sentence with a passive participial phrase at the end position, making it adverbial. Make sure that you punctuate it correctly and that it is not misplaced or dangling.

Chapter 11
Nominal Phrase Clarifications: Nominal Appositives and Nominal Complements

The structures in this chapter, nominal appositives and nominal complements, follow an NP:Head. However, unlike structures such as relative clauses and participial phrases, nominal appositives and nominal complements do not have an adjectival function. Rather, these structures rename or clarify the NP:Head.

Nominal Appositives

Nominal appositives (**NP:App**) follow and rename or clarify an NP:Head. The NP:Head may be functioning in the sentence as a subject, direct object, indirect object, object of a preposition, object complement, or predicate nominative.

To recognize a nominal appositive, you might try to insert mentally a BE verb or an *equals* sign (=) between the NP:Head and the appositive. Because the appositive renames the head, inserting *is, was, were,* or *are* or an *equals* sign should not change the meaning. (Of course, such insertion would change the structure of the sentence.)

- *At a Jodhpur wedding, the groom wears a diamond-studded sarpech,* **a feather ornament owned by his family for generations.** (sarpech = a feather ornament owned by his family for generations)
- *BIGOT, a code word for a security classification beyond Top Secret, was used for D-Day plans.* (BIGOT = a code word for a security classification beyond Top Secret)

The NP:Appositive could be a noun cluster, a noun clause, a gerund phrase, or an infinitive phrase. If it is a noun cluster, you can attach any of the noun cluster expansions to it. For example, a nominal appositive might have a relative clause, adjectival infinitive phrase, or participial phrase attached to the noun cluster.

Sample Structures that can act as NP:App	
NP:App is a single word.	*The Crystal Cave* focuses on the main character **Merlin**.
NP:App is a nominal phrase.	*The king of the Minnesota celebration is named after Boreas,* **the Greek god of the north wind.**
NP:App is a noun cluster with a relative clause attached to it.	*Teofihuan,* **a city that had palaces, monuments, and pyramids,** *is arguably the hemisphere's first true urban center.*
NP:App is a noun cluster with an adjectival infinitive phrase attached to it.	*The Grand Canyon,* **scenery to savor,** *is best experienced when few people are around.*
NP:App is a noun cluster with a passive participial phrase attached to it.	*Edinburgh Castle,* **a massive stone structure built hundreds of years ago,** *was the next destination on the study tour.*
NP:App is a nominal phrase with an active participial phrase attached to it.	*His house,* **a towering edifice overlooking the valley,** *was a monument to extravagance.*
NP:App is a gerund phrase.	*Her goal,* **finishing her second Master's Degree,** *might be a good idea for her career.*
NP:App is a noun clause.	*The ultimate disappointment,* **that the black rhinos of the zoo would not mate,** *was confirmed that next year.*
NP:App is an infinitive phrase.	*The object,* **to eat as many pieces of candy as they could,** *was all part of the fun of the party.*

We assume that the NP structure that comes first is the NP:Head and that the structure that comes second is the NP:Appositive. However, sometimes it seems as if the appositive has been moved to a position in front of the head.

- **Master mimics,** *starlings were taught by the Romans to imitate human speech.*

It seems that *starlings* is the NP:Head, and *master mimics* is the NP:App.

Nominal Appositives and Nominal Complements

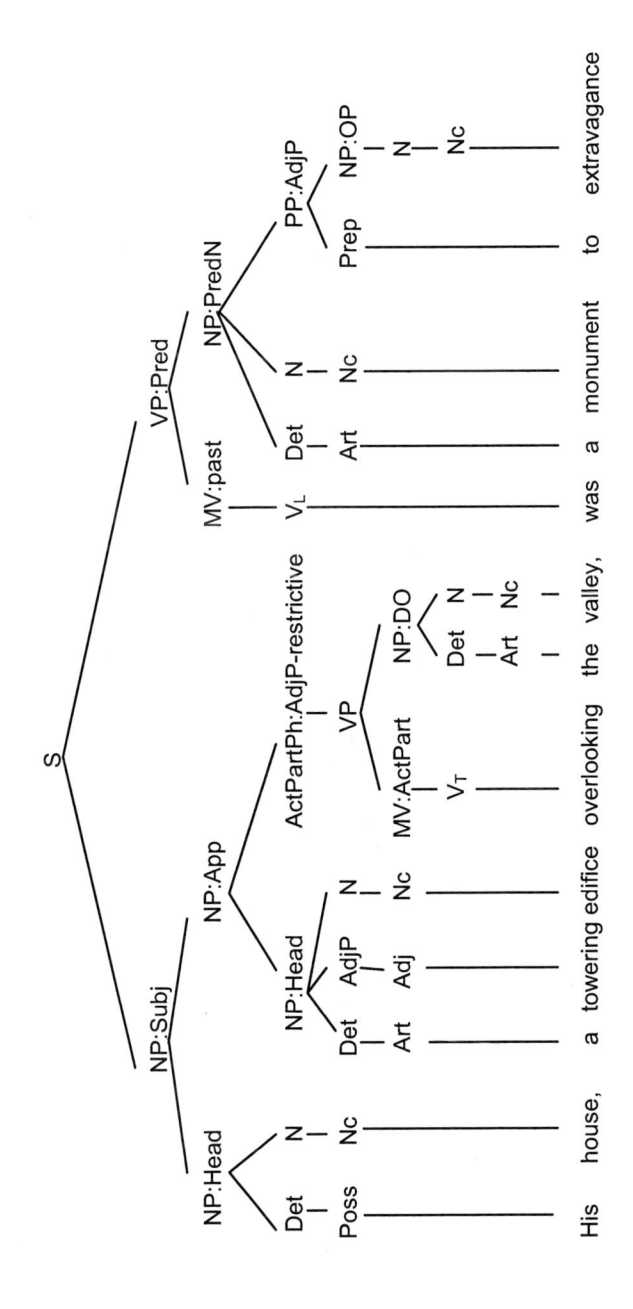

His house, a towering edifice overlooking the valley, was a monument to extravagance

Intensive Pronouns

A unique type of NP:Appositive is an **intensive pronoun (Pro$_{Intensive}$)**. Intensive pronouns end in *–self* or *–selves*, as do the reflexive pronouns (*myself, yourself, himself, herself, itself, ourselves, yourselves, themselves*). However, intensive pronouns follow another NP and intensify it by renaming it. Reflexive pronouns generally function as direct objects, indirect objects, or objects of prepositions.

Intensive Pronoun	Reflexive Pronoun
*You **yourself** know why Penelope took the key.*	*You gave **yourself** the problem by agreeing to the date.*
*The president **himself** ordered the covert operation.*	*He nominated **himself** for the job.*

*The president **herself** had given the speech.*

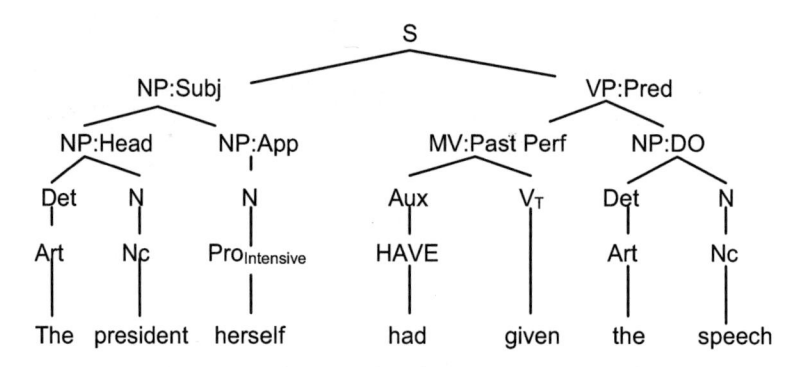

```
                              S
           ┌──────────────────┴──────────────────┐
        NP:Subj                               VP:Pred
      ┌─────┴─────┐                   ┌──────────┴──────────┐
   NP:Head      NP:App             MV:Past Perf           NP:DO
   ┌───┴───┐      │                ┌────┴────┐          ┌───┴───┐
  Det      N      N               Aux        V_T        Det     N
   │       │      │                │          │          │      │
  Art      Nc  Pro_Intensive     HAVE         │         Art     Nc
   │       │      │                │          │          │      │
  The  president herself          had       given       the   speech
```

Pronouns that Become Adverbial

Sometimes pronouns that end in *–self* or *–selves* appear in a location other than NP:App, DO, IO, or OP. When this happens, the pronoun can become adverbial. In the following example, the pronoun is a reflexive adverb of manner.

ProIntensive as Appositive	ProReflexive as NP:AdvP-manner
*The president **herself** gave the speech.*	*The president gave the speech **herself**.*

Nominal Appositives and Nominal Complements

```
                            S
            ┌───────────────┴──────────────┐
         NP:Subj                        VP:Pred
         ┌──┴──┐              ┌───────────┼──────────────┐
        Det    N           MV:past      NP:DO         NP:AdvP-manner
         │     │              │          ┌─┴─┐            │
        Art    Nc             V_T       Det   N           N
         │     │              │          │    │           │
         │     │              │         Art   Nc         Pro_REF
         │     │              │          │    │           │
        The  president      gave        the speech      herself
```

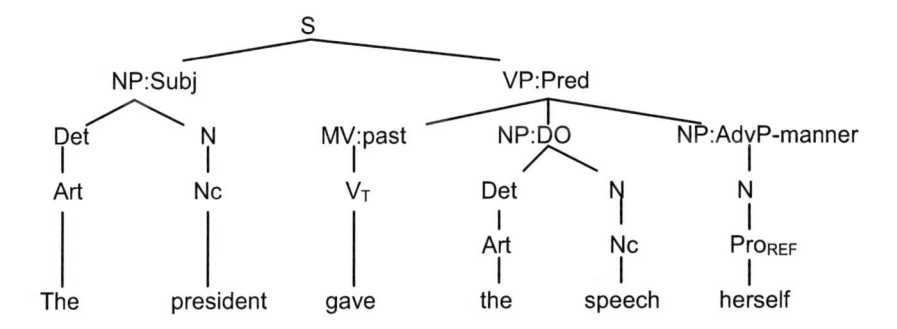

Nominal Complement Infinitive Phrases

Sometimes an infinitive phrase following an NP:Head is so closely connected to the head that it completes the idea. This is a nominal complement infinitive phrase (**InfPh:NomComp**). Nominal complement infinitive phrases are named that way because they <u>complete</u> the idea of the NP:Head. Therefore, they are restrictive and <u>are not set off by commas</u>. In this way, they differ slightly from nominal appositives, which, unless they are very short in length, are generally set off by commas or dashes. The NP:Head that the nominal complement infinitive directly follows is an abstract noun. <u>The infinitive phrase clarifies the abstract noun by defining it.</u>

To test for this type of infinitive, try the following steps.

- Identify the head. (If an InfPh:NomComp follows, the head will be an abstract noun. If the head is an NP but is not abstract, the infinitive phrase that follows it will probably be adjectival or could be a true NP:Appositive.)

- Insert the NP:Head into the blank in the following question.
  What _____ *is/was it?*
  If the infinitive phrase answers that question, it is a nominal complement infinitive phrase.

Sentences with Nominal Complement Infinitive Phrases

Sentence	Test for InfPh:NomComp
Herbert has the stupidity to jump without a parachute.	What stupidity is it? To jump without a parachute
The government has issued a request for the cult members to pay taxes.	What request is it? For the cult members to pay taxes
A reluctance to see blood was the biology student's undoing.	What reluctance was it? To see blood
The painter had the ability to design a landscape.	What ability was it? To design a landscape
His dream to be a cartographer was broken that day.	What dream was it? To be a cartographer
The dancer's inclination to be forgetful drove the rest of the dancers crazy.	What inclination was it? To be forgetful

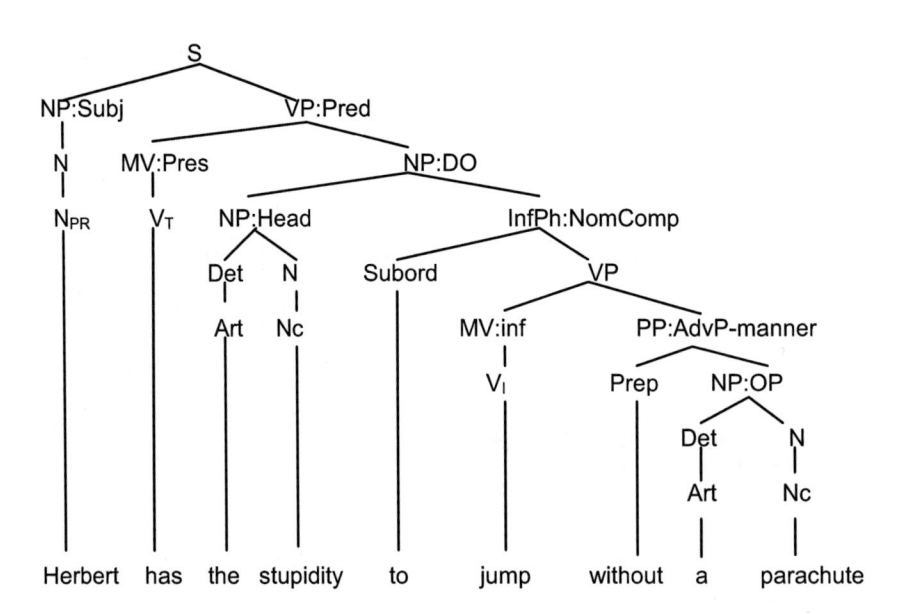

```
                                S
                   ┌────────────┴──────────┐
               NP:Subj                  VP:Pred
                 │            ┌────────────┴────────┐
                 N          MV:Pres                NP:DO
                 │            │         ┌────────────┴────────┐
                N_PR          V_T    NP:Head             InfPh:NomComp
                              │     ┌──┴──┐          ┌────────┴────────┐
                              │    Det    N       Subord              VP
                              │     │     │          │         ┌───────┴────────┐
                              │    Art   Nc          │       MV:inf      PP:AdvP-manner
                              │                      │         │         ┌──────┴──────┐
                              │                      │         V_I      Prep         NP:OP
                              │                      │                                ┌──┴──┐
                              │                      │                               Det    N
                              │                      │                                │     │
                              │                      │                               Art   Nc
                              │                      │                                │     │
                           Herbert  has   the  stupidity   to      jump    without    a   parachute
```

Nominal Appositives and Nominal Complements

Review of Infinitive Phrase Structure

Remember, an infinitive phrase consists of a subordinator and a VP structure. The VP structure does not function as a predicate since there is no subject, but it can have any of the VP elements in it. Also, remember that infinitive phrases can begin with a *for* prepositional phrase as in the second sentence in the chart on the last page: *for the cult members to pay taxes*. The prepositional phrase *for the cult members* functions as an adverb of agency, telling by whom the action (to pay taxes) is being done. Therefore, we also label the OP (*the cult members*) as the logical subject. If this infinitive phrase were a clause, *the cult members* would be the NP:Subject and *pay taxes* would be the VP:Pred. So, in the infinitive phrase form, we label *the cult members* as both the object of the preposition and the logical subject.

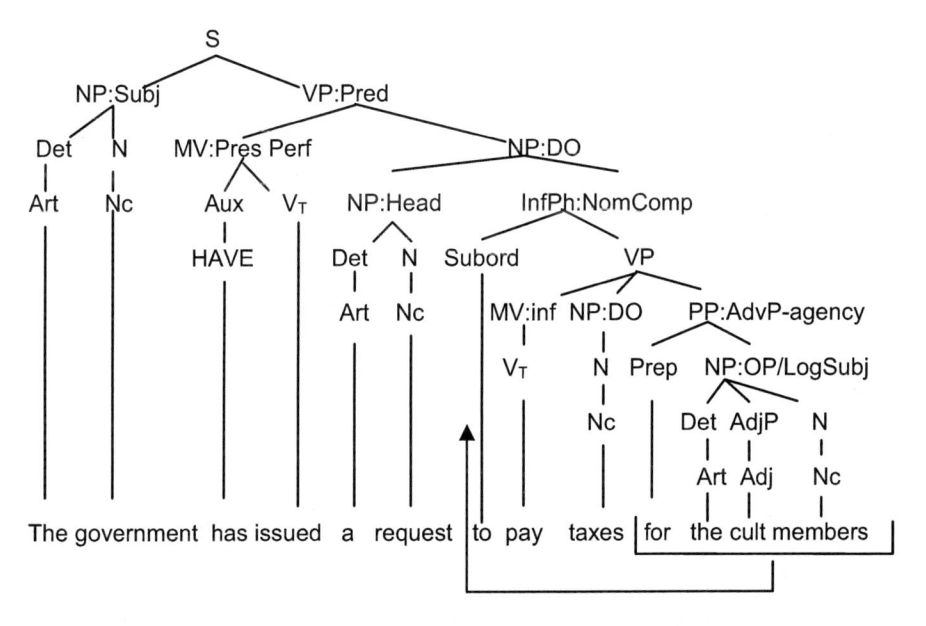

```
                          S
              ┌───────────┴───────────┐
          NP:Subj                  VP:Pred
          ┌───┴──┐        ┌───────────┼─────────────┐
         Det     N    MV:Pres Perf                NP:DO
          │      │     ┌────┴───┐          ┌────────┴────────┐
         Art    Nc    Aux       V_T     NP:Head         InfPh:NomComp
          │      │     │                 ┌──┴──┐        ┌───┼────────┐
                      HAVE              Det    N     Subord         VP
                                         │     │                ┌────┼──────────┐
                                        Art   Nc            MV:inf NP:DO   PP:AdvP-agency
                                                              │     │      ┌────┴─────┐
                                                              V_T   N    Prep    NP:OP/LogSubj
                                                                    │           ┌────┼────┐
                                                                    Nc         Det  AdjP   N
                                                                                │    │     │
                                                                               Art  Adj    Nc

The government   has issued   a   request   to   pay   taxes   for   the   cult   members
```

Infinitives with an Auxiliary

An infinitive can also have an auxiliary. Consider the following nominal complement infinitive phrase.

- *He has a tendency to be always asking dumb questions.*

The form of the verb here is progressive infinitive. The infinitive phrase in this sentence would be treed as follows.

```
                    InfPh:NomComp
                   ╱              ╲
         Subord                      VP
           │              ╱          │              ╲
           │      MV:Prog Inf      NP:DO        AdvP-frequency
           │       ╱      ╲        ╱    ╲            │
           │     Aux       V_T   AdjP    N          Adv
           │      │         │     │      │           │
           │     BE         │    Adj     Nc          │
           │      │         │     │      │           │
           to    be    ⌊asking  dumb questions⌋  ⌊always⌋
                        ▲_____|
```

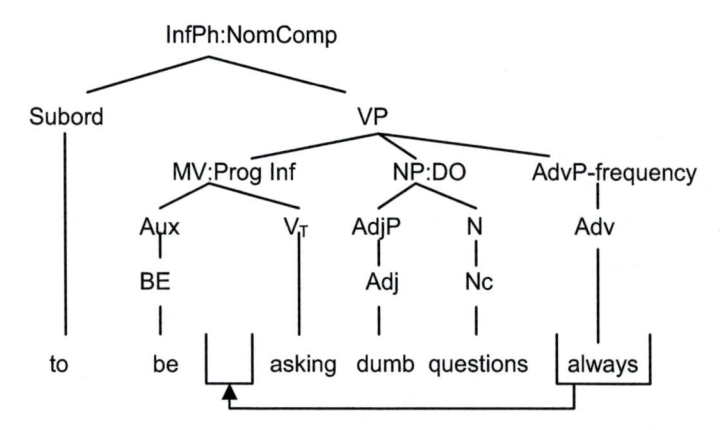

Other infinitives can have an Aux as well. These infinitives may be in sentences with other infinitive phrase functions as well as nominal complement infinitives.

The verb in the following infinitive phrase has a perfect infinitive form. The Aux is HAVE.
- *to have discovered*

The next infinitive is a passive infinitive. The *be* is the Aux (BE), and the MV label would be passive infinitive.
- *to be analyzed*

Nominal Complement Clauses

In the same way that an infinitive phrase can complete an NP:Head, it seems as if a noun clause can complete an NP:Head. This happens, I believe, when the noun clause is not set off by commas. Consider the following examples.
- *The fact that an eagle made of stones was on the bedrock proved that this was sacred ground.*
- *Mungo was aware of the fact that driving a car is difficult for someone who is 6'9".*
- *We had doubted the assertion that wild tigers were in that province of China.*

If the clause should be set off by commas, it is an NP:Appositive; if there are no commas, it is a nominal complement clause.

```
                              S
        NP:Subj           VP:Pred
         |         _____|_____
         N   MV:past perf        NP:DO
         |    ___|___      _____|_____
        Prop Aux  Vᴛ   NP:Head      Cl:NomComp
         |    |         ___|___    _____|_____
        HAVE Det  N  Subord NP:Subj     VP:Pred
              |   |         __|__      ____|____
             Art  Nc      AdjP  N   MV:past PP:AdvP-place
                           |    |     |      ___|___
                          Adj   Nc    Vɪ  Prep   NP:OP
                                              ____|____
                                             Det  N   PP:AdjP
                                              |   |   ___|___
                                             Dem  Nc Prep NP:OP
                                                          |
                                                          N
                                                          |
                                                         Nᴾᴿ

We  had doubted the  assertion that wild tigers  were in  that province of China
```

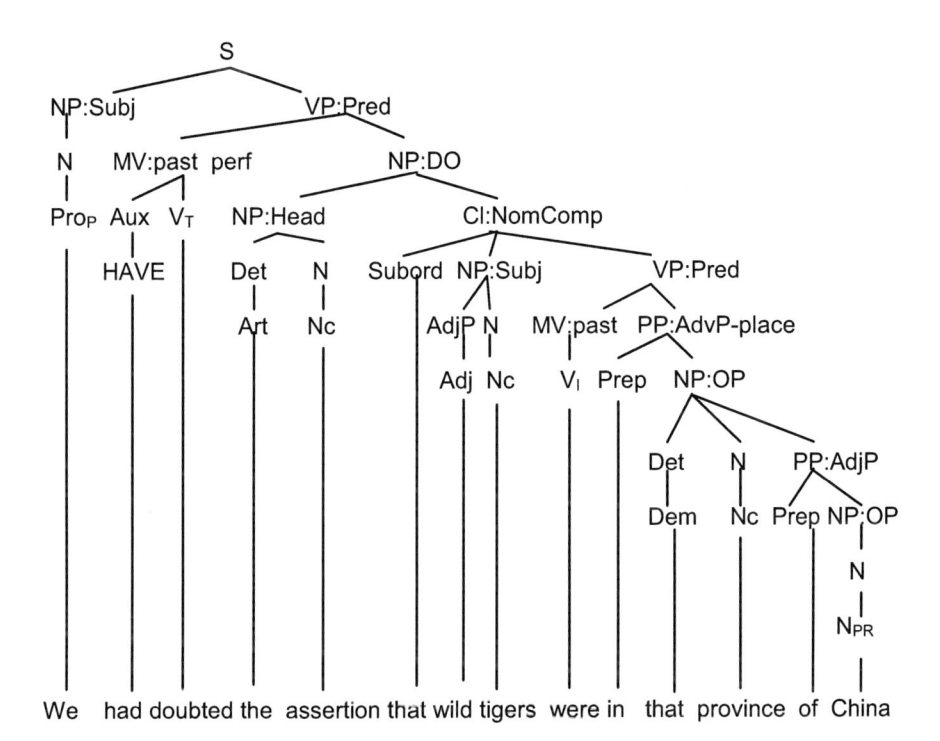

Nominal Appositives and Writing Style

Nominal appositives can affect your writing style.

- First, they can slow the pace of your sentence and so vary the rhythm of your writing.
- Also, nominal appositives can focus the attention of the reader on the NP:Head. If you would like to emphasize an NP, you might consider using an appositive after it.
- Finally, as is true of the other structures we have learned, using appositives can give variety to the types of sentences you are using. For even more sentence variety, when you write with appositives, also vary the type of appositive you use.

Look at the chart on the second page of this chapter. Read the sentences with appositives to see that this type of structure can affect writing style in these three ways. Also, review the different structures that can be appositives.

Nominal Appositives and Punctuation

Commas or Dashes

Appositives are generally set off from the rest of the sentence with commas or dashes. Very short appositives, such as the intensive pronouns, do not need commas even though they are nonrestrictive. Single-word appositives do not generally need commas. Nominal complement infinitive phrases and nominal complement clauses are not set off by commas.

Fragments

Nominal appositives can also end up as fragments. Be sure that they directly follow their heads within the same sentence.

- The article is about Martha Stewart. **A woman who was facing arraignment on criminal charges of securities fraud and obstruction of justice.**

Notice that a nominal appositive fragment, like other types of fragments, will fail the "complete sentence test." If it is a sentence and not a fragment, it should make sense if you insert it into a test frame such as the following: *I told them that _____.*

Our nominal appositive fragment does not make sense in the test frame.

- *I told them that a woman who was facing arraignment on criminal charges of securities fraud and obstruction of justice.*

The full sentence would make sense in the test frame.

- *I told them that the article is about Martha Stewart, a woman who was facing arraignment on criminal charges of securities fraud and obstruction of justice.*

A Review of Phrases and Clauses

Continuing onto the next pages are tables to help you review the various phrases and clauses we have learned so far. To use the charts, first eliminate prepositional phrases since those are fairly easy to recognize. If you need to review prepositions, see the list in Chapter 2. They are not included on the diagrams.

Nominal Appositives and Nominal Complements

After you have checked for prepositional phrases, you need to check to see if the structure in question has a head. Look right in front of the structure; heads usually come first. However, the attachment might have been "moved" to a position in front of the head, so also look for a head right after the structure.

If the structure is attached to a head, determine which type of head it is.

Structure has a Head

	Head is an NP	
Description of Structure	**Function**	**Name of Structure**
The structure begins with a ProRel (*who, whose, which, whom, that*) or a preposition followed by a ProRel.	Structure describes or gives more information about the NP:Head	**Relative Clause (RelCl)**
The structure begins with the word *to* followed by a verb, or it has a *for*-phrase in front of it.	Structure describes or gives more information about the NP:Head	**Infinitive Phrase: Adjectival (InfPh:AdjP)**
The structure begins with the word *to* followed by a verb, or it has a *for*-phrase in front of it.	Structure defines the NP:Head	**Infinitive Phrase: NomComp (InfPh:NomComp)**
The structure begins with an –ing verb form.	Structure describes or gives more information about the NP:Head	**Active Participial Phrase: Adjectival (ActPartPh:AdjP)**
The structure starts with an –en verb form.	Structure describes or gives more information about the NP:Head	**Passive Participial Phrase: Adjectival (PassPartPh:AdjP)**

Head is an Adjective		
Description of Structure	**Function**	**Name of Structure**
The structure starts with the word *to* followed by a VP or has a *for*-phrase before the *to*.	Structure completes the adjective	**Infinitive Phrase: Adjectival Complement (InfPh:AdjComp)**
The structure has a Subord, NP:Subj, VP:Pred; may have parts ellipted.	Structure completes the adjective	**Clause: Adjectival Complement (Cl:AdjComp)**

Head is an Adverb		
Description of Structure	**Function**	**Name of Structure**
The structure has a Subord, NP:Subj, VP:Pred; may have parts ellipted.	Structure completes the adverb	**Clause: Adverbial Complement (Cl:AdvComp)**

If the structure does not have a head, look at the function of the structure.

The Structure does not have a Head

Nominal Function	
(Look especially for Subject, DO, or PredN)	
Description of Structure	**Name of Structure**
The structure beings with an –ing word.	**Gerund Phrase (GerPh)**
The structure starts with the word *to* followed by a VP or has a *for*-phrase before the *to*.	**Infinitive Phrase: Nominal (InfPh:Nominal)**
The structure has a subordinator, NP:Subj, VP:Pred.	**Noun Clause (NClause)**

Nominal Appositives and Nominal Complements

Adverbial Function	
Description of Structure	**Name of Structure**
The structure starts with the word *to* followed by a VP or has a *for-* phrase before the *to*.	**Infinitive Phrase: Adverbial (InfPh:AdvP)**
Structure has a subordinator, NP:Subj, VP:Pred	**Adverb Clause (Cl:AdvP)**
The structure starts with an –ing or –en verb form.	**Adverbial Participial Phrase (PartPh:AdvP)**

Practice Sentences

I. Tree the following sentences. (As always, there are review sentences included. Not all the sentences have the new structures from this chapter in them.)

1. A Greek term *telos*, meaning *mature* or *complete,* is used throughout the text.
2. He had the guts to call her silly.
3. By 1943 scientists warned that the probability that Germany would have several weapons available by the end of the year was high.
4. Her smile continued to reflect her determined effort to be polite.
5. The queen set weary eyes on Scotland Yard's chief inspector, Lawrence Macarthur.
6. Master mimics, starlings were taught by the Romans to imitate human speech.
7. Convinced this career hiatus would be the start to a fruitful writing career, the one she dreamed of in college, she used her time back home to write.
8. Scientists continue to find new ways to insert genes for specific traits into plant and animal DNA.
9. At a Jodhpur wedding, the groom wears a diamond-studded sarpech, a feather ornament owned by his family for generations.
10. We had been listening to the blues, music to move to.
11. The golf ball is arriving in stores with the audacious claim that it rolls straighter than other balls.
12. The competition among the seals to become a beach master was fierce.

13. The English, Bede's own people, settled in the eastern part of the island.
14. The site, a wilderness of broken stone and undulating sand, was soon excavated by the treasure-hunting archaeologists, Tia and Laura.
15. An unwillingness to discuss her problems was the girl's biggest shortcoming.
16. The parents, victims of accidents, wanted the DWI limit lower.
17. Frankenstein had an irrational desire to animate a dead body composed of various parts.
18. I had the right to control their actions and question them about their plans.
19. What you have here is an ostentatious jewel, a symbol of vanity.
20. Her refusal to leave the dorm on a bad hair day made Janelle late for class.
21. The queen tries to kill the princess with two devices: a poisoned comb and a poisoned apple.
22. As time passed, the young queen surprised the people of Great Britain by how well she handled the responsibilities that went with wearing the crown and by the fact that she communicated better than the old king.
23. What Laura needs, taking a dose of Nyquil, would be impossible under the circumstances.
24. The prisoner's desire to come home outweighed all other thoughts.
25. The queen herself issued a decree to free all of the prisoners.
26. Zeke's ambition to get married by August was unrealistic.
27. President Truman considered many factors in his quest to make the right decision.
28. Javelinos--collared peccaries--have spread north from Mexico throughout the century.
29. Bob, Frank, and Harry took their dog, the one that gets car-sick, with them on a road trip.
30. He had the audacity to jump in front of the train.
31. The fact that Laura looks like Julia Roberts has become well known among her friends.
32. The only way to get out of the box was to use the boy's pocketknife to cut through the sides.

33. Mary's reason for putting on makeup and cutting her hair, wanting to look older, was not sufficient for her mother.
34. Her compulsion to hug her teddy bear made her aware of her security needs.
35. Whoever left the wrappers in the grass taught my little brother that some people don't believe that the earth is worthy of preserving.
36. The policemen and firefighters should be praised for their efforts to save innocent lives.
37. George W. Bush himself found the words to calm a nation in chaos.
38. Everyone should have the opportunity to see the Statue of Liberty in New York City.
39. She had the nerve to leave toothpaste in the sink on inspection night.
40. Being confident in our victory is the best way to defeat our rivals.
41. The character Merlin may have been derived from a Welsh bard named Myrddin.
42. Druids, the priests of Iron Age Britain, were associated with human sacrifice.
43. The Roman historian Ammianus Marcellinus said the fourth-century Picts were composed of two groups, the Dicalydones and the Verturiones.
44. The race between seal and fisherman to catch the fish was intense.
45. Taliesin, the most revered of the early Welsh bards, lived in the sixth century.
46. The suggestion that the leader do the work she is assigned is a good one.
47. George, science director of the Wildlife Conservation Society, has spent four decades studying wildlife and fighting for its survival.
48. Mother herself tells me it is something like the way that warm apple butter smells.
49. Paying attention to people who are not the faintest risk as a security threat is one way to defuse the charge of profiling.
50. In the extended Arctic daylight, he spends weeks recovering the bones of woolly mammoths, the lumbering precursors of today's elephants, which long ago wandered the bitterly cold landscape.

II. Write original sentences as directed below. Make sure that you use commas around most nominal appositives but not around nominal complement infinitive phrases. Circle the heads and underline the nominal appositives or nominal complement infinitive phrases.

1. Using the chart of appositive structures on the second page of this chapter, write an original sentence for each of the 9 examples on the chart. Label each one.

2. Write three original sentences with nominal complement infinitive phrases.
    a. Use the subject of the sentence as the head. Use this pattern for the head and infinitive phrase: A/the _____(N)_____ to _(infinitive verb form)_ X_

    b. Use the DO as the head. Use this pattern: _(Subj)___ (main verb) a/the _(N)_ to _(infinitive verb form)_ X_____

    c. Use either the subject or the DO as the head. Use this pattern: a/an/the ___(N)___ to __be__ _(NP or AdjP)___

3. Write a sentence with a nominal complement clause. Remember, nominal complement clauses are not set with commas.

III. Review Phrases and Clauses.

1. Write one sentence for each of the phrases and clauses on the chart in this chapter. You will have 14 sentences in all. <u>Label the phrases and clauses</u>.

2. Practice using these phrases and clauses in your writing. If you will be a teacher, create sentences without these structures and then add the structures. You can use this writing to show your students how effective these structures can be.

Chapter 12
Whole-Sentence Modifiers and Variations

We have looked at variations and expansions of the major parts of a sentence in English. In this chapter, we will look at structures that expand or modify whole sentences or substitute for more than one element in a sentence.

Compound Sentences

We have seen that almost any element in an English sentence can be joined to a like element with the use of a coordinating conjunction (Cjc). We can also join an independent clause (sentence) to another independent clause with a coordinating conjunction. In traditional grammar, these are called <u>compound sentences</u>. To join compound sentences, the following are used as Cjc: *for, and, nor, but, or, yet, so.* Some students remember these by the acronym FANBOYS.

- *This poem is frequently anthologized,* **and** *readers usually take it to mean that humans should choose their own paths.*
- *In the eyes of Frost, society is not a nurturing place,* **but** *it is a place of hostility and potential danger.*
- *Crane was vehemently against any form of preaching in his writing,* **yet** *he was not opposed to making a point.*

Two sentences (independent clauses) can also be joined by a correlative conjunction (Cjcorr).

- *In this story,* **either** *the women's efforts were ignored,* **or** *the males ridiculed their activity.*
- *Frost* **not only** *appears to question if God cares about the world,* **but** *he* **also** *seems to entertain the thought of a negative creator.*

The grammar tree for a compound sentence is fairly straightforward. We have a Cjc (or Cjcorr) triangle with the S. Tree each "sentence" or main clause separately under the appropriate S.

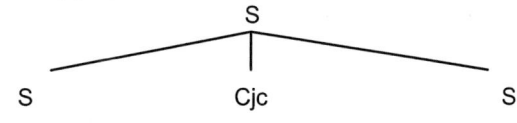

```
              S
      _____|_____
     /        |        \
    S        Cjc        S
```

Sometimes two sentences are joined by a semicolon rather than a Cjc.
- *This poem is frequently anthologized; readers usually take it to mean that humans should choose their own paths.*

Since the semicolon replaces the comma and coordinating conjunction, I would tree the semicolon as an ellipted Cjc.

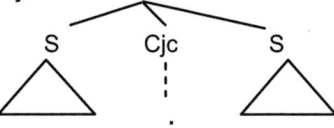

Absolutes

Absolutes are a unique structure in English. They modify the entire sentence. The easiest way to think about an absolute is to think about how it was formed.

- An absolute "started" as a sentence that usually included a form of the verb *BE* in it. (*Her legs **were** pumping with exertion.*)
- Then the **BE** verb is dropped. (*Her legs pumping with exertion.*)
- Then the absolute is attached to another complete sentence (independent clause). We will call this independent clause the **main clause (MC)**. (*Her legs pumping with exertion, the runner would cross the finish line.*)
- The absolute can appear in various locations before, within, or after the main clause. (*The runner, her legs pumping with exertion, would cross the finish line.*) (*The runner would cross the finish line, her legs pumping with exertion.*)
- Often a writer will use two absolutes together. (*Her legs pumping with exertion and her arms swinging at her sides, the runner would cross the finish line.*)

Here is how we tree a sentence with an absolute. Remember, an absolute modifies the entire sentence, so we will label it simply *modifier;* we write "absolute functioning as a modifier" **(Abs:Mod)**. As we have done with other structures, we will tree the missing *BE* element with a dotted line and parentheses around the word.

Whole-Sentence Modifiers and Variations 205

Her legs pumping with exertion, the runner would cross the finish line.

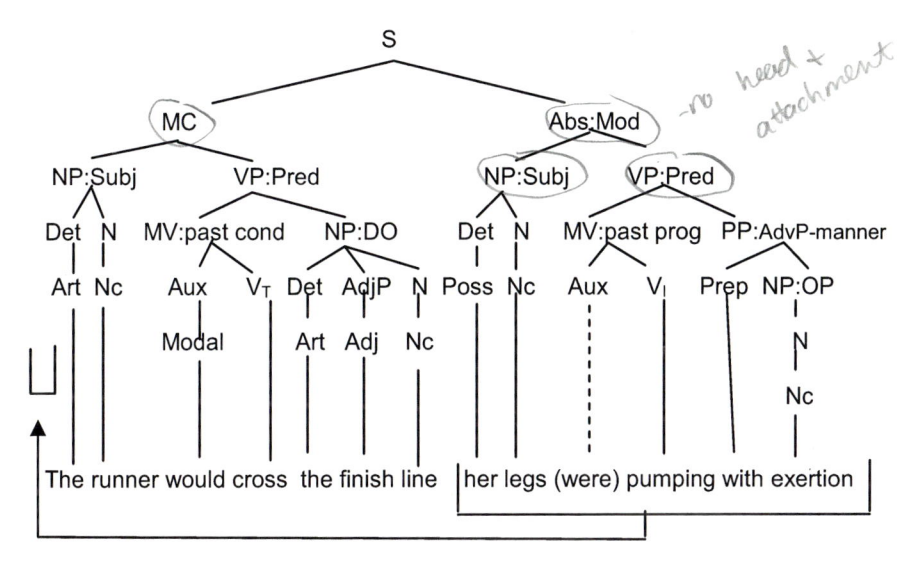

[Sentence diagram with annotations: "—no head + attachment" pointing to Abs:Mod. Tree structure shows S branching into MC and Abs:Mod. MC branches into NP:Subj (Det/Art, N/Nc — "The runner") and VP:Pred (MV:past cond with Aux/Modal "would" and V_T "cross"; NP:DO with Det/Art "the", AdjP/Adj "finish", N/Nc "line"). Abs:Mod branches into NP:Subj (Det/Poss "her", N/Nc "legs") and VP:Pred (MV:past prog with Aux "(were)" and V_I "pumping"; PP:AdvP-manner with Prep "with", NP:OP N/Nc "exertion"). Bottom lines read: "The runner would cross the finish line" and "her legs (were) pumping with exertion".]

Adverbial Conjunctions

Another grammar structure that modifies the entire sentence is an adverbial conjunction (**Cj_Adv**). These types of conjunctions join one sentence to the sentence that comes before or after it. They express relationships such as addition, contrast, result, space, or time. Adverbial conjunctions differ from subordinating conjunctions (Cjs) in that they join sentences while a Cjs begins an adverb clause within a sentence.

Some Words that Can Function as Adverbial Conjunctions		
eventually	accordingly	first
nonetheless	notwithstanding	finally
however	besides	rather
then	also	too
hence	furthermore	last
likewise	moreover	next
otherwise	nevertheless	still
similarly		

Like absolutes, adverbial conjunctions are set off from the rest of the sentence, most often with a comma. Whole-sentence modifiers are generally set off from the rest of the sentence with punctuation.

Like absolutes, they can appear in various positions at the beginning, within, or at the end of a sentence.

- ***However**, they could provide no evidence that she had done anything wrong.*
- *They could**, however**, provide no evidence that she had done anything wrong.*
- *They could provide**, however**, no evidence that she had done anything wrong.*
- *They could provide no evidence**, however**, that she had done anything wrong.*
- *They could provide no evidence that she had done anything wrong**, however**.*

Some Phrases that Can Function as Adverbial Conjunctions		
on the other hand	for example	in other words
all things considered	for the most part	in brief
in the first place	in addition	in short
in summary	in contrast	on the contrary
in the meantime	in fact	

Note: Some words seem as if they can be either a coordinating conjunction (Cjc) or adverbial conjunction (Cj$_{Adv}$), depending upon how they are used. For example, the words *yet* and *so* are coordinating conjunctions when they join two independent clauses. However, they seem to be adverbial conjunctions when they introduce a sentence or main clause and substitute for *however* or *therefore*.

- ***Yet**, Jimmy and Maggie are rarely pictured as participating in the activities that boys and girls of their age usually find amusing.*
- *The choice holds little importance, and **so,** a man does not demonstrate the necessary power to make choices that would truly affect his life.*

In the first sentence, the *yet* is substituting for *however,* and in the second sentence, the *so* is substituting for *therefore.* In these instances, these words are adverbial conjunctions.

We will tree these as we did absolutes, set off from the main clause (MC). If necessary, we will then show that they have been moved to another location within the sentence. Tree phrases functioning as adverbial conjunctions as a unit; do not tree individual words in this case.

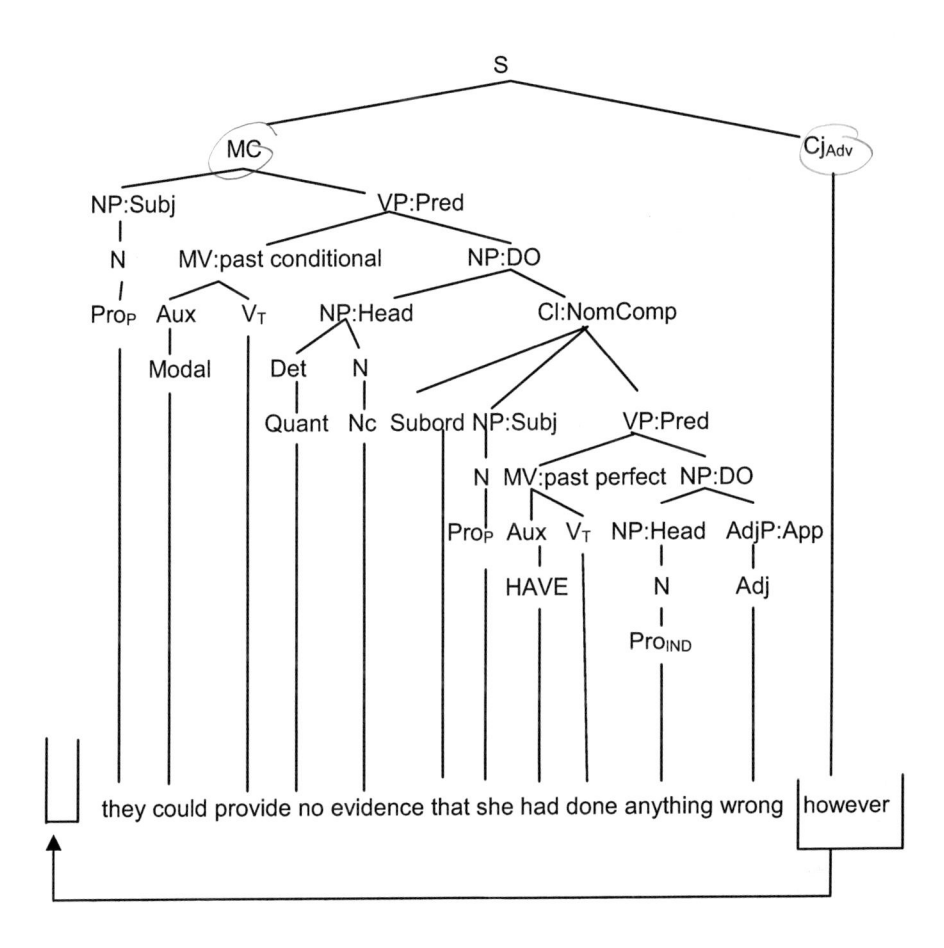

Whole-Sentence Modifiers and Variations 207

[Tree diagram:

S
├── MC
│   ├── NP:Subj
│   │   └── N
│   │   └── Prop — they
│   └── VP:Pred
│   ├── MV:past conditional
│   │   ├── Aux
│   │   │   └── Modal — could
│   │   └── V_T — provide
│   └── NP:DO
│   ├── NP:Head
│   │   ├── Det
│   │   │   └── Quant — no
│   │   └── N
│   │   └── Nc — evidence
│   └── Cl:NomComp
│   ├── Subord — that
│   ├── NP:Subj
│   │   └── N
│   │   └── Prop — she
│   └── VP:Pred
│   ├── MV:past perfect
│   │   ├── Aux — HAVE (had)
│   │   └── V_T — done
│   └── NP:DO
│   ├── NP:Head
│   │   └── N
│   │   └── Pro_IND — anything
│   └── AdjP:App
│   └── Adj — wrong
└── Cj_Adv — however

Sentence: they could provide no evidence that she had done anything wrong | however
(Arrow connecting Cj_Adv back to the beginning of the sentence)]

Other Whole-Sentence Modifiers

We sometimes use modifiers for a whole sentence that <u>do not connect to any other sentences as do adverbial conjunctions (Cj_Adv)</u>. Some examples are *obviously, invariably, perhaps, frankly, undoubtedly, unfortunately, luckily, to our amazement, to tell the truth,* and *speaking of* _____. Nouns of direct address, also called <u>vocatives</u>, could also be put in this category.

- **Peter,** *the pictures you sent were terrific.*

We will tree these set off from the main clause, as we have been doing in this chapter.

[Tree diagram:
S
├── MC
└── Modifier]

Whole-Sentence Modifiers and Variations

Fortunately, the Wright brothers began copying the flying toy, building increasingly larger versions.

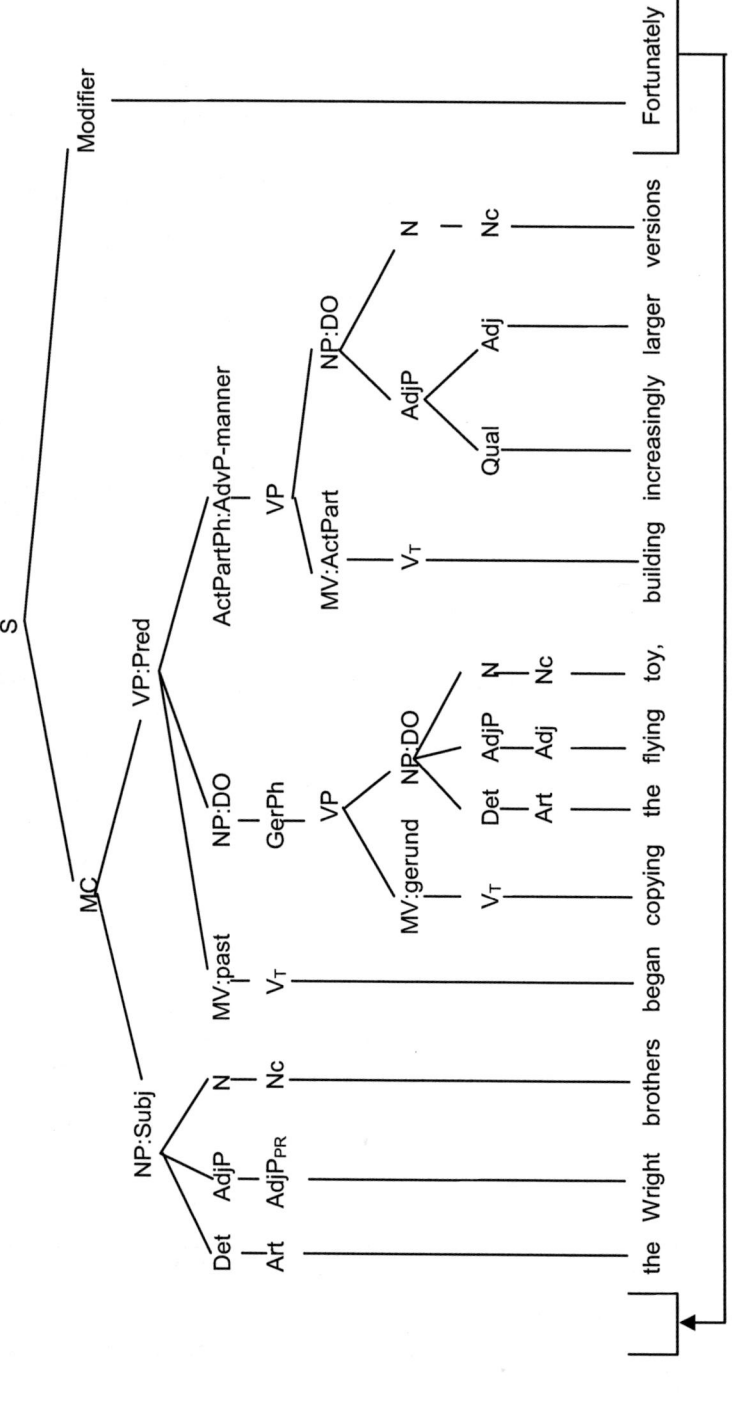

Relative Clauses with Whole-Sentence Heads

Some sentences seem to have a relative clause for which the head is an entire clause.
- Garrett took photographs of the blazing color of the lush coral reefs, **which was an unforgettable experience.**
- Many dinosaur fossils end up in the oceanfront rooms of the grand Pacific coast mansions, **which frustrates paleontologists who would like to study them.**

Notice that in the last example, the first relative clause (*which frustrates paleontologists who would like to study them*) modifies the entire main clause (*Many dinosaur fossils end up in the oceanfront rooms of the grand Pacific coast mansions*) whereas the second relative clause (*who would like to study them*) is adjectival and modifies an NP:Head (*paleontologists*).

(The following tree is not done in detail, so that you can see the relationships of the relative clauses.)

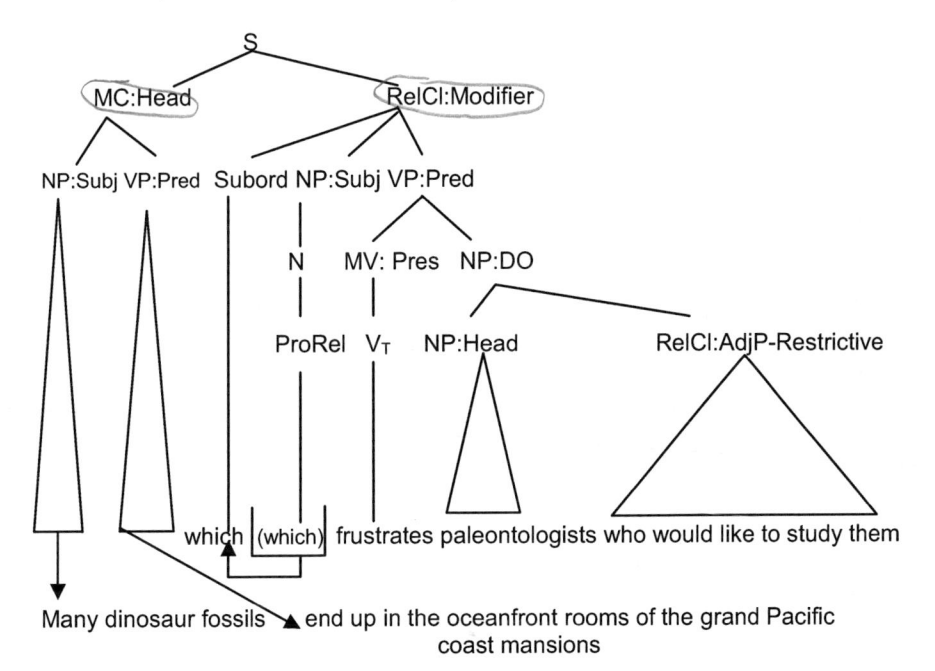

Pro-Forms

The pro-forms are substitutes within a sentence. You are already very familiar with pronouns (noun substitutes), and you have already worked with pro-determiners and pro-adverbs. *Pro-forms* is a general term for words (particularly the word *so* or the phrase *do so*) which can substitute for many types of sentence structures, including entire phrases or clauses.

Sentence with pro-form	Sentence with substituted elements
They predict that spring will soon arrive, and I certainly hope **so**.	They predict that spring will soon arrive, and I certainly hope that spring will soon arrive.
I doubt Hexaba will be promoted, but if **so**, we will make the best of it.	I doubt Hexaba will be promoted, but if she is promoted, we will make the best of it.
They told me to show no emotion, but I was unable to **do so**.	They told me to show no emotion, but I was unable to show no emotion.

In each of the above examples, the pro-form is substituting for a different structure within the sentence.

Sentence with pro-form	Pro-form is substituting for this structure
They predict that spring will soon arrive, and I certainly hope **so**.	Noun clause which is functioning as NP:DO
I doubt Hexaba will be promoted, but if **so**, we will make the best of it.	NP:Subject and VP:Predicate in adverb clause
They told me to show no emotion, but I was unable to **do so**.	VP of infinitive phrase

Also, the words *doing* and *did* can be used as pro-forms if they are substitutes for other words. Watch for these words as well.

Whole-Sentence Modifiers and Variations 211

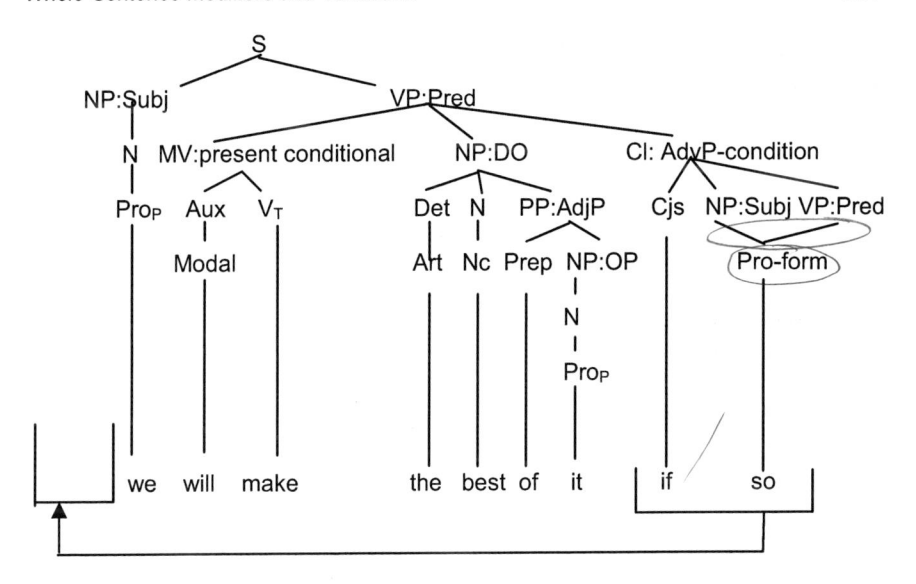

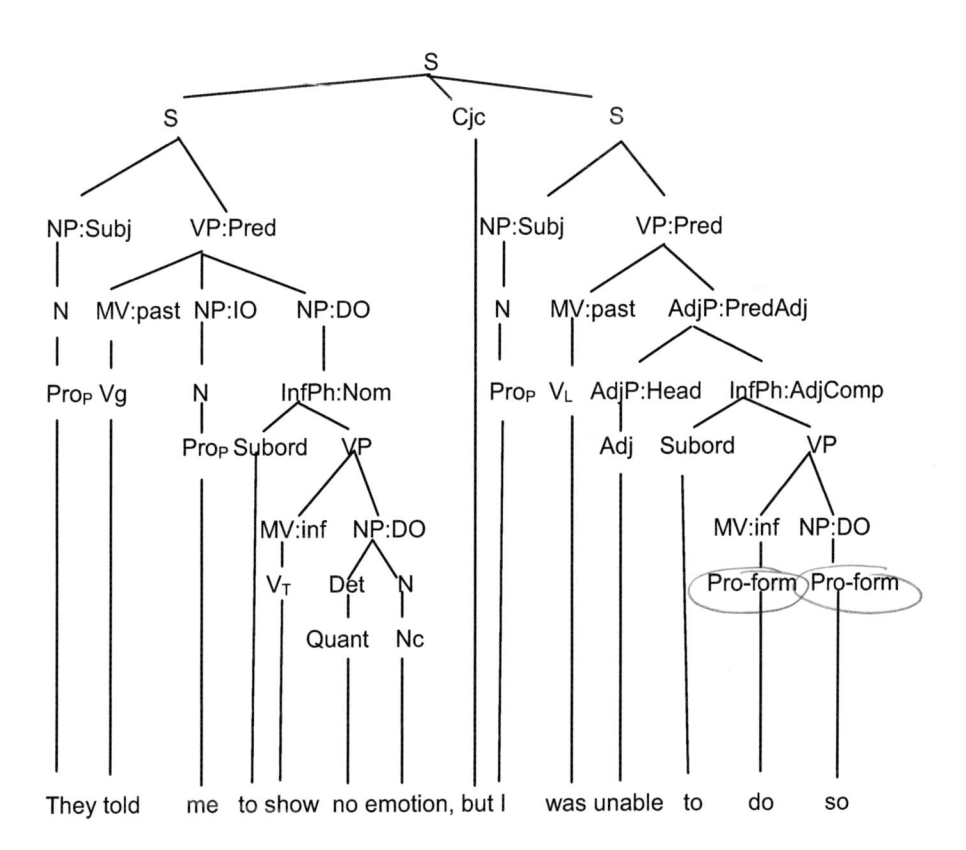

Ellipsis

As we have seen in previous chapters, ellipsis indicates that something has been left out. Especially when we speak, we may leave out part of the sentence. These "left out" elements are still there grammatically; therefore, we will tree them with dotted lines and the words in parentheses. For the missing elements, you may simply indicate the main label. You don't need to do detailed labeling on the parts left out.

Sentence with Ellipsis	Sentence with Elements back in
Although sick of traveling, we packed our two suitcases again.	Although **we were** sick of traveling, we packed our two suitcases again.
Peter loves fish, whether baked or fried.	Peter loves fish, whether **they are** baked or fried.
He was described as energetic and enthusiastic.	He was described as **being** energetic and enthusiastic.
Wanda became a physician and Kathleen a professor.	Wanda became a physician, and Kathleen **became** a professor.

Sometimes the *to* or *for* is dropped in a *for/to* type of infinitive phrase. We delete the *to* or *for* because having it in may sound awkward to us, but it exists grammatically.

Sentence with Ellipsis	Sentence with Elements back in
Fishing is the best way to calm your nerves and enjoy the great outdoors.	Fishing is the best way to calm your nerves and **to** enjoy the great outdoors.
The man wanted his daughter to become an electrician.	The man wanted **for** his daughter to become an electrician.

Remember, tree the "left out" elements with dotted lines and the words in parentheses.

Notes about Punctuation

Structures that Need Punctuation

With the exception of pro-forms (and ellipsis), the structures we have examined in this chapter need to be set off from the rest of the sentence

Whole-Sentence Modifiers and Variations 213

with commas or dashes. Commas are used more commonly, but a dash would indicate a longer pause or a bit less connection to the main clause of the sentence. There might be stylistic reasons for a dash.

Absolute	Set the absolute off from the rest of the sentence with commas or dashes.	*Adam woke with a start—**Kevin's mocking laughter in his ears.***
Adverbial Conjunctions	Set off adverbial conjunctions from the rest of the sentence with commas.	***Nonetheless,** Joanie did not discover that she had a green thumb until she retired.*
Whole-sentence Modifiers	Set off whole-sentence modifiers from the rest of the sentence with commas.	***Undoubtedly,** she is the best teacher that we have.*

Semicolons

One punctuation option for joining two sentences or main clauses is to use a semicolon. When the second main clause has an adverbial conjunction, be sure to include the comma to set that off. If you use this option, the Cjc drops out. <u>Do not use both a Cjc and a semicolon.</u>

- *Since the 1920s astronomers have thought that the expansion of the universe was slowing down; however, recent discoveries show that the energy which counteracts gravity's pull is actually speeding up.*

Coordinating Conjunctions and Commas

Use a comma before a coordinating conjunction (Cjc) only if the Cjc connects two full sentences (independent clauses that could be complete sentences grammatically).

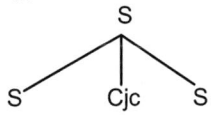

```
        S
       /|\
      / | \
     S  Cjc  S
```

<u>Do not use a comma with the Cjc if it simply connects two like elements</u> (such as two verbs, two noun clusters, two adjectives, or two adverbs).

- *The firefighter never seems to lose the bounce in his step **and** rarely complains even when the fires ravage two billion acres of forest.* (No comma is used with the Cjc.)
- *The firefighter never seems to lose the bounce in his step, **and** he rarely complains even when the fires ravage two billion acres of forest.* (A comma is needed before the Cjc *and*.)
- *Jerry is the supervisor of the department, **yet** he does the chainsaw work himself.* (A comma is needed before the Cjc *yet*.)
- *Jerry is the supervisor of the department **yet** does the chainsaw work himself.* (No comma is used with the Cjc.)

Modifier Usage

Misuse of Ellipsis

Sometimes using ellipsis causes a modifier to be dangling or misplaced. See the following examples.

Sentence with Modifier Problem	Revised Sentence
While fertilizing the bushes, the wheelbarrow broke.	While I was fertilizing the bushes, the wheelbarrow broke.
Riding my bike in the race all day, my shoulders and thighs ached.	Since I rode in the race all day, my shoulders and thighs ached.
Before registering for classes, your advisor should be consulted.	Before you register for classes, you should consult your advisor.
When only a small child, her father took the artist to museums.	When the artist was only a small child, her father took her to museums.
Though needing sugar for her morning coffee, Bev's last cupful was used for making the cookies.	Although she needed sugar for her morning coffee, Bev used the last cupful for making the cookies.
Although an undeniable asset to the neighborhood, they expected her to be the first to break out and make the five-block town famous.	Although an undeniable asset to the neighborhood, she was expected to be the first to break out and make the five-block town famous.

Sentence Modifiers and Style

Transitions

Adverbial conjunctions are more often called **transitions**. For the most effective communication, writers should choose a transition that most precisely represents the relationship of the ideas. Teachers especially should provide student writers with lots of practice using transitions to connect sentences and paragraphs in their writing.

For formal writing style, one should not begin a sentence with a coordinating conjunction such as *and* or *but*. We often begin sentences with *and* or *but* in informal communication, but, as you know from your study of grammar, these conjunctions join elements within a sentence or come between two full sentences. Therefore, although many publications such as newspapers and magazines do so, to be the most formal in a written language situation, one would not start a sentence with one of these words.

Whole-Sentence Modifiers

Some editors think that using a relative clause to modify a whole sentence is not good writing style. They would suggest starting a separate main clause with a reference to the previous one.

- Garrett took photographs of the blazing color of the lush coral reefs, **which was an unforgettable experience.**
- Garrett took photographs of the blazing color of the lush coral reefs; this dive was an unforgettable experience.

- Many dinosaur fossils end up in the oceanfront rooms of the grand Pacific coast mansions, **which frustrates paleontologists who would like to study them.**
- Many dinosaur fossils end up in the oceanfront rooms of the grand Pacific coast mansions; this practice frustrates paleontologists who would like to study them.

Practice Sentences

I. Tree the following sentences. As always, watch for review structures.

1. Coffee cup in hand, the history professor wandered through the offices, looking for someone to whom he could talk.
2. She was interrupted many times to wait on customers, so eventually she had to hurry to get the mail sorted into the various boxes before the post office closed.
3. If disturbed, they give off chemical light.
4. The young man had the ability to succeed, but running down the street to get to work on time was difficult for him.
5. Later, her hair combed and rebound in the braids tossed down her back and her jacket tossed over a chair to dry, she sat on the couch to talk with her mother.
6. Nonetheless, after two decades spent seeking a permit that would allow them to investigate, Jones and her husband, a civil engineer, finally began to study the site in 1994.
7. It wasn't on my lesson plan, but we all learned something that day, all things considered.
8. So far, thirty-five people have died while making the climb.
9. Besides, many communities aren't sure of who is responsible for upkeep of sculpture, so it is never done.
10. She went down to the kitchen, her long skirts trailing on the stone steps.
11. Although an undeniable asset to the neighborhood, she was expected to be the first to break out and make the five-block town famous.
12. As new products hit the market, the biotech industry gathered opposition almost as fast as it did steam.
13. I wanted to go to the play, but I couldn't afford to do so.
14. Likewise, gestures and learned preferences allowed them to tackle the really important stuff like the new Italian restaurant.
15. The goals of that country, however, are opposed to America's goals.
16. The gas prices falling, the IRS had lowered the mileage deduction.
17. Sally was reluctant to write her telephone number on the form, so she was excused from doing so.
18. Besides, his ultimate dream had become to play with the Olympic volleyball team.
19. A preconceived idea of her blind date caused Beth to embarrass herself.

20. For example, this American corporation also had a lot of women in entry-level jobs, a fair number of women in middle management, and a few women in the top ranks, in a pyramid.
21. However, before pointing an accusing finger at the past and branding those involved in the decision as murderers, the public must first sift through the stacks of documents and reports to decipher what information was available to those in vital positions in 1945.
22. I wanted to buy a book to help *for* me *to* sharpen my reading skills but was unable to do so.
23. Therefore, after examining the known information, the motives of those involved, and the results of the bombing, one can confidently claim that the United States made the right decision in dropping the atomic bomb.
24. Her eyes circled by violet shadows, the doctor entered the operating room again.
25. Truman and his military advisors realized that allowing Hirohito to stay would jeopardize future peace plans.
26. Opponents also argue that by the summer of 1945 victory was no longer a possibility for Japan, so the bomb was unnecessary.
27. Ultimately, he straddled the fence between a homeland invasion and the employment of the atomic bomb.
28. In other words, many critics conclude that the bombings were unnecessary and that the United States will forever hold in its conscience the deaths of thousands of innocent Japanese.
29. Researchers have determined that the damage was done by carnivores, including the now extinct hyenas, and publications indicated this.
30. Next, the Eagles, adrenaline pumping, were up to bat.
31. Her gaze fixed on the young gentleman wearing the navy blue suit and blue paisley tie, Amanda worked her way along the corridor.
32. I had drifted into Mitch's bedroom, which smelled like sweaty feet, so I picked up his imitation leather sandals and set them outside the door and pulled open the window.
33. Sheila, her hair blowing in the wind, raced to the car to close the windows.
34. The college student, although only of junior status, was showing definite signs of senioritis.

35. Her parents coming over, the girl scrambled to get the house clean before they arrived.
36. Until she has enough money, she can't go to the mall, or she will overdraw her checkbook.
37. To do so would be a big mistake.
38. Nonetheless, we tried to figure out whether the man running behind the car had the intention to catch it.
39. Elaine was very pale, her blue eyes burning.
40. Jackie's screaming bloody murder caused Mrs. Bisbee to abruptly drop her teacup.
41. Her running the race that was too long also triggered her supposedly cured asthma.
42. She didn't know, when faced with the split second decision, whether to buy the red sweater or the blue one.
43. She sat under the umbrella, the rain touching her fingertips but never her whole hands.
44. He had decided to become a nurse instead of becoming a grammar teacher and then did so.
45. The policemen and firefighters should be praised for their efforts to try to save innocent lives while losing their own.
46. Paul's grinning, when he shouldn't have been, creeped all of the ladies out.
47. The boreal forest—its name derived from the Boreas—comprises one-third of the earth's wooded lands.
48. Sadly, the only support Jim and Maggie receive is from each other.
49. The chimps ought to have enjoyed their freedom but were terrified by their first glimpse of the sun in six years.
50. The U.S. Census Bureau considers Edgar Springs the population center of the country, which surprises everyone.

II. Write sentences.

1. Write 3 sentences, each with an absolute. Follow the description in this chapter about how absolutes are formed when you write your own. Make sure that you set off the absolute correctly with punctuation.

2. Write one sentence with two absolutes together. Punctuate correctly.
3. Write 10 sentences with at least one Cjc each. Then determine for each Cjc whether or not it needs a comma before it. Punctuate appropriately. If you will be a teacher, you can use these sentences with your students when you teach.

III. Practice revision in your writing.

Use a paper you have written for a class. Revise your writing by adding adverbial conjunctions (transitions) and other whole-sentence modifiers. If you have written a piece of fiction, try adding some absolutes.

Chapter 13
Sentence Varieties

We have been looking at sentences that are all declarative sentences. In this chapter, we will look at some additional variations such as interrogative sentences (questions) and imperative sentences (commands). We can label the type of sentence after the main *S* label on top.

Type of Sentence	Label
Statements	S:Declarative
Questions	S:Interrogative
Commands	S:Imperative

Imperative Sentences

Imperatives are commands which use the "understood you" as the subject and have a deleted Aux. To tree the imperative, follow these steps:

- Add the word *you* as the NP:Subj. Use a dotted line and put parentheses around the word.
- Add the word *will* as the Aux. Use a dotted line and put parentheses around the word.
- Label the MV as **MV:Imperative**. There is no other MV label in an imperative.
- Also note that imperatives may be compound: *Shut the door or turn down the music.*

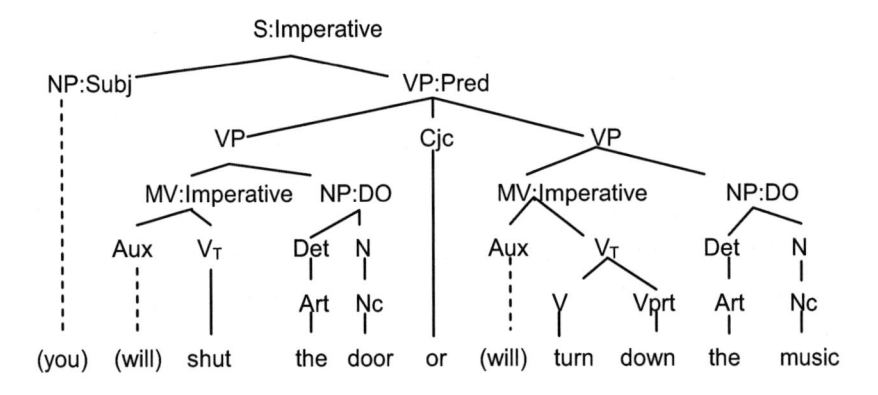

```
                         S:Imperative
         ┌───────────────────┴──────────────────┐
      NP:Subj                                VP:Pred
         ┊              ┌──────────────────┬─┴──────────────┐
         ┊             VP                  Cjc              VP
         ┊         ┌────┴────┐              │        ┌───────┴────┐
         ┊     MV:Imperative NP:DO          │   MV:Imperative   NP:DO
         ┊       ┌──┴──┐    ┌─┴─┐           │     ┌────┴───┐     ┌─┴─┐
         ┊      Aux   V_T   Det  N          │    Aux      V_T    Det  N
         ┊       ┊    │     │    │          │     ┊    ┌──┴──┐   │    │
         ┊       ┊    │     Art  Nc         │     ┊    V     Vprt Art Nc
         ┊       ┊    │     │    │          │     ┊    │     │    │    │
       (you)  (will) shut  the  door        or  (will) turn down  the music
```

Sentence Varieties 221

Note that if you have a compound VP with an imperative sentence, you need to add an Aux (*will*) to both VPs.

Questions

There are two main types of questions: Yes/No questions and *Wh* questions.

Yes/No Questions

To form a yes/no question, we move the first word of the Aux to the front.
- *Naomi is knitting a sweater.*
- *Is Naomi knitting a sweater?*

If the "original statement" did not have an Aux, we need to add a **Supp-DO** as we did with negatives.
- *Thom generally makes his free throws.*
- *Does Thom generally make his free throws?*

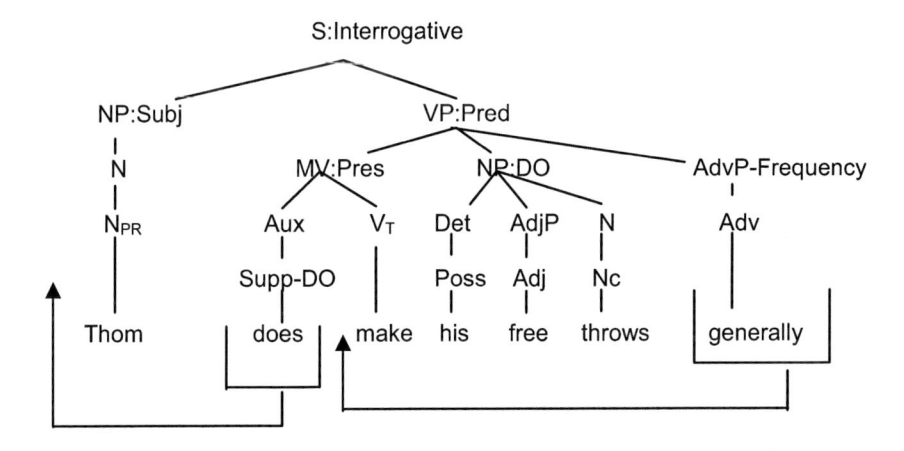

```
                         S:Interrogative
              ┌──────────────┴──────────────┐
          NP:Subj                         VP:Pred
            │              ┌────────────────┼──────────────┐
            N            MV:Pres          NP:DO         AdvP-Frequency
            │           ┌───┴───┐      ┌────┼────┐          │
           N_PR        Aux     V_T    Det  AdjP   N         Adv
            │          │       │      │    │     │          │
            │        Supp-DO   │      │   Adj    Nc         │
            │          │       │      │    │     │          │
          Thom        does   make    his  free  throws   generally
```

Wh Questions

We call these *Wh* questions because many of the "question words" (**interrogatives**) begin with *wh*: *why, when, where, who, whom, what, which,* and *whose*. The word *how* is also an interrogative along with cluster interrogatives such as *how much* or *how many*. We label these words as **Pro**$_\text{Inter}$.

Words which can be interrogative pronouns	*what, who, whom*
Words which can be interrogative pro-adverbs	*when, where, why, how, how often, how far, how long*
Words which can be interrogative pro-determiners	*whose, which*
Words which can be interrogative pro-adjectives	*how much, how many, how**

(*How could be an interrogative pro-adjective in a question such as "*How does rattlesnake taste?*")

Treeing *Wh* Questions

- Find the Pro$_{Inter}$. The interrogative will be at the beginning of the question or with a preposition at the beginning of the question.

- Figure out what type of structure and function the interrogative replaces in the sentence. It will be replacing one of the following:
    - NP
    - AdvP
    - Det
    - AdjP

- Label the interrogative (Wh-word) as Pro$_{Inter}$.

- Tree the interrogative <u>in its grammatical position in the sentence</u>, but use a box and arrow to show that it has been moved to the front of the sentence.

- The first word of the Aux may also have been moved to a position right after the Pro$_{Inter}$. Remember, there might be a Supp-DO if there was no other Aux.

- If required, show the movement of the first word of the Aux with a box and arrow.

Sentence Varieties 223

What do you read when you are at the beach?

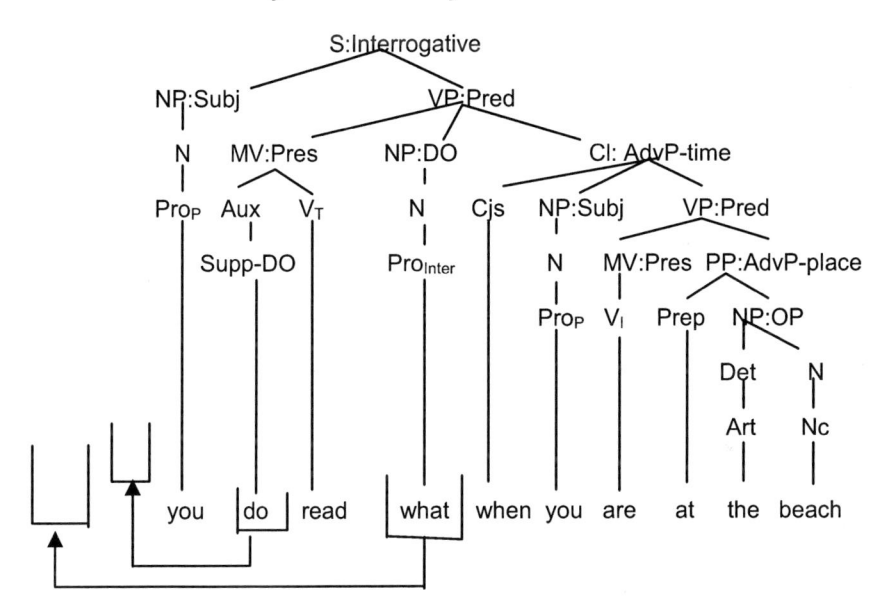

```
                             S:Interrogative
              ┌──────────────────┴──────────────────┐
           NP:Subj                               VP:Pred
             │              ┌──────────────────────┼───────────────────┐
             N           MV:Pres                 NP:DO             Cl: AdvP-time
             │           ┌───┴───┐                 │        ┌─────────┼──────────┐
           Pro_P        Aux     V_T                N       Cjs     NP:Subj    VP:Pred
             │           │       │                 │        │         │    ┌─────┴──────┐
             │        Supp-DO    │              Pro_Inter   │         N  MV:Pres  PP:AdvP-place
             │           │       │                 │        │         │     │    ┌──────┴──────┐
             │           │       │                 │        │       Pro_P   V_I  Prep        NP:OP
             │           │       │                 │        │         │     │    │        ┌────┴────┐
             │           │       │                 │        │         │     │    │       Det        N
             │           │       │                 │        │         │     │    │        │         │
             │           │       │                 │        │         │     │    │       Art       Nc
            you         do     read             what      when      you    are   at      the      beach
```

How does a peccary eat the dense brush?

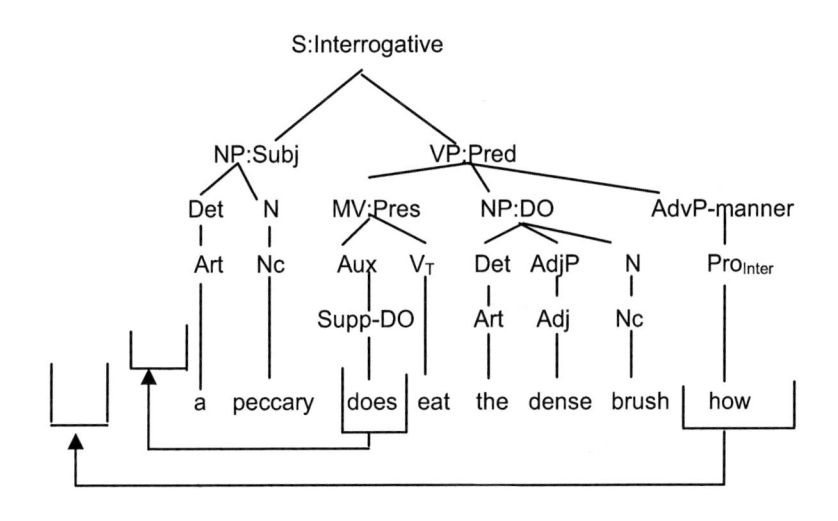

```
                              S:Interrogative
              ┌──────────────────┴──────────────────┐
           NP:Subj                               VP:Pred
          ┌────┴────┐       ┌───────────────────────┼─────────────────┐
         Det        N    MV:Pres                  NP:DO           AdvP-manner
          │         │    ┌───┴───┐         ┌────────┼────────┐          │
         Art       Nc   Aux     V_T       Det     AdjP       N       Pro_Inter
          │         │    │       │         │    ┌───┤        │          │
          │      Supp-DO │         │       Art  Adj Nc        │
          │         │    │       │         │       │        │          │
          a      peccary does    eat      the    dense    brush        how
```

Sentence Varieties

Which library will have the largest collection in the world?

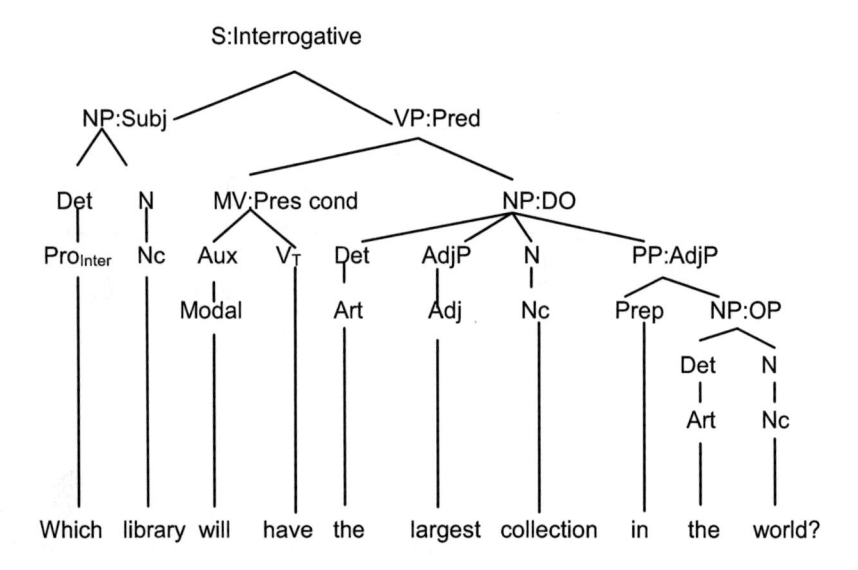

```
                          S:Interrogative
                  ┌──────────────┴──────────────┐
              NP:Subj                        VP:Pred
            ┌────┴────┐          ┌──────────────┴──────────────┐
           Det        N      MV:Pres cond                    NP:DO
            │         │      ┌─────┴─────┐      ┌────┬────┬────┴────┐
         Pro_Inter   Nc     Aux         V_T    Det  AdjP  N       PP:AdjP
            │         │      │           │      │    │    │     ┌────┴────┐
            │         │    Modal         │     Art  Adj  Nc    Prep     NP:OP
            │         │      │           │      │    │    │     │     ┌───┴───┐
            │         │      │           │      │    │    │     │    Det      N
            │         │      │           │      │    │    │     │     │       │
            │         │      │           │      │    │    │     │    Art     Nc
            │         │      │           │      │    │    │     │     │       │
          Which    library  will       have    the largest collection in    the    world?
```

How many acres of land in America are owned by the government?

```
                                    S:Interrogative
                      ┌──────────────────┴──────────────────┐
                 NP:GramSubj                             VP:Pred
          ┌──────────┬──────────┐              ┌────────────┴────────────┐
        AdjP         N       PP:AdjP      MV:Pres passive         PP:AdvP-agency
          │          │      ┌───┴───┐       ┌────┴────┐            ┌────┴────┐
      Pro_Inter     Nc    Prep    NP:OP    Aux       V_I          Prep    NP:OP/LogSubj
          │          │     │    ┌──┴──┐     │         │            │     ┌────┴────┐
          │          │     │    N   PP:AdjP BE        │            │    Det        N
          │          │     │    │   ┌─┴─┐              │            │     │         │
          │          │     │   Nc  Prep NP:OP         │            │    Art       Nc
          │          │     │    │    │   │             │            │     │         │
          │          │     │    │    │   N             │            │     │         │
          │          │     │    │    │   │             │            │     │         │
          │          │     │    │    │  N_PR           │            │     │         │
          │          │     │    │    │   │             │            │     │         │
         How many  acres   of  land  in America       are  owned    by   the    government?
```

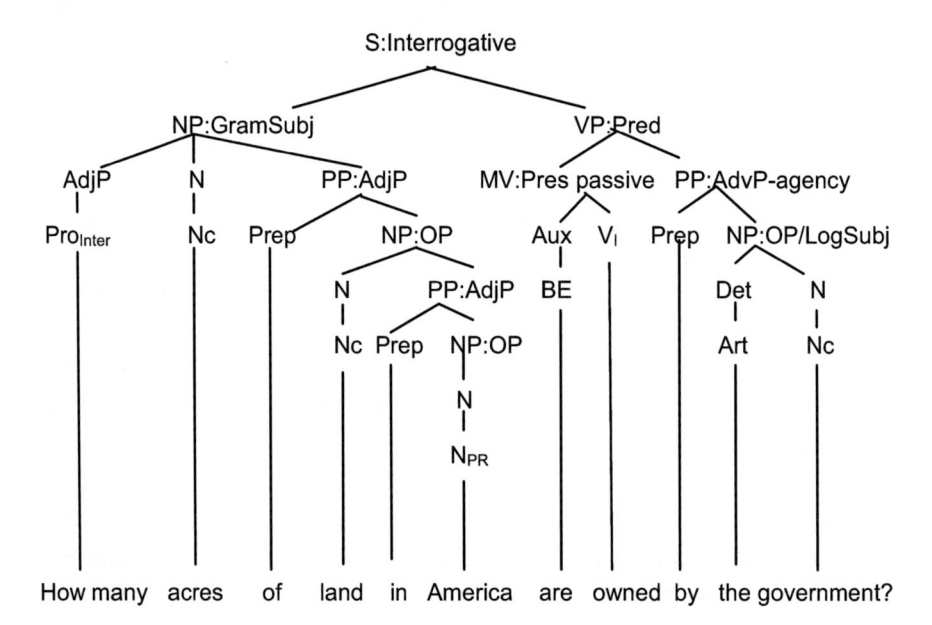

Sentence Varieties

Who had been governing the shire?

```
                    S:Interrogative
         ┌──────────────┴──────────────┐
      NP:Subj                       VP:Pred
         │              ┌──────────────┴──────┐
       Pro_Inter    MV:past perf prog        NP:DO
         │         ┌────┴────┐          ┌─────┴─────┐
         │        Aux        V_T        Det         N
         │      ┌──┴──┐       │          │          │
         │    HAVE    BE      │         Art         Nc
         │     │      │       │          │          │
        Who   had    been  governing    the       shire?
```

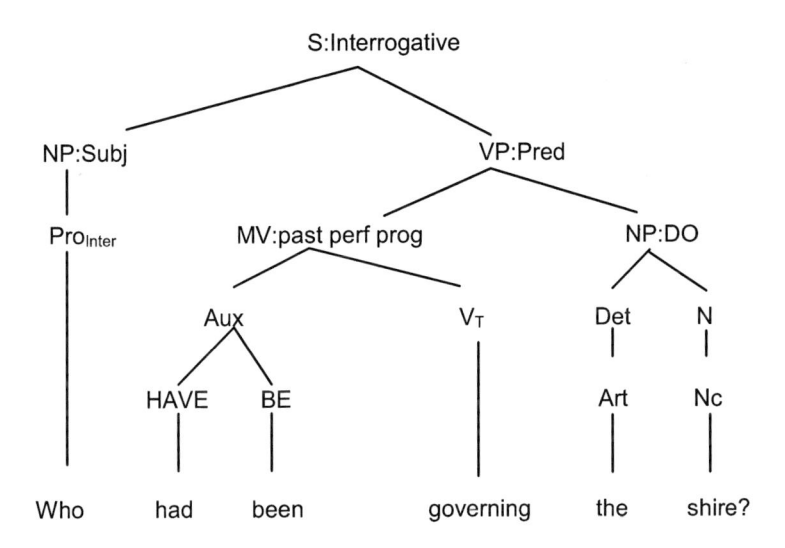

Tag Questions

A tag questions is a short question that we attach to a declarative statement, such as the following:

- *That tomato plant grew really tall, didn't it?*
- *Reg and Ivy are great traveling companions, aren't they?*
- *Attaching the motherboard to the casing is not as easy as it looks, is it?*
- *Carissa has begun an extensive linguistic program, hasn't she?*

Notice that the pronoun in the tag questions refers to the subject of the sentence. Attaching a tag question to a sentence can be a good way to find the subject of that sentence.

I would suggest that we tree tag questions as two independent clauses. See the example that follows.

```
                                    S
                    ┌───────────────┴───────────────┐
             S:Declarative                    S:Interrogative
          ┌──────┴──────┐                     ┌──────┴──────┐
      NP:Subj         VP:Pred              NP:Subj        VP:Pred
         │         ┌────┴────┐                │              │
         N    MV: pres perf  NP:DO            N          MV:Pres
         │      ┌───┴──┐   ┌──┴──┬──────┐     │          ┌───┴──┐
        N_PR   Aux    V_T  Det  AdjP   NP:N  Prop       Aux   V_I
         │     │      │    │    │    ┌──┴──┐  │          │
              HAVE         Art  Adj AdjP   N  Neg
                                     │    │   │
                                    Adj   Nc  not       has
```

Carissa   has   begun   an extensive linguistic program,   she   hasn't

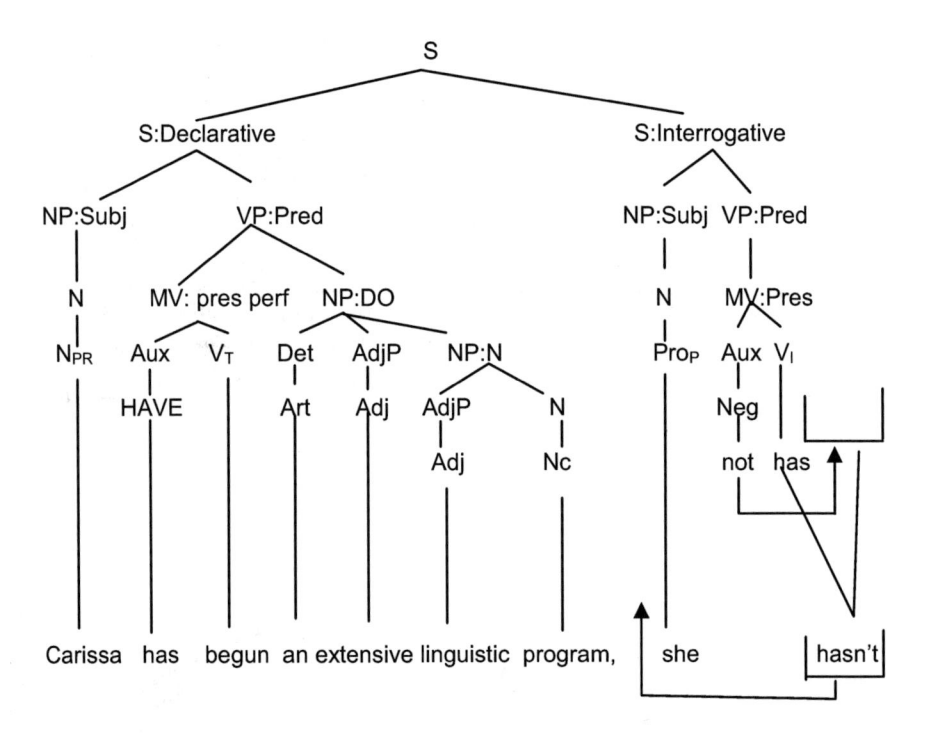

Extraposed Sentences

In an extraposed sentence, the original subject has been moved, and a "place holder word" (usually *there* or *it*) has been put in the subject position. We call this place holder an **expletive**. It doesn't have any meaning in the sentence; it merely holds the place of the subject. Since it is in the subject position, it is called the **grammatical subject (GramSubj)**. The original subject, now generally at the end of the sentence, is labeled as the **logical subject (LogSubj)**.

Extraposed Sentence	"Original" Sentence
*In each drama, **there is** a male's rejection of the feminine contribution to society.*	*A male's rejection of the feminine contribution to society is in each drama.*
*Throughout the whole poem, the main character feels that **there is** something amiss about her farmhouse.*	*Throughout the whole poem, the main character feels that something is amiss about her farmhouse.*

Sentence Varieties

Sometimes when a sentence is extraposed, the original VP:Pred is put into a relative clause.

Extraposed Sentence	"Original" Sentence
It was her struggle for equality in a field dominated by men **that led Schapiro to create "femmage."**	Her struggle for equality in a field dominated by men **led Schapiro to create "femmage."**
It is Fleur, a wild, spirited woman, **who invokes fear in the hearts of the members of the community.**	Fleur, a wild, spirited woman, **invokes fear in the hearts of the members of the community.**

Tree these sentences in this basic pattern.

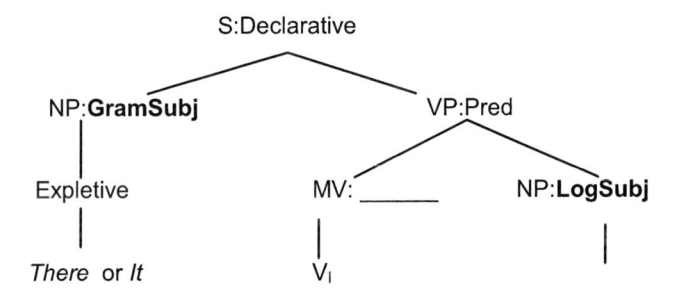

```
                S:Declarative
               /            \
         NP:GramSubj        VP:Pred
              |              /    \
          Expletive        MV:____  NP:LogSubj
              |              |          |
         There or It        V_I
```

The logical subject of an extraposed sentence comes after the verb and after any adverb phrases that may be in the sentence.

Extraposed Sentence	NP:LogSubj
There is something amiss about her farmhouse.	something amiss about her farmhouse
In each drama, there is a male's rejection of the feminine contribution to society.	a male's rejection of the feminine contribution to society
It was her struggle for equality in a field dominated by men that led Schapiro to create "femmage."	her struggle for equality in a field dominated by men that led Schapiro to create "femmage"
It is Fleur, a wild, spirited woman, who invokes fear in the hearts of the members of the community.	Fleur, a wild, spirited woman, who invokes fear in the hearts of the members of the community

Extraposed Sentences with Noun Clauses

In this type of sentence, a noun clause was sometimes the "original" subject. An expletive (*it*) has been put in the subject position and so becomes the GramSubj. The noun clause that was the subject has been moved and labeled as the LogSubj. This type of sentence occurs when the verb in the "original" sentence is a linking verb or a passive verb.

Extraposed Sentence	"Original" Sentence
It is at least understandable that Frost is so bitter about life.	*That Frost is so bitter about life is at least understandable.*
It is prevalent in both texts that Louise Erdich portrays the theme of love.	*That Louise Erdich portrays the theme of love is prevalent in both texts.*
It is said that a picture is worth a thousand words.	*That a picture is worth a thousand words is said.*

It is remarkable that he was able to finish the marathon.

```
                    S:Declarative
              _____|_____
      NP:GramSubj              VP:Pred
         |              _____|_____
         Expl   MV: Pres  AdjP:PredAdj    NP:LogSubj
                    |           |              |
                    V_L        Adj          NClause
                                        _____|_____
                                   Subord  NP:Subj   VP:Pred
                                             |      ____|____
                                             N   MV:past  AdjP:PredAdj
                                             |      |       ____|____
                                            Pro_P  AdjP:Head  InfPh:AdjComp
                                                    |        _____|_____
                                                   V_L Adj  Subord    VP
                                                                   ___|___
                                                                MV:Inf  NP:DO
                                                                  |    __|__
                                                                 V_T  Det  N
                                                                       |   |
                                                                      Art  Nc

   It   is  remarkable   that   he   was   able   to   finish   the  marathon
```

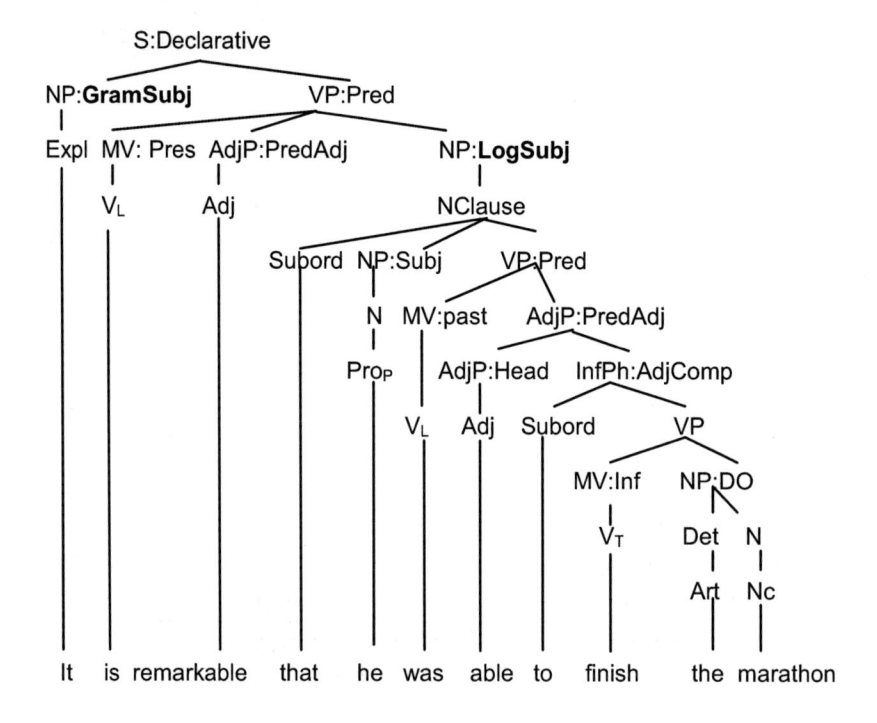

Sentence Varieties

In the sentences we have been looking at, the original verb was linking or passive. In other extraposed sentences with noun clauses, the original sentence had an active verb; in the extraposed version, a noun clause is created.

Extraposed Sentence	"Original" Sentence
It was after this incident that the attraction between the two grew into a relationship.	After this incident, the attraction between the two grew into a relationship.

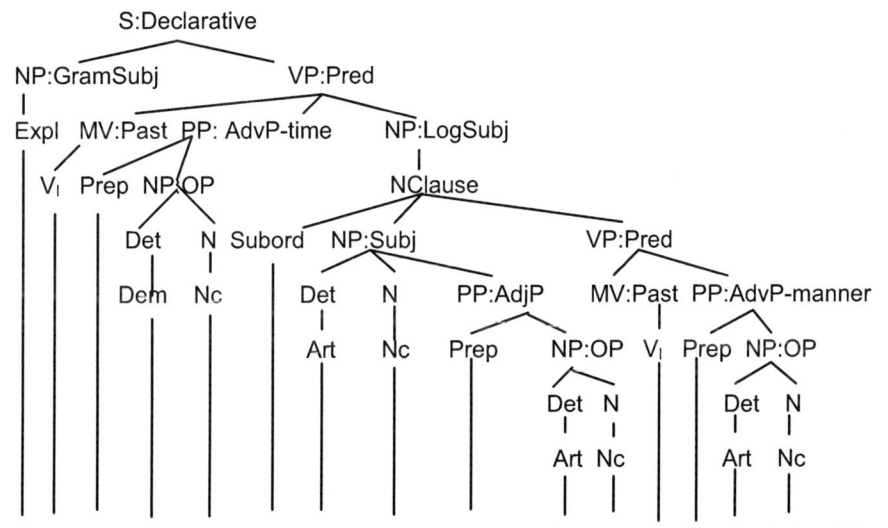

```
              S:Declarative
          _____
      NP:GramSubj        VP:Pred
          |         _____
        Expl   MV:Past  PP: AdvP-time    NP:LogSubj
          |     /      /        \            |
         V₁   Prep    NP:OP                NClause
          |    |    _____          _____
          |    |   Det    N    Subord    NP:Subj           VP:Pred
          |    |    |     |      |    _____   _____
          |    |   Dem   Nc      |   Det    N   PP:AdjP  MV:Past  PP:AdvP-manner
          |    |    |    |       |    |    |    /   \     |       /     \
          |    |    |    |       |   Art  Nc  Prep  NP:OP V₁   Prep    NP:OP
          |    |    |    |       |    |   |    |    / \   |     |      / \
          |    |    |    |       |    |   |    |  Det N   |     |    Det N
          |    |    |    |       |    |   |    |   |  |   |     |     |  |
          |    |    |    |       |    |   |    |  Art Nc  |     |    Art Nc
          |    |    |    |       |    |   |    |   |  |   |     |     |  |
```

It was after this incident that the attraction between the two grew into a relationship

Extraposed Sentences with Infinitive Phrases

In the "original" of this type of sentence, the subject was an infinitive phrase. As we have seen, the original subject has been moved and labeled as the LogSubj; the expletive is labeled as the GramSubj.

Extraposed Sentence	"Original" Sentence
It is the goal of many teenaged girls to look like a model.	To look like a model is the goal of many teenaged girls.
It is unrealistic to expect complete understanding.	To expect complete understanding is unrealistic.

It requires nerves of steel to tree infinitive phrases.

```
                         S:Declarative
                 ┌───────────────┴──────────────┐
          NP:GramSubj                        VP:Pred
              │              ┌──────────────┬──────────────┐
            Expl         MV:Pres         NP:DO          NP:LogSubj
                             │         ┌────┴────┐           │
                             Vᴛ        N       PP:AdjP    InfPh:Nominal
                             │         │      ┌───┴───┐   ┌──────┴──────┐
                             │        Nc    Prep    NP:OP Subord       VP
                             │         │     │       │     │       ┌────┴────┐
                             │         │     │       N     │      MV:Inf    NP:DO
                             │         │     │       │     │       │      ┌──┴──┐
                             │         │     │       Nc    │       Vᴛ    AdjP   N
                             │         │     │       │     │       │      │    │
                             │         │     │       │     │       │     Adj   Nc
                             │         │     │       │     │       │      │    │
                             It     requires nerves  of   steel    to    tree infinitive phrases
```

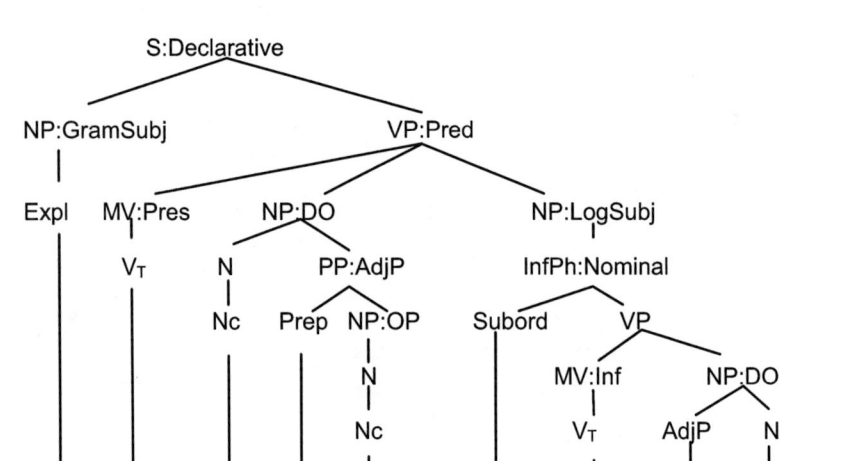

Extraposed Sentences with Gerund Phrases

In the "original" of this type of sentence, the subject was a gerund phrase. As with the other extraposed sentences, the original subject has been moved and labeled as the LogSubj. The expletive *it* is labeled as the GramSubj.

Extraposed Sentence	"Original" Sentence
It is worthwhile getting a degree in English.	*Getting a degree in English is worthwhile.*
Kelina says that it is dangerous driving while eating and talking on a cell phone.	*Kelina says that driving while eating and talking on a cell phone is dangerous.*

Sentence Varieties

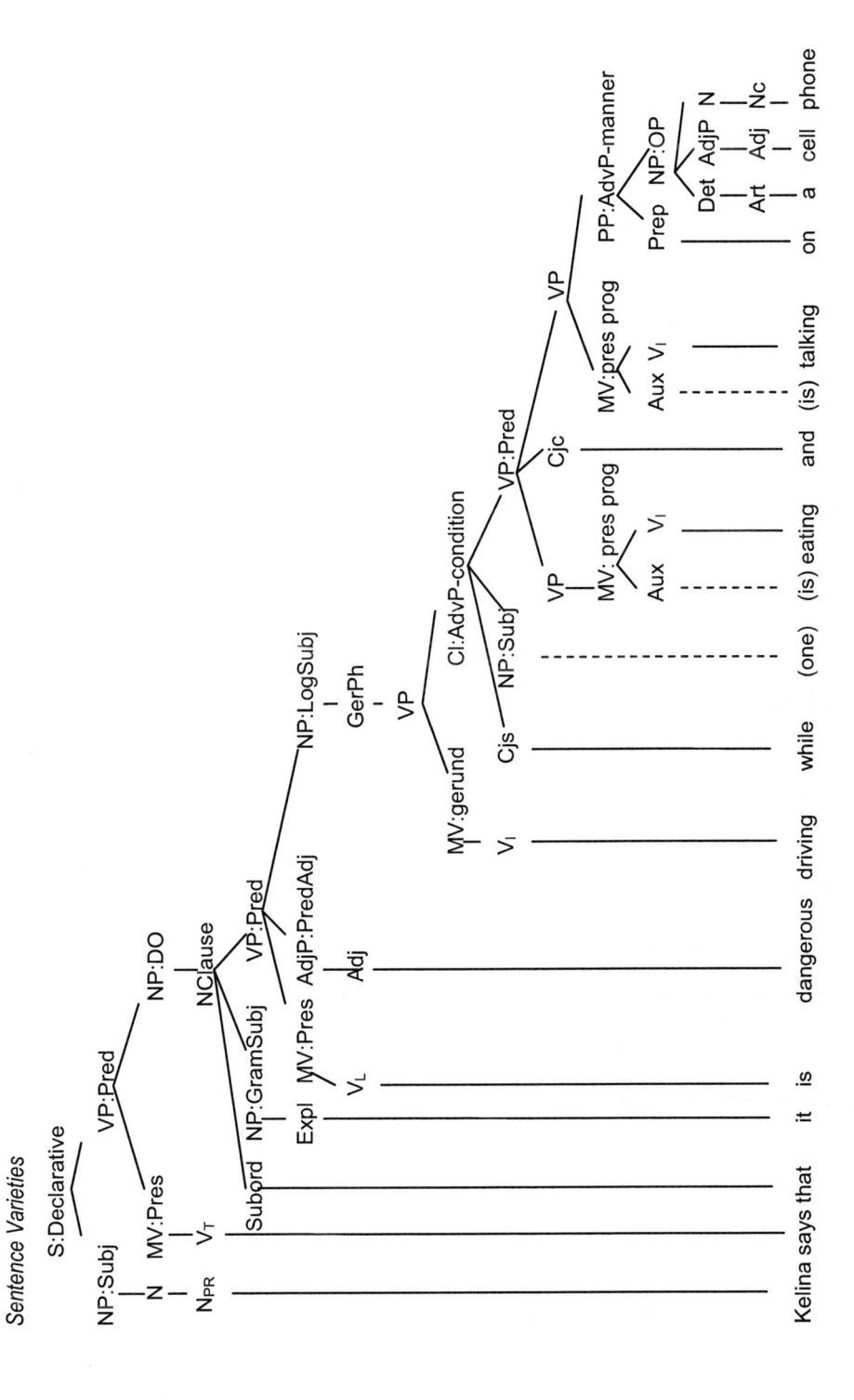

231

Kelina says that it is dangerous driving while (one) (is) eating and (is) talking on a cell phone

Not all sentences which begin with *it* or *there* are extraposed. In the following sentence, the word *it* is a personal pronoun, not an expletive. This time the pronoun <u>does</u> refer to something; it has a **referent**.

- *It is located just south of the isthmus that connected the Greek mainland with the Peloponnese.*

Inverted Sentences

English is highly dependent upon word order. That is the reason we could identify the patterns that we have been working with throughout this book. However, occasionally in English we invert the natural order for stylistic effect. Sometimes this is called poetic inversion.

In cases such as this, we would tree the <u>normal</u> grammatical order and then use <u>arrows</u> to show the inversion.

Inverted Sentence	Tree it like this and show movement.
Blessed are the poor in spirit.	*The poor in spirit are blessed.*
On the desk in the library are the reference materials we will be needing.	*The reference materials we will be needing are on the desk in the library.*
Not only has he cleaned the garage; he has also fixed the sink.	*He has not only cleaned the garage; he has also fixed the sink.*

Notice that the last example has a semicolon. You may tree this example using the semicolon as a type of Pro-form for a Cjcorr.

Sentence Varieties and Usage

Subject/Verb Agreement

With extraposed and inverted sentences, writers must be a bit more careful to make subjects and verbs agree.

- In an inverted sentence, the subject comes <u>after</u> the verb, but an adverb phrase may come before the verb. Make sure that the verb agrees with the subject.
    - *After the rain showers **comes** the rainbow.* (The subject is *the rainbow*, not *the rain showers*.)

- In an extraposed sentence, the verb agrees with the logical subject. However, if the extraposed sentence starts with the expletive *it*, I would think that the verb will always be a singular form of the verb *be*. (At least, I cannot think of any example of an extraposed sentence starting with *it* that doesn't have a singular verb.) If the extraposed sentence begins with the expletive *there*, the verb could be singular or plural. Look at the logical subject.
    - *There are going to be three parties this weekend.*
    - *There is a mix of raisins, chocolate chips, and nuts in this snack.*

Ending a Question with a Preposition

Questions present another challenge to a writer or speaker trying to follow the rule about not ending a sentence with a preposition. Sometimes what seems like a preposition ending a question is actually a verb particle.

- *What are you looking up?*

This is an acceptable question; one would not say "*Up what are you looking?*" merely to avoid ending the question with the word *up*.

However, the following question does end with a preposition and can be rewritten for **formal language use.**

- Question Ending in a Preposition
    - *Whom are you conducting research with?*
- The Question Rewritten
    - *With whom are you conducting research?*

Who vs. Whom

Questions also can give a challenge to writers and speakers who have trouble deciding between *who* and *whom*. The interrogative pronoun *who* is used when the Pro_Inter is substituting for an NP:Subj. The interrogative pronoun *whom* is used when the Pro_Inter is substituting for NP:DO, NP:IO, or NP:OP within the question. When the interrogative pronoun is the object of a preposition, the preposition should stay in a position directly in front of the object of the preposition, as we saw in the example above.

Extraposed Sentences and Modifiers

One danger with extraposed sentences is that a modifier might be incorrectly "attached" to the expletive word. The expletive word is not a head.

- Incorrectly Placed Modifier
    - Coming from such an incredibly hard and unloving family life, it is easy to understand why Maggie would be excited about Pete's interest in her.
- Correctly Placed Modifier
    - It is easy to understand why Maggie, coming from such an incredibly hard and unloving family life, would be excited about Pete's interest in her.

A Note about Style

Most writers think of an extraposed sentence as a weaker one since the expletive is only a placeholder. Extraposed sentences can vary the rhythm of your sentences, and they can add some emphasis to the logical subject that comes at the end of the sentence. However, as a general rule, extraposed sentences are not as concise as they could be. Writers should at least consider rewriting their extraposed sentences to eliminate the "deadwood" words. See the charts earlier in the chapter for ways to rewrite extraposed sentences.

Practice Sentences

I. Tree the following sentences. Watch for review structures.

1. There might be some intriguing problems in the text.
2. It is important to remember that tidal pool creatures should not be removed from the beach.
3. She smiled again and returned to the table, filling her own plate from the leftovers, of which there weren't many.
4. Keep up with the weeds in the vegetable garden and fertilize the flower gardens.
5. Every night parties and receptions were given for the elite guests, weren't they?
6. Behind each order for a sausage and pepper sandwich at the state fair lies a customer's trust that the food will not make him sick.
7. Whom are you calling brain-dead?

Sentence Varieties 235

8. Throughout the whole poem, the main character feels that there is something amiss about her farmhouse.
9. Why do wild Canadian geese walk down the middle of the road?
10. What might be the effect of these engineered plants on the nontarget organisms?
11. It pleased Laura that Tia thought the food was delightful.
12. Thom was anxious for his wife to have the baby, wasn't he?
13. It has been announced who the president will be for the next term.
14. When canoeing, take extra life preservers to be safe.
15. When did Jennifer decide to go downtown and see the new mall?
16. Tell us what you know and how you know it.
17. At the office was the agent in charge to whom he explained what had happened to the little boy's parents.
18. So must the workers of Pharaoh have transported the image of their god king to its original place, chanting as they went.
19. Why would you want to do something like that?
20. It was sad watching the turtle's death on the road.
21. Was the teacher thrilled to see her students learning to tree sentences?
22. Included in the unconditional surrender clause was the deposition of the Japanese emperor, Hirohito.
23. Why can't life be given to me on a silver platter?
24. Do the laundry and the dishes by the time I get home.
25. Stop sulking and try to forget about what happened yesterday when you went to his house.
26. It is ridiculous that an ounce of lead can destroy a life.
27. It was a very nice day until the snowflakes began to fall, ruining our plans.
28. With rights come responsibilities.
29. It is true that whether you believe that God exists is irrelevant to the certainty of his existence.
30. There is no way for us to know the best time for digging potatoes from the garden.
31. Is it necessary to receive nine weeks of training to be a camp counselor?
32. It has been difficult determining why many older people don't move to Florida for the winters.

33. It is Fleur, a wild, spirited woman, who invokes fear in the hearts of the members of the community.
34. What did the girl do when the horse ate her lunch instead of the oats and hay?
35. How did you guess which number was the right one?
36. It was almost impossible for the alligator to eat the frozen mouse floating in the pool.
37. Put the bike where it belongs to keep it in good condition through the winter months.
38. Either fix that run-down car or buy a new one.
39. Is it confusing if you don't read the chapter?
40. It is not imperative that Sally be voted class president.
41. To whom did the company vice president give the plans?
42. How often did that poor man attempt to cross the ocean in a balloon?
43. It is important for us to learn infinitive phrases to be able to teach our students one day.
44. How long will our country be united in this tragic time?
45. It would appear that the police are leaving no stone unturned.
46. How much are the cantaloupes that are on sale at Cub Foods?
47. Is Frost so bitter because he has experienced tragedy in his life?
48. For what were they saving money?
49. Just what a first lieutenant was supposed to do I had no idea.
50. Though it would have been difficult to fault Fatima's arrangements, there were a few household matters to be attended to.

II. Write (or rewrite) sentences as indicated.

1. In the sentences above are some extraposed sentences. Find 4 of them and rewrite them to eliminate the expletive. Remember, some writing style guides say one should never start a sentence with an expletive *there* or *it*.

2. To practice formal Standard English, write 6 questions, 3 which start with *who* and 3 which start with *whom*. For the ones with *whom*, start the question with the following choices: *whom do ..., whom did..., whom will..., whom are..., whom is....* Don't end the question with a preposition.

3. To practice formal Standard English, practice writing three questions beginning with a preposition followed by an interrogative pronoun as the OP.

4. Write 2 sentences that are inverted. Watch for subject/verb agreement. On at least one of them, try for a "poetic" effect!

'no' is Det - Quant

Chapter 14
Launching Out

One of the biggest problems with analyzing English is that people insist on continuing to use (and change) the language! It would be easier if everyone had decided upon an organized system and then kept to that system, but writers and speakers of English have always been and continue to be creative, mostly in word choice but also in sentence structure. Now that you have grasped the basics of the previous chapters, it is time to launch out to try to analyze the sentences that writers actually craft. We now ask the favorite question of advanced grammarians:

> **What is going on in <u>this</u> sentence?**

As you read the following section, try to figure out how you would explain the following sentences grammatically before you read my speculations.

Challenging Sentences

- *Reg had notified the group leaders shortly after the bus broke down.*
- *More than 20 million seahorses are plucked from the world's oceans each year.*
- *The Danube had a dual personality even before the bombing.*
- *Even before the attack on Pearl Harbor, the U.S. was racing Germany to be the first to develop the necessary technology to harness atomic energy into weapons.*

This set of sentences shows a pattern we have not seen before. In early chapters, we looked at qualifiers that came before single-word adjectives and single-word adverbs. In the sentences above, qualifiers are in front of an adverb clause, a cardinal number, and prepositional phrases. The qualifiers are *shortly, more than,* and *even.* One would not have thought that we qualified entire phrases and clauses or that cardinal numbers would be qualified, but that is clearly what is happening here.

- *Engineered crops can help feed the developing world, where poor farming conditions and low-tech prices leave yields far below the potential.*

We saw in Chapter 10 that prepositional phrases can function as predicate adjectives. Here is a sentence in which a prepositional phrase (*below the potential*) is functioning as AdjP:OC. The word *far* is a qualifier in front of a prepositional phrase, as we saw in the sentences above.

- *The chest is worth $200.00.*

Here is another interesting predicate adjective (*worth $200.00*). I would say that *worth* is the AdjP:Head and *$200.00* is the adjectival complement. I think this is a variation of the adjectival phrase *worthy of $200.00,* which would be an adjective with a prepositional phrase adjectival complement. We looked at these in Chapter 9.

- *Laughing while having a mouthful of green jellybeans, I choked and sprayed green spit all over the white couch as my mother watched in horror.*

A couple of interesting things are in this sentence. First of all, we see another qualifier (*all*) in front of an adverbial prepositional phrase. This is similar to the sentences above. Perhaps at this point we would conclude that having qualifiers in front of phrases and clauses is not terribly unusual. The first phrase is more interesting. *Laughing* is a participle, and the phrase *having a mouthful of green jellybeans* also seems like a participial phrase. They are located in front of a head (*I*). However, instead of a Cjc connecting them, we find the word *while,* which is usually a Cjs. We could conclude that *while* is acting as a Cjc between two participial phrases. However, I think a better theory is that the sentence shows ellipsis. We have one participial phrase (*laughing. . .*) and one adverbial clause with words missing: *while **I was** having a mouthful of green jellybeans.*

- *The cross-country skier skied to build endurance for the race next month.*

Of interest here is the NP *next month*. We saw in Chapter 5 that an NP can function as an adverb. At first glance, that is what seems to be happening here. However, *next month* is not adverbial. It is adjectival, describing *the race*. So, *next month* is either an NP functioning as an AdjP:App, or this is a relative clause with ellipsis: *which will take place next month*.

- *I am not sure why Beemer prefers pink puppy snacks.*

There are at least two possible interpretations for this sentence. I think the best explanation is that *sure* is a predicate adjective and *why Beemer prefers pink puppy snacks* is the adjectival complement clause. (Before now, we had not seen a *Wh* clause acting as an adjectival complement.) The other explanation uses ellipsis and hypothesizes a missing preposition of: *I am not sure (of) why Beemer prefers pink puppy snacks.* In this case, there is a prepositional phrase that is acting as the adjectival complement.

- *The book sitting on the shelf is for sale to members only.*

The interesting part of this sentence comes after the linking verb. I think that *for sale to members only* is all acting as a PP:PredAdj. The prepositional phrase *to members only* is adjectival, attached to *sale*, and the word *only* is a post noun.

- *Normally shy and taciturn, David was quite a conversationalist when he was with us.*
- *A century ago, only a few golden seals hunted birds.*

In the first sentence, the *normally* is a qualifier that goes with both *shy* and *taciturn*. The *quite* is a pre-determiner. In the second sentence, the word *ago* is an adjectival appositive. The words *only a few* represent more of a challenge. The word *only* seems to be acting as a qualifier, and we saw above that we are finding qualifiers in front of various types of adjectival and adverbial structures. We have seen that a qualifier can come in front of a cardinal number, for example.

However, that still does not solve our problem because in English we have only one determiner in each NP cluster. Two possible solutions present

Challenging Sentences 241

themselves. One is that we cluster *a few* and make it into an AdjP similar to a cardinal number (such as *a hundred)*; then *only* is the qualifier for that AdjP. The other solution is to say that ellipsis has taken place. Then we would tree *only a few **of the** golden seals.* This is once again a structure that we recognize with *only* as a pre-determiner and *of the golden seals* as an adjectival prepositional phrase following the N *few*.

- *Sarah felt too restless doing her homework to persevere when the cute boy gave her the look.*

We can see first that there is an adverb clause at the end (*when the cute boy gave her the look*), and we might think that the infinitive phrase (*to persevere*) is adverbial because of its location. However, it is actually an adjectival complement infinitive phrase going with the adjective *restless*. The active participial phrase *doing her homework* is adverbial and has been inserted between the adjective and adjective complement. Finally, we see that *felt* in this sentence is a linking verb and that the predicate adjective *restless* has a qualifier in front (*too*).

- *A ship can stir up so many dinoflagellates that its wake can be seen for miles.*
- *The sea turtle was wrapped so tightly in fishing line that its left flipper had to be amputated.*

These sentences have a feature in common with the one we just looked at. In the first sentence, the N (*dinoflagellates*) comes between an AdjP:Head (*so many*) and the clause functioning as an adjectival complement clause (*that its wake can be seen for miles*). The word *so* is a qualifier. In the second sentence, the PP:AdvP-place (*in the fishing line*) comes between the AdvP:Head (*so tightly*) and the noun clause functioning as an adverbial complement clause (*that its left flipper had to be amputated*). Therefore, these last sentences have shown us that in English we sometimes separate an adjectival complement or adverbial complement from its head.

- *If a driver passes a truck on a two-lane highway, she may have to quickly speed up to avoid a head-on collision.*

Some of this sentence we can easily identify. *If a driver passes a truck on a two-lane highway* is an adverb clause of condition; *quickly* is an adverb of manner; *speed up* contains a verb particle, and *to avoid a head-on collision* is an adverbial infinitive. It is the verb cluster that is interesting. It looks as if we have a modal (*may*) and a quasi-modal (*have to*). However, in English we use only one modal in a verb cluster. The explanation I would give is that *may have to* is a cluster quasi-modal, similar to *must*.

- *The sea birds will have to get past the hungry seals.*

I think this is another case of a cluster quasi-modal (*will have to*). *Get* is used as a slang substitute for *go*, and *past the hungry seals* is an adverbial prepositional phrase.

- *The breaking news story on Channel Nine is Johnson's being traded.*
- *Being bought out will have a big impact on the company.*

The interesting part of these sentences is in the gerund phrase (*Johnson's being traded* and *being bought out*). These are passive gerunds. They would have the *being* as an Aux, and the MV label would be passive gerund. The second sentence has a verb particle (*out*).

- *Having jumped in the well, Timmy was now stuck.*

The active participial phrase in this sentence has an auxiliary. The *having* would be the Aux, and the MV label would be perfect active participle.

- *They baked bread to make the bakery smell wonderful.*

This sentence looks simple, but it can be puzzling. The infinitive phrase is adverbial (AdvP-reason). Within the infinitive phrase, *the bakery smell wonderful* all seems to be the direct object. We could say that *the bakery* is the direct object and *smell wonderful* is an object complement infinitive with the *to* dropped: *make the bakery **to** smell wonderful.* It could even be argued that both the *to* and the *for* have been dropped: *they baked bread to make **for** the bakery **to** smell wonderful.* That makes *for the bakery to smell wonderful* into a nominative infinitive acting as the direct object. This

Challenging Sentences 243

second version sounds strange, and we don't talk that way, but it seems to me that this could be what is going on grammatically.

- *Her calling to the mission field made her want to go.*
- *He had let her keep her daughter.*
- *We had to force my brother to eat the squash.*
- *Let me give you some advice.*
- *These stories almost make you feel sympathy for them.*

These sentences are like the one we just discussed. In the first one, the word *to* seems to be missing from the infinitive (*made her **to** want to go*). Either the direct object is *her* with *(to) want to go* as an object complement, or the *for* has also been dropped, and the whole phrase (***for** her **to** want to go*) is the direct object. A similar analysis would apply for the other sentences.

- *Scientists have known for decades about human and animal bones, some as old as 40,000 years, in limestone caves of Ukraine and Siberia.*

The most interesting part of this sentence is *some as old as 40,000 years*. *Some* here is a quantifier pronoun acting as an NP:App. Attached to the NP:App is an AdjP:App (*as old as 40,000 years*). *As old* is the AdjP:Head, with *as* the qualifier. The Cl:AdjComp is *as 40,000 years **is old**,* with *as* acting as the subordinator. See Chapter 10 for a review of this part.

- *They ride bikes to save the environment, even though they are not quite sure it deserves to be saved.*

We have an adverbial infinitive (*to save the environment*) and an adverb clause (*even though they are not quite sure it deserves to be saved*). Within the adverb clause, we have a cluster Cjs (*even though*) and a qualifier (*quite*) in front of the predicate adjective (*sure*). After the predicate adjective comes a that/whether noun clause with the *that* dropped (***that** it deserves to be saved*) acting as an adjectival complement to the predicate adjective. The phrase *to be saved* is a nominal infinitive phrase acting as the direct object to the verb *deserves*.

- *Progress in managing the trade has been made because of the university biologist who founded the project.*

The word *because* is usually a subordinating conjunction (Cjs), and *of* is a preposition. Since what follows these two words is an NP (with a relative clause attached), I would say that *because of* is a cluster preposition.

- *Whether or not the tent leaked didn't matter to Lisa.*

It seems as if *whether or not* should be added to the *that/whether* type noun clause. It is a cluster subordinator.

- *The waves rose from shore to shore.*

We could consider this simply as an adverb of origin followed by an adverb of destination. However, it is fun to speculate on the existence of a correlative preposition *from/to*.

- *The book was kept largely intact at Kells until 1654, when it was removed to Dublin for safety.*

The interesting part of this sentence is that the year, 1654, has a relative clause attached. This relative clause begins with *when* rather than one of the "normal" relative pronouns.

- *Sara is trying to decide whether to take summer classes.*
- *That idiot Anthony was wondering how far to drive to get to the store.*
- *In addition to Roosevelt's promise of unconditional surrender, Truman also inherited the incredibly daunting decision of whether or not to use the atomic bombs against Japan.*

In these sentences, the writer starts a noun clause (*whether...*, *how far...*, *whether or not* ...). Then, at the point one expects to read "*she should*" or "*he should*," the writer uses an infinitive. This mixed construction makes these sentences hard to analyze, and generally mixed construction is considered nonstandard English   To tree these, we would have to use

Challenging Sentences

ellipsis and a quasi-modal: *Sara is trying to decide whether (she needs) to take summer classes; That idiot Anthony was wondering how far (he needs) to drive to get to the store; Truman also inherited the incredibly daunting decision of whether or not (he has) to use the atomic bombs against Japan.* The quasi-modal is *needs to* or *has to*.

Final Tree Assignment

Bring it on!

I. Using the article provided or another current publication, select three sentences to tree. Follow these guidelines.

- Each sentence you select must have at least one embedded phrase or clause (in addition to any prepositional phrases).

- Don't tree a fragment.

- There might be grammatical situations that you have not seen yet. <u>Don't automatically choose another sentence because of this.</u> Instead, follow the models in this chapter and use your knowledge as an advanced grammarian to tree the structure the way that you think it should be analyzed.

- Then, if you are using an original interpretation, write me a note explaining why you analyzed the sentence the way you did.

II. Did you find an interesting sentence that could be included in Chapter 14? To continue to advance as a grammarian, look for additional structures that we didn't cover in the previous chapters. If you find some unique ones, send them to kmb@nwc.edu.

Chapter 15
Applications of Grammar

I hope that you have found some joy at your grammar understanding (what my students and I call "grammar moments") and that you now have some appreciation of our language's operating system. It is okay to both be in awe of our language and to really like doing grammar trees. Beyond that, the study of grammar has allowed you to further understand the human mind. Large areas of our brains are used for language, and when we study language, we are studying in part what it means to be human.

Beyond the enjoyment, the understanding, and the appreciation of the intricacies of our language-using human brains, however, there are other uses for your knowledge of syntax.

We have been answering the question "What is going on in *this* sentence?" There is another question that advancing grammarians might ask:

> What can I do with all of this knowledge of English syntax?

Applications for Writers and Students of Literature

The study that you have done using this textbook will help you think about what you write and read. It enables you to think about your language use and that of others and gives you a vocabulary to talk about it. Finally, a conscious knowledge of grammatical structures potentially gives you more control over your writing.

Punctuation Decisions

Make Punctuation Decisions in your Writing.

We punctuate in English according to structure. Therefore, being able to recognize the various structures will enable you to make punctuation decisions.

Applications of Grammar 247

- See the commentary at the end of many of the chapters for punctuation tips based upon your knowledge of English grammar structure.
- Also, knowing the structures should help you avoid awkward or mixed constructions, fragments, comma splices, or run-ons.

Analyze the Punctuation of a Published Author.

The work of published authors has generally been edited for standard punctuation. Therefore, if you find punctuation that is different from that, it may be a conscious decision on the part of the author. Examine the varied punctuation. Does it have any effect on the text? Also, written English is punctuated differently in America than it is in Britain, for example. When you see differences, consider the place of publication.

Usage Considerations

Reread the sections at the ends of chapters to review the implications for usage. If you plan for standard usage for your audience, use your knowledge gained in reading this book to make decisions as you write.

- However, review the sections on usage and note the comments on formality and informality. Some of the usage admonitions (such as agreement of subjects and verbs) would apply in any situation, but many of the traditional Standard English "rules" apply only in very formal situations. Make your usage choices based upon the rhetorical elements of audience and purpose. The point is that having learned the structures, you now understand those choices.
- You can also judge whether a published author has made decisions on usage which appropriately match the audience and purpose. In an evaluation of rhetoric, if usage does not match the rhetorical elements, the text must be judged to be less effective.

Style Considerations

Make Style Decisions in your Writing.

Many writers find it helpful to work on their style revision after they have written for content. A style analysis such as the one given in the "Applied Grammar Assignment" at the end of this chapter will help you see your basic writing syntax style. Then you can consider style revision. To get you started, at the end of several of the chapters is a discussion of style considerations. Reread these sections. Other ideas are listed below.

Remember, your study of grammar has given you options. Use these ideas for writing style.

- Studies have shown that readers think that writers who use only simple clauses or compound sentences or many prepositional phrases have an immature style. As a writer, you are judged both by what you say and by how you say it. Readers think more highly of a writer who uses various structures and who can embed and combine sentences in various ways. For example, the use of nonrestrictive modifiers is seen as a sign of more mature writing. With your current grammatical knowledge, you should have a large repertoire to use in your writing.

- You can make many decisions based on your knowledge to change the emphasis in your writing. For example, the use of the Emph-DO emphasizes a verb and the use of an appositive or other NP attachment emphasizes the NP:Head.

- You can make decisions to vary the rhythm of your sentences. Some structures slow the pace, and others speed it up.

- You can make decisions to make sure that your forms fit the meaning of the sentence.
    - For example, using a present participial might suggest an ongoing process.
    - Using an active participial phrase in front of the main clause might suggest movement toward the ideas in the main clause, while putting the phrase behind the main clause might suggest movement away.
    - Symmetry in a sentence might emphasize the idea of order, whereas a sentence with a large variety of structures might emphasize an unusual idea in a sentence or a sense of unrest.
    - Examine your use of subordination and coordination of elements in your sentences. Changing the structure can subtly affect the meaning.

- Lots of embedded phrases and clauses might enhance a sense of activity, many things happening at once, or a complexity of human experience that is being portrayed.
- Some structures might reinforce a sense of serenity.

- You can make decisions to affect the clarity or conciseness of your prose.
  - Passives with no adverb of agency phrase are less clear, particularly for journalism and expository writing such as directions.
  - Noun clauses might be harder for the reader to process.
  - Abstract NPs and vague verbs should be rewritten.
  - Adverb infinitives should be placed carefully for maximum clarity.

Do a Style Analysis of Published Authors.

A writer's style is a consistency or pattern of the language choices that have been made. Look first for any punctuation anomalies or nonstandard usage. Use the previous sections to give you ideas for anything interesting that may be present in the author's work. There might not be any deviant punctuation, but the usage might suggest something about intended audience, for example.

Then look at the grammatical structures an author typically uses, under what circumstances, and how often. Look for patterns. Also look for different structures under different circumstances. For example, in fiction, is the passive used to describe apathetic characters? Are more complex patterns used to show the complex thoughts of a character or a complex situation? If the author uses "interior dialogue" for the thoughts of a character, is the style there the same as it is for the narration? Does style differ between the characters?

Specifically, use the ideas presented in the previous section "Make Style Decisions in your Writing" to analyze another author's style. Draw conclusions based on the patterns you see.

You can do various options of a style analysis.
- You can look at an author's early versus late style.

- You can do a historical study of style. What grammatical style did typical authors of a particular time period use? Figure out what structures are used, how often, and where in the sentences. Also, check out sentence length.
- You can compare and contrast the style of two different authors.
- You can analyze the style of a typical genre or within a particular profession or group.
- By looking at dialogue, you can analyze the style of different characters within a single novel or story.

Applications for Teachers

As a teacher of English language arts or a teacher of ESL, you will probably not have the time for a full course in grammar syntax nor will most of your students be able to understand the material as well as college students. Also, most research shows little automatic transference of direct grammar instruction to their skills of reading or writing. Students improve in their writing and reading by <u>doing</u> writing and reading. So, I do not recommend that you teach your students as you have just been taught. Rather, you should <u>use your understanding of English grammar to teach skill lessons</u> to your students that will enable them to more directly benefit. For example, the point is not whether your students can identify participial phrases, but whether they can use them effectively and punctuate them correctly.

Here are some general guidelines or principles that you can use as a teacher of English.

Guidelines for Teachers

- **Make sure that you have a purpose for everything that you teach.** Be particularly careful with lessons that have students label (such as verb types or parts of speech). There might not be a good reason to have them ever learn to label verb types, for example. They don't **need** to learn the names of all grammatical structures. Make sure that <u>you</u> think through the reason for everything that you are teaching before you start work on any teaching plans and materials.

- **Always tell them the reason they are learning something.** You might even start mini-lessons with the reason they will be glad that they know what you are about to teach. Therefore, you will not be having them merely identify structures for no purpose, and you will at least occasionally be able to avoid the whining ("Why do we have to know this?").

- **Teach within the context of their writing or reading.** You are teaching **applied grammar.** They should be using their own writing and that of their classmates as much as possible. Studies have shown that doing exercises and quizzes does not cause students to transfer the learning to their own language use. Instead, newly learned skills should be practiced on their own writing at the time they are learning them.

- **Base the learning as much as possible on student discovery.** Let your students be language "investigators" and really <u>look</u> at language use. If you have <u>guided</u> them into understanding rather than simply told them something, they will be more apt to really learn and apply that knowledge to their own language use. I would recommend that you teach inductively as much as possible. Give them the examples of the language style, usage or punctuation that you want them to learn and then guide them in discovery of the concepts. Of course, make sure that your students have discovered the concepts and that the concepts are clearly stated by the end of the lesson. Make the concepts explicit at that point.

- **Use lots of examples.** The discovery learning should be based on as many examples as possible, including student examples. It is also really motivating for them if you use examples of the concepts you are teaching from their favorite authors.

- **Don't make the learning technical, detailed, or complicated.** Your students don't need a thorough understanding of grammar theory. They do need to be able to <u>use</u> the grammatical structures. I would suggest that you use a few of the basic grammatical terms, but there is no reason to use all of them with younger students.

Therefore, you can call them "ing chunks" (or "ing clusters," if your students have "issues" with the word *chunks*!) rather than gerunds or active participial phrases. Technical language merely scares off the typical ninth grader. As long as they learn to use them for more effective writing, they don't need to know the technical terms. Present any structures you want to teach <u>in groups by their function</u>. Make sure that you always discuss the function of any structure that you teach.

- Have them learn to use **simple structures to begin with**. Then have them move to more complex structures.

- **Make sure that your students are <u>using, not identifying.</u>** You are teaching **applied grammar.** You are using your knowledge of grammar to make application lessons for their writing. It will not help them to do worksheet after worksheet of identifying the structures. They need to be able to use them and punctuate them.

- **Let your students experiment and practice.** Help them to see all the options and provide as much variety as you can. You are teaching them locations, choices or forms, and effects. Let them practice those. Discuss the various options with them and the effects of these sentence options.

- **Most students enjoy games.** When you are teaching these concepts, try to develop a learning game for your students to do in teams. Sentence baseball or Jeopardy would work, for example. Also, most group work can be developed into a game. However, make sure that your students do not lose sight of the application or reason they are doing the game.

- **Use the term "Standard English"** to explain what contemporary uses of English (people with power and money, at least) usually do. Explain that there are other ways of using English that are appropriate in different situations with different audiences.

- **Celebrate language use and style.** Be enthusiastic about the sentences with the new structures. Tell your students how

Applications of Grammar 253

wonderful these structures can be. Have a bulletin board area in which you display "great sentences" that your students have written themselves or have found in magazines or novels.

Writing Style Lessons

Sentence Combining. Show them new ways of combining, using all of the choices you now know about from your study of grammar.
- Give them long lists of simple sentences of coherent text. Use current topics of interest to them for your sentences. Ideally, you can include some interesting pieces of information and words that they didn't know before. You might even get ideas for sentences from textbooks in their other subjects (history or science, for example). Make sure that the sentences really communicate something significant.
- Tell them to combine the sentences into longer ones. This can be done in small groups, if you like.
- With the whole class, discuss the various combinations that are possible. Students in your class have probably combined the sentences differently, but if they have all done it the same way, you should show them other possibilities, using your knowledge of English syntax.
- Teach them how to use coordinating conjunctions (Cjc) and subordinating conjunctions (Cjs).
- Show them that it makes a difference on emphasis which ideas they subordinate using embedded phrases and clauses (less important ones) or where the adverb clause comes in the sentence. Remember, don't use technical language to do this illustrating.
- Be sure to point out appropriate punctuation for the combinations they are using.

Learning to Use New Structures. In small doses, teach them to use the grammar structures that you have learned. This method can be used with any of the structures you know. Depending upon the age and ability of your students, you might want to do only one new structure at a time.
- Show them samples of sentences with the structure you want to teach. Be sure to illustrate how effective the structures make the

sentences, and avoid using technical names that will scare your students off.
- If you have older students and will be discussing more than one structure, give them the same information written with different structures (gerund, noun clause, or nominal infinitive, for example) or written as an extraposed sentence. Discuss the effects of these variations.
- Then give them base sentences. Don't have them write the sentences. Give them some interesting sentences with which to work. Tell them to add the type of structure that you illustrated in step one of this lesson. You might want to do one or two with the whole class and then have them do others in small groups. They will get ideas from each other in small groups and will enjoy using language more.
- With the whole class, discuss the sentences they wrote in small groups. Celebrate how impressive they are!
- Go back to the writing they have done previously. (Save previous writing from each student in folders in your classroom.) Have students now add the structure they learned to appropriate places in previous writing.
- Have students share their new sentences. Discuss them. (Which sentences have been improved? Can you add too many of these to be effective?) Celebrate their new, good sentences.
- Be sure to include in your discussion the appropriate punctuation (or lack of punctuation) for the structure you are teaching them.
- You also might have them do a "grammar hunt" to find examples of the new structure in magazines and newspapers.

Imitation.
- Find some particularly effective passages of unique prose style from various authors. I would recommend that these be about a paragraph in length so that your students get a sense of the rhythm, but you could do a single sentence.
- Share these with your students and discuss them in class.
- Then give your students an idea for a short topic or narrative with which they can **imitate** the author. Have them write sentences that exactly mimic the structures, punctuation, and length of the original.

Applications of Grammar

- Have them share their writing. Your students will probably enjoy the results of their imitation writing, and they will have learned more style options. Some of these finished assignments would make good bulletin board display items. Celebrate their writing!

Parallelism. As you know, items in a series should be parallel in form for most effective writing style. Also, tell your students that effective parallelism can make them seem really smart to their readers, and yet it is quite easy for them to learn.
- For an initial discussion of the concept, you might try giving them sentences that aren't parallel and ones that are to see if they can notice the difference. Remember, you don't need to use the technical names for the structures themselves.
- Provide them with opportunities to rewrite sentences to make them parallel, using their own sentences or other student sentences if possible. You should provide these sentences. The best approach is to have collected nonparallel sentences from their previous writing and then use these in class (without the student names, of course).
- Provide them with opportunities to write sentences with parallel elements. Give them appropriate "base sentences" to work from.
- Include in your discussion the appropriate use of commas for parallel elements.

Transitions. Students often don't add transitions to their prose.
- Give them a list of single-word adverbial conjunctions and cluster adverbial conjunctions. You don't need to call them adverbial conjunctions. Use the term *transitions* or even *connecting words* (for younger students).
- Discuss these transitions and when a writer would use each of them. Don't use technical language to explain the transitions, but do use examples to illustrate the ones with which students might not be familiar.
- Have them practice adding these to a page or two of writing from which all transitions have been removed. You could have them do this in groups and then get them together again as a large class to discuss the additions.

- Finally, if they have previous writing of their own that could use transitions, have them add them to their own writing.

Active vs. Passive.
- Before you start this lesson, review the sections of this book that discuss passive verbs and under what circumstances they might be used.
- Find (or write) examples of sentences with passive verbs and active verbs. Find sentences written in various fields, such as government, journalism, and science. Take sentences from reports and instruction manuals as well as narratives.
- Share these examples with your students. Discuss the possible uses and differing effects of passive or active verbs. Make this into a good lesson on <u>audience and purpose.</u>
- Have them practice changing sentences back and forth between active and passive. You should provide the sentences so that they don't have to think up ideas and can concentrate on the new skill. Make sure that you give them many sentences to practice on so that they can do this switch fairly easily.
- Let them practice writing text, using various scenarios in which active or passive would be better. For example, give them a specific assignment which would call for the use of active rather than passive verbs (writing something for a newspaper would be a good chance for them to practice active verb constructions).

Other Style Lessons. Look at the discussions throughout the chapters in this book for other style lesson ideas. Follow the types of procedures I have given in the other lessons in this section.

Lessons to Add Detail to Writing

Learning Nouns, Verbs, and Adjectives.
- I would suggest that you teach these only so that you make your students aware of how they can <u>use</u> them when they write. For example, you teach nouns, not so that they can underline or circle them on a worksheet, but so that you can discuss, for example, the effect of having specific nouns rather than vague ones. You teach adjectives so that they can improve their description. If you

are asked to teach "parts of speech," make sure that you give your students a use for that knowledge.
- Review Chapter 2. If you are teaching identification, use the methods in that chapter. Use the "clues" provided with your students, but use only the clues that are most effective for that function. Don't ever give your students a list of words and ask them to label them as a certain part of speech. Words can often function as different parts of speech in different sentences.
- **However, always move quickly from the identification to application.** The application for these lessons would be style lessons, perhaps involving the use of a thesaurus. Have your students choose more effective nouns and verbs or have them add effective adjectives.

Types and Placement of Adverb Phrases. You know various structures that we use for adverbs in English, and you know the adverb questions. You also know that adverbs are highly mobile! Introduce your students to the "wonderful world of adverbs."
- Start with a set of simple sentences that you have written and give them the list of adverb questions.
- With the whole class, add some adverbs to your simple sentences that answer some of the adverb questions. At this point, don't worry about the structure (whether they are using all single words or all prepositional phrases, for example). Discuss with your students how adverbs can really help a writer to add detail for the reader.
- In small groups, have them practice adding adverbs, using the adverb questions. They will, of course, need more base sentences for this.
- As a whole class, discuss their new sentences. Are there any of the adverb structures they aren't using? Have prepared before class some of the base sentences to which you have added adverbial infinitive phrases or adverb clauses, for example. Then you can share these to expand their repertoire of adverb structures.
- Now, have them play around with various locations of adverbs in the sentences. Show them examples of how the emphasis

changes when the adverb moves to a different location in the sentence. Tell them that adverbs (unlike most of the other structures in English) are highly mobile. Make sure that they see all of the options and some possible effects.
- If they have previously written stories, for example, this would be a good time to get those out of the folders and have your students add adverb structures to their own writing.

Types and Positions of Adjectival or Nominal Additions. This lesson will work best with older students. The lesson includes more than one structure, and some of the structures may confuse younger students. It could be simplified for younger students.
- Start with simple sentences that you provide.
- Show your students the various structures that we can add to simple nouns or nominal phrases that describe or rename (Chapters 8. 9, and 11). Try to get students to give you suggestions for additions to your simple sentences. Make sure you are illustrating that the same adjectival or appositive information can be given in various ways. Emphasize the choices that they have.
- Don't use all the technical terms. Choose the structures you want to name (perhaps relative clauses, for example), but present the other structures with informal explanations. You could use the concept of "head" to teach these structures.
- Discuss the effectiveness of these structures for readers. Discuss not using the same type all the time (all relative clauses, for example).
- Have them practice by adding adjectival structures in small groups to sentences which you provide. You might write sentences about a school event or other topic which they might be interested in.
- Discuss the various locations of adjective structures (in front of N, after linking verb, after the NP). Show them that adjectival appositives or nominal appositives go after the NP.
- Have them (as individuals) go back to their previous writing and add adjectival structures to improve their detail for the reader.
- Celebrate their effective new sentences with the class.

Grammar to Help Organize Material into Paragraphs

Paragraphing. If your students are trying to cover too many topics in a paragraph, you might try this lesson during revision sessions.
- Have the students circle or highlight the subjects of the sentences in a paragraph.
- Then discuss the subjects. Are they related? Is the paragraph coherent? Should some of these subjects be in a paragraph of their own?
- Students would then reorganize and even develop some topics more fully.

Usage Lessons

Standard English Language Formations. You can teach students (particularly younger ones) how we "do things" (plurals, possessives, verb forms, comparisons or superlatives, etc.) in English. Any of these lessons would be vital for ESL education, of course.
- Show them lots of examples and guide them into discovery of the principles behind the language skill that you want to teach.
- Don't use technical terms such as "progressive" and "perfect." Your goal is not to have them identify these verb types but to be aware of all the possibilities we use in Standard English.
- Make sure that you include a discussion of dialects and that some speakers of English say things a bit differently. Tell them that one method of language use is not better than another linguistically. However, tell your students that they are now practicing Standard English, which is the usage that people with power (and money) use. Tell them that they are learning another option for their speaking and writing.

Misplaced Modifier.
Review the discussion of misplaced modifiers, particularly in Chapter 10.
- Find or write examples of sentences with misplaced modifiers. These sentences can often be humorous. Enjoy the humor with your class.
- As you share these examples with the class, teach them the basic concept of a head. A misplaced adjectival modifier may have "wandered" from its head. A dangling modifier has no head. (If

your students are in middle school, they will probably like the concept of a detached head!)
- With the class, have them rewrite the sentences to fix the modifier problem.
- If possible, collect sentences from their own writing which have misplaced modifiers. Have them work in small groups to correct these.
- Add misplaced modifiers to their personal lists of usage they now know and can look for when they edit their writing or the writing of classmates.

Subject and Verb Agreement. Teach this lesson if you see that they are having trouble with this, particularly in their writing. This is a problem generally when their sentences get longer, and it becomes harder for them to see the subject and verb.
- Before you begin this lesson, discuss with them that not all dialects handle subject and verbs in the same way. You are teaching them standard usage because in most writing situations, it is appropriate to use Standard English for subject and verb agreement. If they learn this, they will have the option to use Standard English.
- They need to find these elements to make them agree. Teach them to recognize prepositional phrases. Have them draw parentheses around the prepositional phrases and then ignore them to figure out the subject and verb. As you know, neither the subject nor the verb will be in a prepositional phrase. Therefore, being able to recognize these phrases (and then temporarily to ignore them) will be helpful for your students. Since we use so many prepositional phrases in English, this method alone might help them find the subject and verb.
- Try to have them use tag questions to find the subject. Review Chapter 13 for a discussion of tag questions. If a tag question is added to a statement, the pronoun at the end of the tag question will refer to the subject. This might help them find the subject of the sentence.
- Teach them that the noun "substitutes" (including demonstrative pronouns, personal pronouns, quantitative pronouns, and indefinite pronouns, as well as gerunds, noun clauses, and

Applications of Grammar 261

nominative infinitives) can be subjects. Remember, don't use technical names for these structures and don't ask your students to identify which structure is which. All you want them to do is be able to find the subject so that it agrees with the verb.
- One idea for helping them find the verb of the sentence is to have them make the sentence negative. Chapter 6 covers the use of the negative verb. If they add *did not/don't*, the verb will be after the negative addition. If they add *not*, the verb cluster will start with the word in front of *not* and will continue after *not* (unless it is a BE-verb).
- Some teachers have had success having them find the verb first, using the method above, and then insert the verb into the following question: *Who or what _____?* The answer should be the subject.
- Once they have identified the subject and verb, they need to make them agree. At this point, you will need to teach them about how verbs in English are inflected for number. Again, give them many examples, and I do not recommend that you use a phrase such as "inflected for number" with your students.
- You might have them substitute an appropriate pronoun for the subject. This substitution makes subject-verb agreement easier.
- Have them practice reading sentences, some of which are standard for subject and verb agreement and some of which are not. Have them identify and correct the nonstandard ones. This can be done in groups or individually. Be sure that you discuss the standard answers in class.

Pronoun Usage. See Chapter 4 for some specific ideas for lessons. Teach any of these lessons if you see that your students are having trouble with this when they are trying to write or speak in Standard English. Some teachers have had success using colors to teach pronoun case. (The subject forms can be red, for example, and the object forms can be blue.) This way, students can grasp the concept without the terminology.
- Be sure to tell them the reason you want them to learn this. This would be a good time to discuss the idea that English has several dialects but that knowing Standard English, as well as other dialects they might know, can be an advantage to them in life.

- For any of these concepts, you might try to have them discover the pattern by providing many examples of standard usage. Have them work in groups to see if they can discover the rule for Standard English. Guide the discovery process by telling them what part of the sentence they should be looking at.
- Discuss what they find. Be ready to explain the concept if they have not been able to discover it.
- Give them enough practice, preferably with sentences you have taken from their own writing (without their names).
- You could also give them a "language detective" assignment and have them listen to conversations outside of your classroom and record instances of nonstandard usage and standard usage. In a future class session, you can discuss what they discovered, when Standard English was used and when it was not.

Other Usage Lessons. Look at the discussions throughout the chapters in this book for other usage lesson ideas. Follow the guidelines and model the lessons after the other usage lessons in this section.

Punctuation Lessons

Sentences and Fragments. Follow the guidelines and pattern this lesson like a usage lesson. Teach this lesson if they have been having trouble with fragments in their writing. Make sure that you tell them that fragments are acceptable under some circumstances. You are teaching them this lesson so that they can use full sentences when they want to use Standard English.
- Find or write sentences with which they can practice. Don't have them write fragments for the purpose of correcting. It is best if the sentences are in sustained text rather than in a list. That is more realistic, and it also makes the correction more valid, because it is within a context.
- Try to have them change the piece of text into a yes/no question. If they can do this, chances are they had a sentence rather than a fragment.
- Complete sentences (rather than fragments) should fit into a test frame and make sense:
    They explained the idea that _____.

- Have them try to put the piece of text they are figuring out into the blank. If it makes sense, it is a full sentence and not a fragment.
- Fragments might fit into one of the test frames for the parts of speech. If a piece of text fits into one of these other test frames, it is fragment, not a complete sentence.
- Make sure that you show them various ways of fixing a fragment to make complete sentences. You can combine it with another sentence or add material to it. Always have them fix fragments as part of the lesson.
- You can have them check every sentence in a piece of their previous writing by using the "sentence clues" given above. Even if they have no fragments, this will be practice in a useful skill for proofreading in the future.

Commas. Teach them "chunks that need to be set off by commas." Instead of giving comma rules, try the following.
- Show them lots of examples of structures that are being set off by commas and ask them to see a pattern. Use Chapters 5, 8, 9, 10, and 11 to find these structures.
- Lead them to see that **introducers** and **interrupters** are set off from the rest of the sentence with commas. Note that you can use these terms rather than the technical labels. <u>Do not have your students label the various structures</u>. You want to teach them to punctuate, not to label.
- Discuss the effect of commas versus dashes.
- Give them simple or base sentences and have them add introducers and interrupters, punctuating them correctly.
- Have them go back to their previous writing, looking for introducers and interrupters to set off, or have them add these structures to their writing.
- Remember, don't have them write for the purpose of punctuating. Have them punctuate writing they have already done for an assignment that had an audience and purpose.

Reading Lessons

Your knowledge of syntax will aid you in helping your students read better.

Reading Complex Sentences. To aid your students in reading difficult sentences, teach them to "find the clusters." Use sentences from their reading (perhaps textbooks for other classes) and show them the pieces of the sentence. Don't teach the technical names for the pieces. The idea here is that their comprehension will be improved if they can learn to see the major clusters of the sentence and process the clusters, rather than the individual words.

- Show them how to recognize the "introductory pieces" of a sentence, which precede the subject.
- Teach them at least three of the basic sentence patterns from Chapter 3 (linking verbs, intransitive verbs, and basic transitive verbs). Then show them these patterns at work in their reading. Their reading comprehension will be improved as they see these basic patterns as they read. In a difficult sentence, it is imperative for them to find the subject, verb, and, if there is one, the object, predicate nominative, or predicate adjective.
- Show them the pieces of a sentence that can come at the end.
- Teach them about "interrupters" which come somewhere inside a sentence.

Better Understanding of Parts of a Sentence. This could be a lesson on the idea that words can function as various parts of speech. For example, contemporary English is showing a growing tendency to use words generally considered nouns or even adjectives as verbs in a sentence. If this type of usage occurs in their reading, a short lesson on this can improve their understanding, particularly if you discuss the connotations involved when an author uses a word to jump grammatical categories.

Recognizing Common Expressions. These might be like the whole-sentence modifiers discussed in Chapter 12. The point is that there are common expressions that occur, particularly in specialized prose and more formal or academic prose. Teaching these specific expressions will help students process their reading more quickly.

Doing Close Reading to Appreciate Literature. With some of the literary texts they are reading, you can lead them in a close reading. Point out to them what happens in the sentence and what effects the author has achieved. Include the rhythm of the sentence. If you don't scare them off with the technical terms, they should come to appreciate the author a bit more.

Applications for Students of Other Languages

As we saw in Chapter 1, early language scholars used Latin grammar to study English. Then, however, linguists found that since English grammar is not the same as the grammar of Latin, this approach had several problems. Most modern linguists would say that a language should be studied without trying to impose another grammatical structure onto it.

Nonetheless, there are some similarities in the grammar of all languages. (All languages have nouns, for example.) I believe that your study of English grammar will benefit your study of other languages because you have been practicing thinking consciously about grammar. Grammar analysis is a skill that can transfer <u>(as a skill, not as a body of knowledge)</u> to your study of another language. Your best use of your knowledge of English grammar is to compare its similarities and contrast its differences to the grammar of the language you are learning.

Applied Grammar Assignments

Writing Majors

Using your knowledge of syntax, do a style analysis of your own prose.

- Find a sample of your own prose that has little or no dialogue or quotations from others. You must have at least 25 sentences (excluding dialogue or quotes) with which to work. Use consecutive sentences, skipping the ones with quotes.
- Complete charts like the one at the end of this chapter, using as many sheets as you need for all of the sentences. Analyze each of your sentences carefully so that the chart is accurate. If you don't recognize some structures, use your textbook, especially the review section in Chapter 11.
- Review the sections of the chapters of this book dealing with usage, punctuation, and style. Make sure that you have read this chapter for ideas as well.

- Then, take some notes about what you discovered about your writing. What do you see in your writing style? What tendencies do you notice? Are there any patterns? What structures do you never use? Where do you put adverb structures? List the effects of the various structures within your sentences. What did you learn about your writing style?
- Rewrite this same passage in a different way, using different grammatical structures and combining ideas in different ways. As you rewrite, use your chart. Use structures that you didn't have before. Experiment with your syntax.
- Fill out charts for your rewritten version. There should be distinct changes!
- Take some notes about your rewritten passage. What changes did you make? What is the effect of these changes? How did the rewriting change the effect of your prose? Which changes were effective and why? Which changes were not effective and why not? What else did you notice or decide?
- Write a short paper (minimum of 750 words) about your analysis. Be specific in the support of your conclusions. Use specific examples from your writing to illustrate your insights.
- Hand in everything, including the original sample of your writing.

Literature Majors

Choose a prose author in whom you are interested and do a simple style analysis using your knowledge of syntax. Follow the steps below.

- Find a sample of this author's prose. You must have at least 25 sentences (excluding dialogue) with which to work. (A more complete and valid style analysis would involve more sentences.) Use consecutive sentences, skipping the ones with quotes.
- Complete charts like the one at the end of this chapter, using as many sheets as you need for all of the sentences. Analyze each of your sentences carefully so that the chart is accurate. If you don't recognize some structures, use your textbook, especially the review section in Chapter 11.
- Review the sections of the chapters of this book dealing with usage, punctuation, and style. Also, make sure that you have read this chapter for ideas.

Applications of Grammar

- Then, take some notes about what you discovered about your author's writing. What do you see in the writing style? What tendencies do you notice? Are there any patterns? What structures does the author never use? Where does the author put adverb structures? List the effects of the various structures within the sentences. What have you learned so far about the writing style of your author?
- Try writing some of the sentences in a way that is different from the original. Use different structures and combine ideas in different ways. Type this up. Playing with an author's work in this way might show you more about the original work.
- Write up an analysis of this writer's style, using your data. Draw conclusions about the patterns you are seeing and their implications upon the style of writing. What do you notice? How do these grammatical structures influence the style? What effect do they have? (Make sure that you have read this chapter and the style sections of the other chapters for ideas.)
- Write a short paper (minimum of 750 words) about your analysis. Make sure you use your notes and organize your thoughts into paragraphs. Use specific examples to illustrate your insights.
- Hand in everything, including the sample of your chosen author's prose.

Education Majors

Using your knowledge of grammar and the ideas in this chapter, create three different lesson plans and materials for your future students. Use the lesson ideas I have included in this chapter or create similar ones of your own. Make sure that you are following the guidelines for teachers given in this chapter. Another teacher should be able to teach your lesson without having to add any other preparation. Everything must be complete.

- At the top of each lesson, list your major (ESL Ed, ENG Ed, EL Ed) and the grade level of the students of whom you are thinking for this lesson.
- Then write down the purpose of your lesson. Why do you want your students to learn this?
- Make a list of the activities you will do to teach the lesson. Estimate how much time each part will take. Make sure that you

are giving them <u>enough practice</u> to master any skills you want them to learn. Describe what will be happening in each part of the lesson. Be specific. For this lesson, assume a 50-minute class.
- You must include all materials:
    o All discussion questions, along with speculation about their possible answers
    o All handouts (with samples included)
    o All overheads (on paper)
    o All notes to be written on the board or on the overhead
    o All practice materials for your students
    o All "explanation" material you will present to your students, everything you will say to them

Language Majors

Find and explain (with illustrations) a minimum of 20 total comparisons and contrasts between the grammar of the language you are studying or another language that you know and English grammar. Make this into a list with a short paragraph of explanation for each comparison or contrast.

Applications of Grammar

Sentence Style Analysis

Sentence #								
S-V								
S-LV-PredN								
S-LV-PredAdj								
S-V-DO								
S-Cjc-S								
Compound Elements								
Extraposed Sentence								
Inverted Sentence								
Adverb Clause								
PP:Adverb								
NP:Adverb								
Infinitive Phrase: Adverb								
Adv Word (w/ opt. Qual)								
Adv Active Part Phrase								
Adv Passive Part Phrase								
Adv Complement Clause								
Passive Main Verb								
Nominal Infinitive Phrase								
Gerund Phrase								
Noun Clause								
Nominal Appositive								
Nominal Comp Inf Ph								
Adj word (w/ opt. Qual)								
PP: Adjective								
Relative Clause								
Adj Infinitive Phrase								
Adj Active Part Phrase								
Adj Passive Part Phrase								
Adj Appositive								
Adj Complement Inf Ph								
PP:Adj Complement								
Adj Complement Clause								
Absolute								
Adverbial Conjunction								

Index

absolute, 204, 213
active participial phrase, 152, 161, 197
adjectival complement, 156, 157, 171–74, 197
adjective, 4, 32–33, 177
   proper, 56
   usage, 85
adjective phrase, 55–56
   grouping, 61
adverb, 4, 33–35
   mobility, 75
   questions, 34, 74
   usage, 85
adverb clause, 8, 82–83, 198, 257
adverb phrase, 45, 46, 257
   noun clusters, 78
adverbial complement clause, 177–79, 198
adverbial complement phrase, 177
apostrophe. *See* punctuation, apostrophe
appositive, 8
   adjectival, 156, 174, 177
   nominal, 187–88
article. *See* determiner article
auxiliary, 16
Bloomfield, Leonard, 15
Boas, Franz, 15
Campbell, George, 3
cardinal number, 55
Chomsky, Noam, 18, 19, 24
clause, 8
   independent, 8
   subordinate, 8
closed class, 17
comma. *See* punctuation, comma
common case, 4

competence, 19
compound elements, 62, 63, 83, 84, 103–4, 141, 157, 158, 159
conjugation, 31, 102
conjunction, 16
   adverbial, 205–7, 213
   coordinating, 4, 62, 103
   correlative, 4, 63, 85, 104
   subordinating, 4, 82, 83
deep structure, 19
demonstrative. *See* determiner demonstrative
demonstrative pronoun. *See* pronoun demonstrative
deSaussure, Ferdinand, 15
determiner, 16, 27–28, 54
   article, 55
   demonstrative, 55
   genitive noun, 55, 110
   possessive, 6, 55, 110
   quantifier, 55
direct object, 45, 47
distinctive feature matrix, 21
ellipsis, 171, 178, 212
embedded structures, 121–22
expletive, 226
extraposed sentences, 232
form class words, 16
Fries, Charles, 15
function words, 16
genitive case, 4
genitive noun. *See* determiner genitive noun
gerund phrase, 7, 110–12, 121, 161, 198, 230
grammar definition, 1

grammatical subject, 226
Grimm, Jacob, 14
head, 130, 138, 139, 141, 209
headword., 17
hyphen. *See* punctuation, hyphen
immediate constituent analysis, 17
imperative mood, 5
indefinite pronoun. *See* pronoun
   indefinite
indicative mood, 5
indirect object, 47, 48
infinitive phrase, 8
   adjectival, 141–42, 143, 197
   adjectival complement, 167–70, 197
   adverbial, 79–82, 121, 143, 168, 198
   for/to, 119–20, 170
   nominal, 119, 121, 143, 198, 229
   nominal complement, 191–94, 197
   passive, 120
   perfect, 194
   progressive, 193
   pseudo-adjectival-complement, 169
interjection, 5
intransitive verb, 5, 44–45, 51
inverted sentence, 232
Johnson, Samuel, 3
lexical insertion, 21
linguistics
   cognitive, 25
   comparative, 14
   descriptive, 14, 15
   historical, 14
   prescriptive, 14
linking verb, 41–44, 47, 51
logical subject, 120, 226, 227
Lowth, Robert, 3

misplaced modifier, 182, 214, 234, 259, 260
modal, 95
modifier, 130, 163
   whole-sentence, 207, 213
morphology, 15
Murray, Lindley, 3
nominal, 27
nominal complement clause, 194
nominal grouping, 61
nominal phrase, 45, 54, 64
nonrestrictive modifier, 138–39, 154, 155, 157
noun, 4, 27–29, 56, 57
noun clause, 8, 112–19, 121, 143, 198, 228
object complement, 49
   adjectival, 49, 176, 177
   nominal, 49
open class, 17
ordinal number, 55
parallelism, 106–7, 126, 255
participial phrase, 7
   adverbial, 180, 198
parts of speech, 4–7
passive participial phrase, 153, 197
performance, 19
periphrastic comparison, 4
phonology, 15
phrase, 7
phrase structure rules, 19–20
post-noun, 60
pre-determiner, 60
predicate adjective, 43, 102, 176, 177
predicate nominative, 42, 49
preposition, 4, 16, 58, 59, 60, 94
   object of preposition, 59

prepositional phrase, 4, 7, 35, 58, 77, 176
  adjectival, 77, 78
  adverbial, 77, 78
Priestly, Joseph, 3
Priscian, 2
pro-form, 114, 115, 210
pronoun, 6
  demonstrative, 7, 30, 57
  indefinite, 7, 30, 57
  intensive, 190
  interrogative, 7
  personal, 6, 29, 57, 58
  possessive. *See* determiner possessive
  quantifier, 30, 58, 59
  reflexive, 7, 29, 57, 58, 190
  relative, 6, 130–32
  usage, 68, 69, 70
punctuation, 247
  apostrophe, 71
  comma, 87, 145, 161, 183, 196, 213, 214, 263
  dash, 145, 161, 196, 213
  hyphen, 62, 70
  parentheses, 145, 161
  semicolon, 213
qualifier, 16, 43, 55, 70, 75
quasi-modal, 95
question. *See* sentence, interrogative
Rask, Rasmus, 14
relative clause, 8, 130–41, 143, 197, 209
relative pronoun, 130–32, 134
restrictive modifier, 138–39, 154, 157
Sapir, Edward, 15
semantics, 25
sentence
  complex, 9
  compound, 9, 203

  compound complex, 9
  declarative, 8, 220
  exclamatory, 8
  extraposed. *See* extraposed sentence
  imperative, 8, 220
  interrogative, 8, 220, 225
  inverted. *See* inverted sentence
  simple, 8
sentence formula, 17
sentence fragment, 86, 125, 161, 196, 262
structural grammar
  description, 15–17
  history, 14–15
  uses and limitations, 18, 17–18
subject/verb agreement, 105, 123, 232, 260, 261
subjunctive mood, 5, 83
subordinator, 80, 113, 114, 131
  missing, 137–38
substantive, 4
surface structure, 19
Sweet, Henry, 15
syntactic features, 20–22
syntax, 15
tag question, 225
teaching
  guidelines, 250–53
  lesson ideas, 253–65
Thrax, Dionysius, 2
traditional grammar
  advantages and disadvantages, 12–14
  description, 3–9
  history, 1–3
transformational grammar
  description, 18–24
  uses and limitations, 24
transformations, 24

transitions, 215, 255
transitive verb, 5, 45–50, 51
universal grammar, 19, 24
usage, 36, 247, 259
   adverb, 85
   complement clause, 183
   misplaced modifier, 163
   noun clause, 123–24
   preposition, 144, 233
   pronoun, 68, 69, 70, 261
   qualifier, 70
   subject/verb agreement. *See* subject/verb agreement
   subordinating conjunction, 86
   verb, 105
   who/whom, 123, 144, 233
Vc verb, 50, 100, 101

verb, 5, 30–32
   active, 5, 99, 256
   auxiliary, 5, 31
   conditional, 95
   copulative, 5
   emphatic, 5, 98
   irregular, 105
   negative, 98
   passive, 5, 99–102, 256
   perfect, 5, 96
   progressive, 5, 97
   verb particle, 93–95
Vg verb, 47–48, 100, 101
Wallis, John, 3
writing style, 36, 87–88, 106, 125, 146, 161–63, 195, 215, 234, 247–50, 253–55, 265–67